FATHER GEORGE CALCIU
INTERVIEWS, HOMILIES, AND TALKS

Fr. George Calciu.

FATHER GEORGE CALCIU

INTERVIEWS, HOMILIES, AND TALKS

*Compiled and edited by
the St. Herman of Alaska Brotherhood*

SAINT HERMAN OF ALASKA BROTHERHOOD
2015

Copyright © 2010, 2015 by the
St. Herman of Alaska Brotherhood
P. O. Box 70
Platina, CA 96076

website: sainthermanpress.com

email: stherman@stherman.com

A free catalog of titles is available upon request.

Front and back covers: Fr. George Calciu.

First printing: 2010
Second printing: 2015

Printed in the United States of America.

Some materials in this book were published in Fr. George Calciu, *Christ Is Calling You!* (Platina, Calif.: St. Herman of Alaska Brotherhood, 1997).

Publishers Cataloging in Publication

Calciu, Gheorghe.

    Father George Calciu : interviews, homilies, and talks / Fr. George Calciu; compiled and edited by the St. Herman of Alaska Brotherhood.—Platina, CA: Saint Herman of Alaska Brotherhood, c2010, 2015. 2nd printing.
    p. ; cm.

      ISBN: 978-1-887904-21-6
      Includes bibliographical references and index.

      1. Calciu, Gheorghe—Sermons. 2. Orthodox Eastern Church—Romania—Clergy—Biography. 3. Political prisoners—Romania—Biography. 4. Youth sermons—Romania. 5. Christian life—Orthodox Eastern authors. I. Saint Herman of Alaska Brotherhood. II. Title.

BX597.C35 C35 2010   2010938538
281.9092—dc22   1011

CONTENTS

INTRODUCTION *by Frederica Mathewes-Green*   9

PART ONE: THE LIFE AND REPOSE OF FR. GEORGE   23
   A Brief Autobiography of Fr. George   25
   The Last Years and Repose of Fr. George
      by Ryassaphore-monk Adrian   43

PART TWO: AN INTERVIEW WITH FR. GEORGE   59
   Introduction *by Nun Nina*   61
   An Interview with Fr. George   63

PART THREE: HOMILIES TO THE YOUTH   151
   Introduction *by Hieromonk Seraphim Rose*   153
   First Homily: The Call   157
   Second Homily: Let us Build Churches   161
   Third Homily: Heaven and Earth   165
   Fourth Homily: Faith and Friendship   170
   Fifth Homily: The Priesthood and Human Suffering   175
   Sixth Homily: About Death and Resurrection   181
   Seventh Homily: Forgiveness   188
   An Additional Homily to the Youth: A Homily to
      Theologians   196
   A New Word to Youth: Christ Has Risen within
      Your Heart   205

PART FOUR: DIVINE LIGHT IN THE DEVIL'S LAIR   213
   Lecture One: From Holy Romania to the Devil's Lair   215
   Lecture Two: Return to the Devil's Lair   237
   Lecture Three: Uncreated Light   263

PART FIVE: OTHER TALKS, HOMILIES,
        AND INTERVIEWS   279
   The Inner Church   281

Contents

A Word on Pious Prayer 301
A Word on Anger 308
A Word on the "Spirit of the Times" 314
Walking on the Sea of Life 316
How to Battle against the Demons 318
On the Importance of Holy Tradition 320
The Centurion's Faith and the Healing of the Heart 322
Thomas Sunday 325
The Healing of the Paralytic and the Loneliness
   of Contemporary Man 329
On the Meaning of Suffering 332
The Great Supper 334
On the Communion of the Soul with God 335
Prayer Is a Struggle 338
The Church and the Spirit of the World 341
A Word on the Feast of the Holy
   Great-martyr George 343
An Interview on the Fall of Communism and the
   Future of Romania 349
An Interview on Ecumenism 356

Appendices 359
   Appendix One: Fr. George's Letter to the CIEL 361
   Appendix Two: Fr. George's Preface to *Pitesti* by
      Dumitru Bacu 364
   Appendix Three: A Redeemer of the Time: Razvan
      Codrescu's Introduction to the Romanian Edition
      of Fr. George's *Seven Homilies to the Youth* 375

Index 383

Map of Romania showing places mentioned in this book.

Fr. George Calciu.

INTRODUCTION

by Frederica Mathewes-Green

It is hard to write, or even think, of Fr. George without being flooded with memories. His presence was so tender and strong, and so indomitably jovial, that he will not, for any of us who knew him, recede into the past. He lives.

And yet the years keep accumulating since the last time I saw his face. In my parish, Holy Cross Antiochian Orthodox Church, just outside Baltimore, Maryland, there are several other people who were his spiritual sons and daughters. We were at the hospital on the night he died; we gazed on his peaceful face and prayed beside his coffin on the night before his funeral; we were privileged to be part of the crowd that came to his funeral, an immense crowd which overflowed the church and the parking lot and trailed down the highway for a block.

On the third anniversary of his death some of us, his children, gave a presentation after the Sunday morning Liturgy on his life and magnificent witness—to Christ, to life, to the power of God's love. Rather than compose a literary introduction for this book, I'd like to simply repeat what I said that day. This is how we remember him, in one of the many communities that knew and loved him.

***

This weekend we are remembering the repose of Fr. George Calciu, who died on November 21, 2006, just two days before his eighty-first birthday. He died of pancreatic cancer, a fast-moving and painful cancer, and had barely survived long enough to complete one last trip to his homeland, Romania.

The news reached us on a Sunday evening that he had taken a turn for the worse. Fr. Gregory and I were hosting a gathering for Orthodox young people at our home that night, but I left our guests and went with Chris Vladimir to the hospital. Other members of Holy Cross were already there, and numerous parishioners and spiritual children from all over. We filled the waiting room and, whenever possible, took a turn slipping into his crowded hospital room for a final prayer at his side and a moment to kiss his hand.

I came to know Fr. George because I had been searching for a spiritual father for some time, and asking everyone I knew for recommendations. When I asked Bishop Basil (Essey) if he had any recommendations, he said, "Fr. George Calciu is not far from you, in Alexandria, Virginia. Why not ask him?" I was astounded to hear this; I had read Fr. George's book, *Christ Is Calling You!*,[1] but I didn't have any idea that he was even on this continent. So I drove over to meet him at his church, Holy Cross Romanian Orthodox Church, at Bailey's Crossroads in Alexandria. I had noted this church many times before, because it is a small white clapboard church, an old church, and it looks incongruous in the midst of the shopping malls and office towers that make up the area. It was in March 1999 that I met him for the first time, and he agreed to be my spiritual father.

Since his parish was named "Holy Cross" too, it gave us another thing in common. He was our preacher here on our patronal feast one year, and in December 2000 he gave our Advent retreat. Something else that stands out in my memory is that I had an appointment for Confession on September 12, 2001. I drove past the Pentagon to get to his church, and saw it still in ruins, hasty tarps dragged into place and flapping. When I got there he asked me, "Why do you think that happened yesterday?" I hadn't thought about "why." He replied that he had opened his Bible at random the night before and read, "Unless the Lord guard the city, the watchmen watch in vain" (Ps. 126:1). The Lord had to have deliberately allowed this to happen, he told me: think

---

[1] A previous version of the present book, published in 1997.—ED.

INTRODUCTION

how many "watchmen" the perpetrators had gotten past. It was an observation that gave me much to think about.

If you don't know much about Fr. George, the one thing you know is that he was a survivor of terrible torture in Communist prisons, in Romania. He was imprisoned twice, from 1948 to 1964, and from 1979 to 1984, for a total of twenty-one years.

And yet his most distinctive feature was his smile; he had a beaming smile. He was often amused by life, and ready to laugh. As I read about Elder Paisios,[2] it seems like he too had this quality of amusement and delight. Orthodox ascetics are often characterized by their joy. Fr. George was joyful, and, although he was married and lived in the world, he was an ascetic. He fasted voluntarily on Mondays, to make an offering to God from his free will, something not required by the Church. And I was told that he did not eat before 3:00 PM—though I think someone else told me, not before sunset. He was a champion of long church services and felt, for example, that you really couldn't pray an Akathist with your whole heart without preparing by praying an entire Vespers service first.

Yet he was hardly dour. He was naturally affectionate, and would hold my hand, or anyone's; the first time he met my husband, he stood there in the aisle of his church holding his hand for some time, and just beaming with a radiant smile. I'm a smiler too, and when the two of us held hands in his church, just smiling away, I would think, "Now the angels are rejoicing. Now the demons gnash their teeth." Joy, like love, is a powerful force to spread God's presence in the world.

Fr. George was the youngest of eleven children and, as the baby of the family, was his mother's favorite. When I saw his smile I would think, "That's the reflection of his mother's smile—that's the same smile he saw looking down into his cradle." His mother's love for him shone out through him all his life.

---

[2] Elder Paisios (Eznepidis) of Mount Athos (1924–94).—ED.

FATHER GEORGE CALCIU

Fr. George on his last visit to Romania, in 2006.

You would not guess, when you saw that smile, that he had suffered terrible things. In 1948, when he was twenty-three years old and attending medical school, he was imprisoned by the Communists and subjected to brainwashing, that is, "reeducation." Only young men were chosen for this process, because the goal was to make a sharp break with the past and begin fresh, with a new generation of leaders. In the entire Communist world, the preeminent place for this form of mental and emotional torture was the prison in the town of Pitesti, near Bucharest.

At Pitesti, the goal was to break down a prisoner's mind and sense of self, and rebuild him into the ideal Communist man. When a new group of prisoners came in, they were beaten by guards, and by prisoners who had been there longer. A few of them would be killed—whoever appeared to be a leader. They would be tortured and humiliated in many ways, and in particular forced

INTRODUCTION

to watch or participate in blasphemy. Fr. Roman Braga, a fellow prisoner who is now at Holy Dormition Monastery in Michigan, told me that, with no calendar, they could not know what season of the year it was, but could take their cues from the guards' songs; if they were singing a blasphemous version of a Nativity hymn, they would know Nativity was nigh. Fr. Roman also told me that one of the things guards said to torture them was that the Lord Jesus had had an affair with St. Mary Magdalene. He commented to me that, in Communist prison, this constituted torture; in America, people will pay money to read it in a book, like *The Da Vinci Code*, or watch it in a movie.

The psychological dimension of the process was called "unmasking," in which prisoners were required under torture to renounce everything they believed. Fr. George recalled being compelled to say, for example, "I lied when I said 'I believe in God.' I lied when I said, 'I love my mother and my father.'" With time, the exhausted prisoners would come to doubt their memories, and no longer know what was true about their own past. The intention was to undermine the prisoner's memory and personality, to infiltrate his consciousness with lies until he came to believe them.

This experiment lasted only a few years, because, when word began to leak out to the outside world, the Communists abruptly reversed course, and began to condemn "reeducation." They began to claim that they knew nothing about it, and started identifying and executing scapegoats.

And what happened to the prisoners? It seems that, once the torture stopped, many people began spontaneously to heal. With time they would recover their memories and sense of self and, hard as it is to believe, gradually return to normal. This healing could begin even though they were still in prison, simply because the brainwashing methods had stopped. Not all recovered, though. Some went insane, or died, sometimes by suicide.

When people hear of this torture they think, "I could never be that brave. I would just give in and say whatever they wanted."

But what Fr. George said was that this was true of many prisoners, including himself.

In an interview conducted by Nun Nina, Fr. George speaks at length about his experiences.[3] In talking about Pitesti he said, "It was a spiritual fight, between good spirits and evil spirits. And we failed on the field of battle; we failed, many of us, because it was beyond our ability to resist.... The limit of the human soul's resistance was tried there by the devil."

He also told Mother Nina, "When you were tortured, after one or two hours of suffering, the pain would not be so strong. But after denying God and knowing yourself to be a blasphemer—that was the pain that lasted ... We forgive the torturers. But it is very difficult to forgive ourselves."

But afterward, when at last alone, Fr. George would feel tears of repentance, and that would bring healing. Being able to turn to God at night and repent after the torture and failures of the day was very consoling. Fr. George said, "You knew very well that the next day you would again say something against God. But a few moments in the night, when you started to cry and to pray to God to forgive you and help you, were very good."

There was yet one more stage of "brainwashing," the worst of all. The mentally and physically broken prisoner would ultimately be forced to torture someone else. This was what completed the destruction of their personalities. Fr. George said, "Under terror and torture one can say, 'yes, yes, yes.' But now, to have to act? It was very difficult. It was during this part that the majority of us tried to kill ourselves." Fr. George says he tried to throw himself off a three-story staircase, and was saved only when another prisoner grabbed him and pulled him back.

The Romanian poet Razvan Codrescu wrote about Fr. George:

All the life of this man after the tragic Pitesti episode was

---

[3] See Part Two, pp. 63–149 below.—ED.

one of confession and sacrifice. In his soul and in his flesh he measured the distance between hell and heaven. Perhaps no survivors of Pitesti achieved a moral victory as brilliant and as enduring as his. Because the case of George Calciu exists, it can be said that the Pitesti experiment was a failure.

In 1964 there was a general amnesty, and Fr. George was released. He had lost sixteen years of his life, and, at this point, getting a medical degree would have taken too many more years. So Fr. George studied for a doctorate in French, and also attended seminary, being ordained a priest in 1973. During this period of freedom he also married his preoteasa,[4] Adriana, and they had a son, Andrei. Fr. George taught French and theology at the Orthodox seminary in Bucharest, and there were a few years of rest. But in the seventies the Communist government began attacking the Church (for example, demolishing buildings), and Fr. George felt he had to speak out. Many of the Church and seminary leaders, however, felt that protests only made things worse, and urged Fr. George to be silent.

In 1978, Fr. George felt called by God to deliver a series of seven sermons, one for each week of Lent, addressed to young people and calling them to transformation in Christ.[5] For the first four weeks Fr. George gave the sermon in the seminary church, but there was hostility from government observers, and Church leaders felt threatened. In the fifth week they locked the church, trying to deprive Fr. George and the students of a place to meet, but he simply gave his sermon in the courtyard. In the sixth week, they locked the seminary gates, but the students climbed over the walls to hear Fr. George's sermon.

After the seventh and last sermon in the series, the Paschal holidays[6] began, and during that time Fr. George began to receive

---

[4] *Preoteasa:* the Romanian title of a priest's wife.—ED.
[5] See Part Three, pp. 157–95 below.—ED.
[6] *Pascha:* the Feast of the Resurrection of Christ.—ED.

death threats against himself, his wife, and their son (who was then twelve years old). His reaction, characteristically, was to plan a new series of sermons to make public what was happening. But he didn't get the opportunity, because the seminary expelled him from its faculty. Fr. George told Nun Nina that God was telling him, "You asked for seven sermons, seven weeks, and I gave this to you. There is no need to explain and defend yourself. These sermons were not for the purpose of defending yourself, but to bring My word to the students and to worship God."

Within a year Fr. George was again arrested and confined to prison. However, the seven sermons had been recorded, and cassette tapes and typed transcripts were carried to Jerusalem and from there translated into other languages and spread throughout the West. Fr. George became internationally known as a political prisoner, and many organizations called for his release, as did prominent Romanian expatriates like Mircea Eliade and Eugene Ionescu. When George Bush, Sr., was vice president, he called on the president of Romania, Nicolae Ceausescu, and urged him to set Fr. George free. Instead, Ceausescu tried to arrange for Fr. George's murder in prison, but his plans failed and in the end he was compelled to release him from prison. Fr. George reunited with his wife and child, and in 1985 they immigrated to America.

This was how I found him, fifteen years later, when I was searching for a spiritual father. In light of everything he had been through, it was amazing to me that this living martyr, a survivor of torture, at that point in the latter half of his seventies, was still working full-time as a parish priest. It was obvious that there would be no retirement for him, that he would work until the day he died, and he did. As I went regularly to see him for Confession (he told me to come every forty days), I could observe how hard he worked, ministering not just to church members but also to people in need who had no ties to the church. He was always ready to give. I knew of a Romanian immigrant, a non-churchgoer, to whom he regularly gave groceries, and whom he cared for as

INTRODUCTION

Fr. George with parishioners.

if she were his parishioner, his responsibility. I knew of a young man, non-Orthodox, angry at God and belligerent, with whom Fr. George met regularly to talk. He told me that he kept telling the young man just one thing, over and over: "I love you."

Despite his age, Fr. George was always vigorous, strong in body as well as mind and spirit. He would fly back from Europe on a red-eye flight, then go right to church and stand through four hours of worship. Nothing stopped him. He was small, not a great deal taller than I am, but so vital and alive that I always thought of him as a "little lion." And, as I've said, he had a radiant smile. He seemed always ready to be amused.

Fr. George could be stern, however, for example, when dealing with Orthodox Christians who were careless about fasting and church attendance, or who reveled in religious emotionalism rather than maintaining a deep commitment to God.

And he was brilliant. As I mentioned, he first trained to be a doctor, and after his release from prison earned a degree (in addition to his seminary degree) in French literature. When exploring the nature of memory he would make an allusion to Proust, for example. Once I told him about an evangelical church in Canada where worshippers, believing that they are under the power of the Holy Spirit, laugh uncontrollably or bark like dogs. He gave a big smile and said, "It is the spirit of Anubis!" It took me a minute to remember that Anubis was the dog-headed god of the ancient Egyptians. The range of Fr. George's knowledge was vast.

English was not his best language, however. I'm afraid there were many times that I was not sure what he was saying. One time I asked him whether I should pray "deliver us from evil" or, "deliver us from *the* evil" (that is, "the evil one"), as it says in the New Testament Greek, only to find that he didn't understand that there was a difference. Though it was wrenching to lose him, in a way I feel closer to him now, because there is no more language barrier.

As he lay dying in the hospital, after he had (to all appearances) passed beyond awareness of his surroundings, he nevertheless knew, somehow, when those around his bed began to sing the Akathist to St. George. He tried to sing along, and his right hand swept upward in an attempt to make the sign of the Cross.

I'd like to conclude with a few stories and examples of his eldership.

1. The first time I met with him I asked him for advice in saying the Jesus Prayer. I had a three-hundred-knot prayer rope and had been saying three hundred Jesus Prayers each night. He told me that he did not believe in praying great amounts of the prayer, and I should cut it back to one hundred. He also showed me that when praying the Jesus Prayer you should form your right hand as you do when making the sign of the Cross, and then rest it over your heart. He also showed me that if you then cover your right hand with your left, as he said, "It makes a barrier that the devil cannot get through."

2. I was telling him once how badly my mind wanders in

church. He looked surprised and said, "Well, when that happens, you just change your position." He showed me—like standing with your arms by your sides, and then folding your hands together. If you change your posture a little bit, it automatically puts your mind back into the presence of God. Needless to say I'd never experienced that, but he thought it was common knowledge.

3. Fr. George was blessed to see the Uncreated Light on several occasions. The first time was when he eight years old, and looking at a field of wheat while thinking of God as Creator, and of what his mother and the priest had said about God. He said, "In a moment, I realized that the field was full of light. I could not understand what it was: this light had no shadow and no perspective. Perhaps because I was accustomed to the image of natural light on the land, I could see all the details, but only in light, not in shadow. I was as if petrified. I don't know how long I was like that: and when I recovered the field was normal."

President Ceausescu tried to have Fr. George murdered in prison, and in one case assigned him two sadistic criminals as cellmates with orders to kill him. But instead Fr. George changed their hearts. One Sunday Fr. George served the Holy Liturgy in the cell—an act strictly forbidden in the prison. After he had partaken of Holy Communion, he turned to his cellmates and found them kneeling in prayer. Fr. George said, "They were in this Light, visible Light, Uncreated Light but visible.... The whole cell was full of Light."

4. In a 1997 talk[7] at St. Paisius Monastery in Forestville, California,[8] Fr. George talked about another experience with the Uncreated Light; and this one is especially interesting to me because Fr. George says that later that day he did something that spoiled it. One morning in prison he heard the church bells and knew that it was Pascha. When a guard came into his cell for the usual inspection, Fr. George said, "I didn't turn my face to

---

[7] See pp. 263–77 below.—ED.

[8] The St. Paisius Monastery is now located in Safford, Arizona.—ED.

the wall as I was supposed to, but said to him, 'Christ is Risen!' He looked at me and at the other guards. [This] was the most sadistic man I had ever met in my life. He could not accomplish his eight-hour shift without beating and torturing the inmates. His face was like that of an angel, very beautiful, very elegant, but I never saw such cruelty in a man. Nevertheless he answered me, 'In Truth He is Risen!' This shocked me very much. He shut the door and I was petrified because of what he had said."

Fr. George goes on: "And little by little, I saw myself full of Light. The board against the wall was shining like the sun; everything in my cell was full of light. I cannot explain in words the happiness that invaded me then. I can explain nothing. It simply happened. I have no merit. I was perhaps the biggest sinner in that section, but nevertheless God gave me this Light…. In a short time this Light disappeared, but the happiness lasted many hours."

But later that same day a colonel came and Fr. George began to speak with him about the Faith, and use his intelligence to argue.

> I heard [the colonel's] steps in the corridor, and I knew that the guard was about to tell him what happened in the cell. He was approaching the cell … and I prepared my answer. Now it was like in a theater, in a play or a movie: I knew he would come, I knew his question, and he knew my answers. He opened the door and, as I had done with the guard, I looked at him and said, "Christ is Risen!" He looked at me and said, "Did you see Him?"
>
> "No, I did not see him, but I believe that Christ is risen because of those who testified: the apostles, the martyrs, the bishops, the patriarchs, and all the Christians who for two thousand years affirmed that Christ is risen and who answered, 'In Truth He is Risen!' You believe in things you have never seen. Did you see the North Pole? It exists, and you believe in it on the authority of the men of science. Did you see Marx

INTRODUCTION

and Engels? You didn't see them, but you believe in them because people of authority told you that they existed. You didn't even see Stalin, our contemporary. But you know that he existed because someone told you. Because of this authority concerning the Resurrection of Jesus Christ, I believe in His Resurrection."

He did not have an answer for me. But I felt something false in myself. No argument is able to convince somebody about Jesus Christ—it is a single argument to say, "Christ is Risen!" Can you bring forward some proofs that Christ is risen? No. Only faith.

I remember reading something in a Russian newspaper or book, how at the beginning of the revolution in Russia, the Communists sent people of science, people with higher education, from village to village to speak to the peasants and show them with scientific arguments that Jesus could not have risen from the dead. Trotsky, with a group of such devoted Communist scientists, came into a certain village on Pascha. The police obligated the people and the priest, on the day of Pascha, to come to a big hall to hear the scientific arguments that Jesus Christ could not have risen. They said a lot of things, very intelligent, and at the end they asked if there were any questions. Then the priest, who in fact was a peasant, said, "I have a question." They said, "Come here," and he came up to the front and said, "You are very intelligent people: the intelligentsia of Russia. I think what you said is true, but I want to say something. People, CHRIST IS RISEN!" And he heard the answer: "IN TRUTH HE IS RISEN!"

This is the single argument we have for the Resurrection of Jesus Christ. We can invoke the information of the Bible: to the unfaithful it means nothing. We can speak from the Holy Fathers; again, it is nothing to them. Therefore, it was enough for me to say, in front of the colonel, "Christ is Risen!" We need no other proof. Because of just trying to prove to the colonel that Jesus really rose from the dead, I felt something wrong in my orientation. Since then I gave up trying to give proofs to the guards or to the inmates, the criminals. I had learned from experience that people are changed only by the fire of your faith, by the dedication in your attitude to them and to God, because this is the most powerful proof.

As someone who has been writing books and giving speeches about Orthodoxy for many years now, I often turn over those words in my mind. I have been often puzzled and disappointed to see that even Christ-loving Western Christians can hear about the treasure of our Orthodox Faith, can hear about the healing of the inner person, the enlightening of the *nous*,[9] and the possibility of theosis,[10] and simply not care. I'm surprised at how often there are no follow-up questions after a speech. Perhaps they just don't believe me; perhaps I'm a very poor example. But I think there is a basic truth in what Fr. George says here. Explanations and arguments don't persuade people; they provoke, instead, rebuttals. God's way is to woo us, to draw us with cords of love (cf. Hosea 11:4). "People are changed by the fire of your faith," by witnessing the action of God in your life. Wood catches fire from fire, not words. Fr. George lived as a flame, a light that could not be overcome by darkness. We who rejoiced for a time in his presence long for the day we will feel the warmth of that fire again, and see the beauty of his smile.

***Khouria Frederica Mathewes-Green** is the wife of Fr. Gregory Mathewes-Green, the priest of Holy Cross Antiochian Orthodox Church in Linthicum, Maryland. She is the author of numerous popular Orthodox Christian books and a contributor to journals and online magazines.*

---

[9] *Nous:* the highest faculty of the human soul, which, when purified, can come to a knowledge of God.—ED.

[10] *Theosis*: deification, the process and state of being united to God through His Energies.—ED.

PART ONE

The Life and Repose of Fr. George

Fr. George blessing a boy at St. Innocent's Academy in Kodiak, Alaska.

A BRIEF AUTOBIOGRAPHY
OF FR. GEORGE

This account was recorded by Fr. George in 1996 and transcribed at the St. Paisius Monastery, Forestville, California, by an American Orthodox nun, Mother Nina, now of St. Nilus Skete, Alaska. —ED.

I WAS BORN INTO a family of farmers, of peasants.[1] There were eleven of us children. My grandmother lived with us, so there were a total of fourteen people to eat and work, and my poor mother had no time to take care of everyone. So my brother—I was the last in the family—helped me and the other ones to get food, to start work, and to go to school. At the same time, we received an education from our mother and from the firstborn in the family.

There are many things that constitute my faith and my inclination to the Faith. I was born in a small village in the Danube Delta, and we did everything by hand. There were fish, and it was very simple for us to catch them.

There were lots of different birds. From generation to generation we learned not to touch the eggs—not more than one egg from every nest. So the birds were not hurt by us, and the fish were not diminished. Because we considered everything a creation of God and that everything was made for us, we had to protect the animals. There was a kind of holy relationship between us—between children and the people of the Danube Delta and the animals. We lived together; we grew up together. There was sort of an eternity between us and nature and the animals.

---

[1] Fr. George was born to Stefan and Elena Calciu on November 23, 1925, in Mahmudia, Tulcea County, Romania.—ED.

So, we started to love; we learned to love everyone. You can imagine a small village like ours. Everyone knew everyone, and it was not possible for us to do a bad deed and not be discovered. And we knew that above all of us was the eye of God, Who knew everything and Who would discover our bad deeds in time.

There was a priest, a very good priest—an old priest, like a saint. He knew everything about us—about the children, about the people. For a generation everyone was baptized, married, and buried by this priest, so he was like the eye of God in our village. My mother, especially, was very, very faithful. From her I learned many things. Sometimes we could not be in the church; I don't know why, perhaps we were sick, but at the table mother told us about the Liturgy and about the reading from the *Cazania*.[2] Every Sunday and every holy day of the Church, someone in church would read the *Cazania* and the Lives of the saints of the day. Therefore, from the time I was a child I knew a lot about the saints of the day and about the monks. We were not too far from various monasteries. From time to time we went to them to visit the monks and nuns, to bring them food, and to ask them to pray for us, because everyone knew that we needed someone to pray for us.

I was very much inclined to contemplation, and I wanted to be a true Christian. I was perhaps around six or seven years old, and I wanted very much to see a miracle or to be the subject of a miracle. I remember that one time I tried to force God to make a miracle for me. There was a small field with thick nettles, and I decided to go through this field and if the nettles did not harm me, then that would mean that God had done a miracle for me. I was stepping without any care [through the field], and nothing happened. [The nettles did not prick him.] But before I had finished walking through the field, I heard the voice of a man—one

---

[2] *Cazania:* a compilation of sermons originally written in the seventeenth century. In the early twentieth century Romanian priests rarely gave sermons in church. Instead the chanter would read from the *Cazania* or the Lives of the saints.—ED.

Fr. George with his family (his mother is in the center) in 1972.

of our neighbors who would curse frequently. When I heard his voice, I said in my mind, "He is a bad man." At this moment the nettles started to hurt me, and I knew that God was very angry at me because I had an evil thought about my neighbor.

I liked to go out into nature, and I liked to go by the Danube—the Danube was very wide. I had a boat, and I crossed the Danube in this boat. Far into the forests of the Delta there was a family, friends of our family, who were very poor. They lived far away from the village and had no house. They had dug a house under the earth. It was a space with two or three rooms under the earth, covered with leaves, and it was very nice. For me, it was something absolutely like in Paradise. They were young then, with three or four children, and their life was like the life of hermits. Everything around their house had been handmade. Like us, they had fish and eggs, animals and sheep, and so on. And every time I went there, I felt like I was in a monastery. Their hospitality was without limits. When the sun was setting, they accompanied me home, and my parents were very happy to see me return. They knew I had been there. The visits I made from time to time to that family taught me a lot—about God, about God's care of men; and I understood that we can live without striving beyond measure to get everything we need. Yet, in fact, I could not understand everything at that time. Later, I realized how hard my father was working for us and how hard my older sisters and brothers were working to get food and to have everything in our family and our house. I was the only one of eleven children to go to school.

The priest from my village helped me to go to school, because my father had no intention of sending me to high school. But the priest very much insisted. I sang in the church choir and I also chanted prayers under the supervision of the priest. He counseled me to go to seminary, but the seminary was very far away. There was no seminary close to our village, or in the city near our village, so my parents decided to send me to high school. I went to the high school in the city closest to our village; it was about thirty miles distant. In my years there we had a priest who taught us the Orthodox Christian religion. So I was growing in my understanding of Christianity—in prayer, meditation, etc. He was a very good priest and also a philosopher. He knew how to interest the young boys in school about religion, about faith, and even about the understanding of philosophy. I entered into a prayer group with this priest and other young men. There were also people from the city—intellectuals. We knew during this time a small group of the Army of the Lord, as well.[3] We learned some religious songs, how to read the Bible, and how

---

[3] The Army of the Lord was founded by Fr. Joseph Trifa, an Orthodox priest. Seeing that the Protestant sects were winning over more and more Romanian Orthodox Christians, Fr. Joseph started the Army of the Lord in order to keep believers on the true path of salvation in the Orthodox Church. Since the Protestants were attracting people by composing and singing religious songs, Fr. Joseph began doing the same thing, using Orthodox hymns to Jesus Christ, the Mother of God, etc.—ED.

to interpret and understand it. Thus I succeeded in becoming a good Christian.

My priest at school counseled me to go into medicine and to prepare myself to help people. He said, "You can do for people what I am doing for you. You can take care of the body of a person, but a true doctor takes care of the soul, also, because it is not enough to heal the body—you must heal the soul." And he told me, for the first time, about the physicians who healed without pay—the unmercenaries Sts. Cyrus and John and the other holy unmercenary physicians.

Therefore, I decided to become a doctor. I went to Bucharest, the capital of the country, and there I passed the admission exam. The admission exam was very serious; I had prepared for the exam and passed it. I then started to study medicine—the first and second years. It was very difficult for me because, according to what my priest had taught me, I had no right to mutilate the body of my neighbor, so dissection was a big problem for me. In the beginning I did it, but, later, because I was gifted in drawing, I asked my friends, my colleagues there, to make the dissections, and I drew the parts revealed by the dissection—the nerves, arteries, veins, muscles, and so on. Thus, I succeeded in going through the second year without touching a corpse in dissection.

During this time, I discovered that there were many, many religious groups in Bucharest. There were some very famous priests. There was Fr. Chiricutsa; he was a priest in a small but very old and beautiful church. Every Wednesday night we had a Bible study. Now for the first time I understood how deep the Bible was, because, as you can imagine, in elementary school the teacher—the priest—explained a lot of things, but we were too young [to understand]. Now I heard someone interpreting the Bible, explaining it in depth. Thus I was one of his students there.

This put me in conflict with medicine, that is, with the

materialistic direction of the doctors. From time to time I entered into conflict with the medical assistants, because they considered the bodies of our neighbors as objects. I tried to tell them that the body is not an object, but the temple of God; and they laughed at me. But, anyway, I received some respect from them.

Later, I discovered a very spiritual movement called the "Burning Bush."[4] In the Burning Bush movement there were a lot of professors of theology and philosophy—men of science. The most important lectures were in Bucharest. They had a monk; he was a bishop from Russia who had arrived in Bucharest in 1946. He was followed by the KGB, but I don't know why. The monastery in Bucharest, St. Antim Monastery, gave him shelter. They hid him and, little by little, a circle of intellectuals—priests, monks, and professors of theology—gathered around him, because he taught them the Jesus Prayer. In the secluded monasteries of the mountains, the monks were practicing the Jesus Prayer. But the professors of theology, the priests—they knew nothing about the Jesus Prayer. This man taught them about the Jesus Prayer, according to the practice they had in Russia from Elder Basil of Poiana Marului in Romania and St. Paisius Velichkovsky of Neamts. Thus, as they discovered the Jesus Prayer and the beneficial effects of this prayer upon the soul, more and more intellectuals gathered around him.

I came in the beginning of 1948, and discovered this circle. They were delivering speeches, giving lessons on the Prayer, on the *Philokalia* and the Lives of the saints of the desert. I remember

---

[4] The Burning Bush was a renewal movement in the 1940s and '50s centered at Antim Monastery in Bucharest, and based on an interest in hesychast spirituality and the Jesus Prayer. It strove to make the Orthodox Faith come alive in its hesychastic expression among the intellectuals, and to help make scientific research and all human activity a meeting place between God and man. It was stopped by the Communists in 1958, and its leaders were imprisoned.—ED.

a conference led by Fr. Staniloae.⁵ It was a series of conferences called "The Fathers of the Desert: The Lives and Teachings of the Holy Fathers." They were not open to everyone, but were intended for young people. They accepted only people they knew very well, because they were being watched by the Securitate.⁶ In 1944 Communism had been installed in Romania. At the beginning [of Communism], they had started to arrest people and to put intellectuals in prison—priests, monks, and so on, who tried to defend themselves against this intrusion. Therefore, I was not accepted into this intimate group. They knew some young doctors, especially Dr. Nicolau, who was a friend of mine. I was a young man—twenty-two years old. He was around thirty, thirty-five, but he loved me and tried to explain to me many things about the Faith, and especially about the Prayer of Jesus.

In 1948, the first priests from this group, the "Burning Bush," had a special icon painted by a painter of the group. [The icon showed] the Mother of God in the middle of a bush, surrounded by flames that could not consume her or the bush. They would have their meetings in front of this icon. The icon is now in America, in the Monastery of the Dormition of the Mother of God in Michigan, with the priest Roman Braga. He was a student at the time, a theologian and a monk, and was accepted into this group.

In the spring of 1948, I was arrested and sentenced to sixteen years of imprisonment; I finished my punishment in 1964. The rest of the history is known by you, Mother Nina. I was not

---

⁵ Fr. Dumitru Staniloae (1903–93) was a Romanian Orthodox priest and theologian. In addition to translating the *Philokalia* into Romanian, he wrote many books on theology, including commentaries on the works of Sts. Gregory of Nyssa, Maximus the Confessor, and Athanasius the Great. From 1958 to 1963, Fr. Dumitru was imprisoned by the Communist government for his participation in the Burning Bush movement. He is considered to be one of the greatest theologians of the twentieth century.—ED

⁶ *Securitate:* the secret service of Communist Romania.—ED.

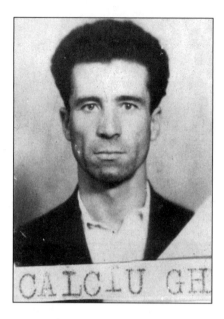

George Calciu, medical student, at the time of his first arrest, in 1948.

arrested in connection with the "Burning Bush." As I have said, I was not a member of the group—I had only taken part in their public gatherings. My connection with them was through Dr. Nicolau. I was put into prison because I had participated with a group of students that made a stand against the introduction of Marxism and Bolshevism as the only philosophy taught in schools—in the university, high schools, and even in elementary schools—because they started with the indoctrination of children when they were five or six years old. The other young people and I were frustrated at not being able to know any other philosophy besides materialism. In fact, we had done nothing bad; we only had one demonstration—when the Securitate tried to arrest our doctor, our professor of anatomy. We blocked the university. We surrounded it and did not allow the Securitate to take away our professor. The professor was saved, but he was very sick, and in a short time he died because of his heart. He was an old man; a very good man, very faithful, very Christian. He never neglected to make the connection between medicine and religion, between the body and the creation, and between the soul and immortality.

But for the Communists, for the Russians who occupied our country, this opposition by the young people seemed very bad. They wanted to make a new generation—a new generation to build Communism. For this, they didn't need enemies, so they arrested the priests and monks, the intellectuals, technicians, and scholars. They wanted to put a big gap between the old generation and the new generation that they wanted to form, so they put everyone in prison. They sentenced people to ten, twenty years, without any justice, just because they wanted to destroy a generation in order to make this gap. Thus I was arrested with the young people, the students, and sentenced with them. And my life in prison—I described a part of this life in prison—it was like everyone else's life in prison.

For our family, for the people who lived outside prison, we were as dead people. No one knew anything about us. We were living in fog, in the night. No one had any idea about us. We had no right to send a letter to our family; we had no right to receive letters or packages. So, in the beginning of the sixteen years, I had only three letters from my family. Then they changed their rules in prison and introduced a regime to exterminate the people. The people who were not exterminated in prison were exterminated in labor camps. So hundreds of thousands of people were killed, and millions were put in prison or put under house arrest or exiled to different areas—small areas. It was like Siberia was for Russia. In a part of the country south of the Danube, people were put on a large plain without anything. They had to dig their houses underground. They built houses from mud, thus starting new villages in this area.

I told you that I went to prison in 1948, on May 21, the commemoration day of Sts. Constantine and Helen. In the beginning I was in Jilava Prison. Jilava is a prison built underground. Above every cell there were seven meters of earth:

trees, animals, and so on. My time there was very bad. Afterwards I was sent to Pitesti, where I stayed from the autumn of 1948 until 1952, when I was moved to Gherla Prison. Gherla is a very tough prison, built by the Austro-Hungarian empire; I stayed there until 1954. In 1954, I was taken from Gherla and sent to Jilava again with fourteen other friends and put in a special kind of extermination area, where Costache Constantine Oprisan[7] died. In 1961, I and my friends who survived this extermination were sent to Aiud Prison—another prison built by the Austro-Hungarian empire. I changed my attitude—I became more and more mystical. I prayed a lot. I was no longer interested in what happened around me. After my experience [at Pitesti], something had changed in my soul. The directors of the administration of the prison wanted to force everyone to be reeducated in order to accept the new situation—to accept that Communism would win the whole world, that there was no other political regime better than Communism, and to recognize that we had made mistakes before Communism.

I told the director of the prison that I was not interested, and that my intention was to leave and, if possible, to become a monk. So he isolated me with another group in a special building in the prison, with another group that refused any reeducation.

The life in Zarka—this special building in Aiud Prison was called Zarka—was not so bad. I mean, it was very bad from the material point of view—food and persecution and beatings and so on—but spiritually we were very, very happy. This building was full of intellectuals, priests, monks, professors of theology, and so on. We communicated among ourselves through signs, through knocking on the walls. We had conferences about icons, about theology, about history, and so on, because the most important intellectuals from Romania were there. So I stayed in this prison until May 1964, when I was set free—but not quite free. I was

---

7 See pp. 109–16 below.—ED

sent into a village built on this plain for exiles. I remained in this village until August 1964, when a general decree of amnesty was applied to everyone and we had the right to go into the world.

It was a very strange situation we encountered as we entered the "real world." It was a Communist world, and we were like ghosts for these people. We could not understand them; they could not understand us.

By the decree of amnesty, we were allowed to start over again. I tried to enter medicine, but they no longer recognized the two years I had studied, so I had to start at the beginning. It was too long—I would have had to study six years; so I decided to study the French and Romanian languages. I passed the admission exam and studied French for three years. After three years, I was approved to teach French in elementary school. I completed the last two years of study: not in class with everyone else, but studying independently to pass the exams.

In 1964 I had been set free, and in 1965 I met my wife. I knew her not just as an individual, for she had two brothers in prison and I had met them there. They were students like me, but older. Through them I met my wife[8] and we decided to get married. We were married in February of 1965. My wife was a biologist, a researcher. I can say that my life was not so difficult because she had a good salary, and I received my salary, too. We had a child, and my decision, as I told you, was to become a priest. I had given up the idea of the monastic life, but I tried to keep my word, my vow to God, that if I succeeded in getting out of prison in good health, mentally and physically, I would become a priest.

So I decided to study theology. I was now a teacher of the French language. I had finished my five years of study, but I was not happy, not at all, because I felt that my life was like a desert. Anyway, as a teacher in an elementary school I did everything that I could just to tell something to my students about Jesus Christ.

---

[8] Adriana Dumitreasa.—ED.

George and Adriana Calciu after their civil marriage ceremony in 1965.

Every year I organized an excursion with my students—actually, my ex-students. They were thirteen or fourteen years old. I would always put the monasteries in our itinerary. Thus they were in touch with the nuns and the monks, who talked to them about Jesus Christ, so I had done something. I cannot say that I accepted not talking to the students about Jesus Christ or God. I did [talk with them about Christ and God]. With prudence, surely. I did not want to go to prison again or to be let go from my job, but I was obsessed with the vow I had taken. So I decided to go to the Patriarch, Patriarch Justinian Marina, and to get admitted into the faculty of theology.

My wife, as I told you, did research in biology. She knew a few things about religion; she had a religious education, but not a very deep one, so I had to work with her and my son. She followed me in everything. She supported me in my decision to go to theology school and to become a priest. She knew that in her work in the field of research, she could be put out if they discovered that I was a priest. But she accepted everything. I told her that if I became a priest, I would have a church and she could leave work and we could work together helping others, and so on, and she accepted this. Happily, nothing happened to her. I had been appointed as a professor of the French language and of the New Testament in the seminary when the Securitate discovered that I was a student of theology. My wife followed me everywhere. She was a shy and timid person, but when the persecution started against me, she was with me. She fought more than I fought. She was even more courageous than I was. For this I am very grateful to her.

In 1979 I was arrested and put in prison,[9] and at first they wanted to sentence me to death. When I came to America, I met some defectors—members of the Securitate—and they told me that Ceausescu really believed that I had organized a plot against him. They told me that after my arrest he had ordered

---

[9] See Appendix One, "Fr. George's Letter to CIEL," pp. 361–63 below, for his explanation of his persecution by the government.—ED.

George Calciu holding his son, Andrei.

an in-depth investigation among the students of the seminary, the young people—eighteen, nineteen, twenty years old. He was very surprised, too. He knew nothing about them—the students of theology. The Securitate told him that the majority of my students were minors, so under the pressure made by the Christian groups abroad, he gave up the intention of executing me. He gave an order to put me in prison, and he left me there. I was sentenced to ten years.

After the arrest by the Securitate, I was initially placed in Aiud Prison. The majority of the time I was alone in a cell in confinement. Sometimes I had some friends, sometimes enemies in my cell. But most of the time I was alone, because the pressure on Ceausescu was very strong. Many congressmen and senators, and even [Vice President] Bush, came to Romania and asked Ceausescu to set me free. They had a list of persecuted people. I was on the top of the list because I was in prison and sentenced to ten years of imprisonment. They knew about my situation, the persecution. And so I suffered in prison. Whenever they came to Romania and asked Ceausescu to set me free, the Securitate brought me to Bucharest. They did not know what had happened to me ... perhaps Ceausescu had set me free. So they brought me into the cell of the Securitate; they allowed my wife to come to me and to bring me food. Thus after months of hunger, I was being fed and was looking better. But never was one of these visitors allowed to come to visit me. I received some news from different congressmen asking me to write a petition to ask Ceausescu to set me free, to exonerate me for the rest of the punishment. They assured me that Ceausescu would accept it. But I refused for two reasons: first of all, I had put my life into the hands of God. Secondly, I did not want to make such a petition because I knew that I was innocent. In writing this petition, I would be acknowledging before Communism and Ceausescu that I was guilty. For this reason I refused, but they tried to convince me. When one of the visitors left Romania, I was sent back to Aiud

Fr. George and family at the time of their immigration to the United States.

or to Galati—another prison. The majority of time that I was in Aiud and Galati Prisons, and part of the time in the Securitate in Bucharest.

Christian groups and even political groups, organizations for human rights, started to apply stronger pressure on Ceausescu, asking him to set me free. They even threatened to not give him the most-favored-nation status, so Ceausescu decided to set me free. I was freed in August 1984 and put under house arrest with my whole family. I had no right to go anywhere without the permission of the Securitate. If I wanted to go to church, I had to tell my guards. My wife was allowed to go back and forth to her job. My son had to go to high school, and later he was obliged to go into the army; everywhere he was watched by the Securitate. He had no right to talk with people, so our life was very hard. Happily, there were many people in the apartment where I was under house arrest. The neighbors could communicate with me, and many people tried to communicate with me through them. I was well known.

My neighbors tried to transmit to my friends abroad what

had happened to me; the persecution and so on. There was a radio station called "Radio Free Europe" which broadcast news about me, and this fight or battle put Ceausescu in a difficult situation. After setting me free, in 1984, he received most-favored-nation status. But then, a year later, the same organization did not give him most-favored-nation status—this status was to be renewed every year.

As a result, Ceausescu decided to force me to leave Romania for America. I knew nothing about it. One day, members of the American embassy entered my house—I was very surprised to see them. There was even a lady among them. The police tried to check her body; she refused and said, "I am immune; I have diplomatic immunity. Let me enter." She told me everything. Then the men said, "Now you have to go with us to the Passport Agency in Bucharest to get your passport." I could not believe it. In the beginning I had supposed that it was a prank by the Securitate, but I then realized that they really were Americans. So we went together, the three of us, to the Passport Service and got a passport. The passport was delivered exactly one year after I was set free from prison (in April 1985), but they kept the passport until August 1985. Afterwards we went to the Embassy, where we swore that everything about us was true, and in two days we left Romania for Rome. In Rome we stayed two more days, and then we came to America, to New York.

My wife, son, and I were received by the delegates of our episcopate, and one American friend said, "I desire to receive Fr. Calciu into my home. He will be given good food, shelter, and so on." I stayed in the house with this American for two months. Afterwards I went to the Transfiguration Monastery,[10] founded by Mother Alexandra, the Princess Ileana of Romania, a member of the royal family. I stayed there for two more months, and afterwards the Church sent me to Ohio and offered me a house.

---

[10] The Orthodox Monastery of the Transfiguration, Ellwood City, Pennsylvania.—ED.

Fr. George in his coffin.

We stayed in Ohio for three years. During this time, I traveled much in America and in Europe—France, Germany, England, Switzerland—and gave lectures on the situation of the Church in Romania. I talked about what had happened in prison; many things happened to me there that were a manifestation of God's love for me. Finally, I was appointed as a priest in the church of the Holy Cross in Alexandria, Virginia, near Washington, D.C.

THE LAST YEARS AND REPOSE OF FR. GEORGE

by Ryassaphore-monk Adrian

Father George Calciu's final years in the United States were marked by the same patient suffering and indefatigable resolve to serve the Lord that had characterized his entire life.

In 1989 Fr. George was appointed pastor of the Holy Cross Romanian Orthodox Church in Alexandria, Virginia. In this capacity, he cared for the growing Romanian émigré community, while bringing many American converts into the Orthodox Faith.

At the altar of God, Fr. George was deeply focused. There were no distractions for him during the Church services. One of his parishioners, Iacovos Ioannou, recalled: "He had a profound respect for the institution of the priesthood, and during services he was exclusively dedicated to God. He spent a lot (if not most) of the time during Vespers kneeling. The sight of him coming out from the Royal Doors with his white beard is an image that has stayed in my mind: imposing, reverent, royal, a representative of Christ Himself. In his sermons (at the end of the Vespers), he spoke with gentleness and kindness, with a soft voice that never showed any signs of anger or worldly emotions. At the same time, he was a priest who would say whatever his flock needed to hear, without shying away from 'difficult' or controversial issues."

Fr. George would hear Confessions late into the night. Despite being in his seventies, with a body that had suffered through twenty-one years of imprisonment and torture, he would remain kneeling while he heard Confessions hour after hour. Another of his spiritual sons, John Lyon, recalled a typical memory of Confession with Fr. George: "I went to Confession that night, being drawn to his amazing grace and spirit. He prayed for me, listened briefly, and looked into my eyes to my soul. That night I experienced an epiphany of healing from deep wounds that had been terribly saddening. He anointed me and blessed me and no doubt changed the course of my life."

Outside of the Church services, everyone who came into contact with him remembers him as radiating the love and joy of Christ. Even in a 1989 *Washington Post* article, the writer commented that his face was "pink as a child's and his eyes [were] an unclouded blue. Something in his gaze [suggested] the triumph of joy over anguish."[1] He tried to impress on all around him the love of Christ that he had experienced. Ho (Symeon) Kim, a young man just coming to the Orthodox Faith during Fr. George's last year, remembered: "Over the one year that I got to know Father before his repose, he told me many times that he loved me very much and God loved me much, much more. He seemed to always want to remind me that he loved me. He would always hold my hand, kiss my head, give me a blessing, and laugh gently each time he saw me. One thing I found out after Father reposed was that when he typically addressed his close spiritual children, he would call them 'sinners' (of course in a spiritual, loving way). But Father only addressed me as 'good boy.' Father would always say to me 'You are a good boy,' or 'God will help you to be a good boy.' Maybe Father always verbally and explicitly reminded me of his love for me and called me a good boy (instead of a sinner) because he knew how weak I was and how prone to doubting I was; because someone with such a weak and constantly doubting heart as I had needed explicit verbal encouragement and positive words."

---

[1] Patricia Sullivan, "Obituary of Anti-Communist Priest Gheorghe Calciu-Dumitreasa," *The Washington Post,* Nov. 26, 2006, p. C9.—ED.

THE LAST YEARS AND REPOSE OF FR. GEORGE

To the end of his life, Fr. George labored in asceticism—something he had been forced to do during his twenty-one years in prison. After his 1964 release from prison, Fr. George began to keep a strict fast every Monday, Wednesday, and Friday, not eating until after sunset. This continued until his last years, when poor health prevented him from fasting. Likewise, his labors of prayer in prison did not cease when he came to the United States. Even outside of services he kept his mind focused on the Jesus Prayer. In a lecture given in 2000, Fr. George said, "Prayer is a connection between man and transcendental reality, a connection between man and the Divine world.... Through prayer man surpasses the human condition and is deified by the grace of Jesus Christ. By prayer we glorify God. We become humble in front of God. We understand the ontological difference between human beings and God, something we cannot overcome. By prayer in front of God, we recognize our sins. We ask for pardon. We promise not to sin again. We put in order our relationship with our neighbors. We place in front of God all of life: spiritual, material, and social relations with the family, with the Church, and with God. There is not a part of us remaining outside the prayer."

After the fall of Communism in Romania in 1989, Fr. George returned to Romania on numerous occasions. And the traditions of Romania were never far from him in the United States. According to Iakavos Ioannou, "He remained faithful to his homeland and its traditions; he considered 'Western values' as harmful to the fabric of our society, and consumerism as inconsistent with the life and tradition of the Orthodox Church. He pointed out that children in the United States are brought up with so much affluence that they do not appreciate what they have. He spoke with fondness about his homeland, his parents, his life as a child, and his modest beginnings, which, however, were more than made up for by warm family relations and closeness to nature."

Fr. George maintained a schedule that would have exhausted most people half his age. In 2004 and 2005, he underwent two heart operations, but he would not allow even these to slow his labors. One parishioner recalled: "We were surprised to find Fr. George at Friday Vespers, immediately after his operation. And not only that, he spent most of his time kneeling in the church!"

For twenty-one years (the same amount of time that Fr. George spent in Romanian prisons) the West was given the great Christian witness of Fr. George Calciu. One of his parishioners said, "I was shocked by his love and said to myself, 'Here is a true Christian; this is the True Faith,' and any doubts I had about Orthodoxy were dissolved."

Fr. George's final call to suffering came in the spring of 2006 when he was diagnosed with pancreatic cancer. For the next six months he kept this a secret from the public, except for his attending physician and spiritual daughter, Dr. Maria Rosana Stoica. He had wanted everyone to remember him as a strong servant of God. And indeed his condition remained unknown to all his parishioners. Dr. Stoica recalled: "He demonstrated incredible endurance, even when celebrating the long Paschal service—despite excruciating pain."

Fr. George was unwilling to undergo surgery, but he had agreed to initiate a course of chemotherapy with the approval of the Church hierarchy. However, when the time drew near to begin the procedure, Fr. George conceived of a different plan. During one of Dr. Stoica's visits to discuss the treatment and its side effects, Fr. George lay down on his favorite couch. "Father placed my hand on his chest, looked me straight in the eye—with his beautiful blue eyes now yellowed by his last trials—and with a very paternal voice he told me, 'Maria Rosana, I love you very much, just like a daughter—however, I do have to go and say good-bye to my people in Romania.' I asked him if he knew that in his condition there were many risks associated with this decision. Father acknowledged the risk and proceeded to say,

THE LAST YEARS AND REPOSE OF FR. GEORGE

Fr. George during his last visit to Romania, with Abbot Justin of Petru Voda Archangels Monastery, October 2006.

'I have lived a long life. I have fought many battles—my time has come. People like you—and so many others that God has brought to the Church—have been sent to help me through this difficult trial.'"

On September 25, 2006, Fr. George flew to Romania for what he knew would be his last trip to his beloved country. While there, he visited all his dearest friends throughout the country and especially those in the monasteries. One of his spiritual sons remarked upon seeing pictures of Fr. George during his stay in Romania that they "looked unlike any I had seen of him before: he seemed to be between heaven and earth, his face had a tired, pained, but unearthly glow to it."

Dr. Stoica also traveled to Romania to monitor Fr. George's health and administer pain medication during the first portion of his trip. At a certain point she was forced to return to her work in the Unite States. It would be the last time that she would see Fr. George with all his powers.

Under a heavy schedule, Fr. George's body was overcome by exhaustion and by the natural effects of the growing cancer. One day, toward the end of October, he suddenly collapsed and was taken to the emergency room. The doctors soon discovered that he had not been able to digest food for the previous three days.

When news of Fr. George's hospitalization became public, a flood of people came to visit him, sensing that this would be their last opportunity. Among his visitors were the president of Romania, the patriarch of Romania, and many of the holy elders who had co-suffered with him in prison. So many people came that the hospital officials had to install two guards by his hospital door, as he was not getting any rest. Part of the "problem" was Fr. George himself, who was overjoyed to see all of the visitors. Despite being close to death, he was in very good spirits, joking and conversing with everyone who came to see him.

Dr. Stoica stayed in constant communication with the Bucharest hospital staff, exchanging medical records and offering her advice. Fr. George's son, Andrei, was in Romania at that time and acted as translator over the phone. Unfortunately, the doctors in Romania decided to perform an operation that proved unnecessary and greatly prolonged his stay in the hospital. Thus, Fr. George lost some of his last vital days before the cancer spread to his liver.

Arrangements were made for Fr. George to fly back to the United States. All the logistics were in place, including an attending doctor for the flight, but Fr. George remained hospitalized with no reports of his progress filtering home. After twenty-six days had passed, Dr. Stoica made the decision to fly to Bucharest. Before she could do so, Fr. George's release form was signed.

On November 16, 2006, when Dr. Stoica finally greeted Fr. George at the door of the Inova Fairfax Hospital in Virginia, she found that he had been reduced to an emaciated version of himself. Still, his clear blue eyes peered out from his failing

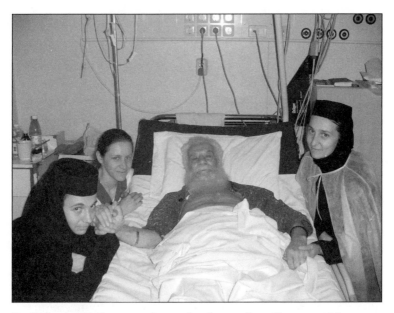

Fr. George in the Romanian hospital with nuns from Diaconesti Monastery. They stayed by his bed until he was flown back to the United States.

body, and extending a frail hand, he whispered, "My daughter, I am back!"

That night, an entire battery of tests and scans were performed on Fr. George. The oncologist confirmed everyone's worst fear: the cancer had spread to Fr. George's liver, and no further treatment was possible. Seeking second, third, and fourth opinions, Dr. Stoica consulted with five doctors in the hope that some treatment might be found. Exhausting all her hopes, she realized that "God had His own plans for Father."

At that point Dr. Stoica took an icon of the Theotokos from her purse and placed it on a stand next to Fr. George's bed. According to Dr. Stoica, "Father saw it, and asked me to give it to him. He kissed the icon with such tenderness, as if he were saying, 'I'm coming.'" During his first days at the hospital, visitors were not permitted, but Dr. Stoica remained by his side without sleep for the whole of his hospitalization. Fr. George shared with her stories from his life and his thankfulness to God for his sufferings in prison, which had helped him become the person he was that day.

On Sunday, November 19, Fr. George received the Holy Mysteries for the last time in his earthly life. Fr. Claudiu Lutai heard Fr. George's Confession, communed him of the Holy Gifts, and performed the Holy Unction service. It had now become clear that Fr. George would soon repose, and a steady stream of visitors entered his hospital room, a few at a time, to receive a blessing and bid their beloved pastor farewell. One of his parishioners remembered: "Fr. George had prepared me for his repose, a year before, when he was going to have risky heart surgery. He had instructed me that if he were to repose, I was not to cry. He asked me on another occasion, at the funeral of a dear friend of ours, 'Are you sad?' I said, 'Yes.' He told me, 'Don't be sad: that is from the devil. The Christian always has hope that the person will be saved.' With this in mind, I was able to have a sense of joy as I entered the ninth floor of the hospital. When it came time for me to enter the room, I went over to Father's bed, got his blessing and he told me several times what he always told me, 'I love you.'"

Another parishioner present that night related: "I arrived just after Fr. George stopped receiving visitors (he needed to sleep) on that Sunday evening at the Inova Fairfax Hospital. I didn't have the chance to talk with him, and only saw him with his eyes open once more after that. Even though his gaze was turned away from where I was standing, towards his wife, Preoteasa Adriana, I did perceive a deep peace in his eyes, and also a sorrowful compassion—I felt that he was looking with pity on her and all of us, knowing how we would miss him. Although we would gain an intercessor in the heavens, we were losing a true friend in the flesh. Fr. George seemed to be more concerned about the sorrow of those closest to him (like our Lord on the Cross who cared for his dearest friend, St.

John the Theologian, and his Mother the Theotokos) than about his own sufferings. He had sacrificed a lot to come back for those few days, which must have been physically painful for him, but which was emotionally and spiritually healing for us."

Outside the room many of Fr. George's spiritual children were gathered, praying and singing Canons and Akathists to the saints and the Theotokos. The crowd became so great that by 6:00 PM the hospital staff was forced to call the police, who sent everyone downstairs. Only the clergy, the Psalter-readers, Dr. Stoica, and the guard at the door (one of Fr. George's parishioners) were allowed to remain. Fr. George called for a deacon who was present, and everyone thought that he would repose at any moment.

At around 9:00 PM, the deacon had to leave for the night. Before he departed he told the people assembled outside the room that while he was in the room, he saw Fr. George's face glowing "like on the icons." In all, three people related seeing Fr. George in Uncreated Light during his final days.

After the deacon left, the Psalter continued to be read in Romanian and English. Fr. George was sleeping and no one knew if he would awaken again. A little later a local Romanian priest served a Paraklesis [Supplicatory Canon]. By 10:00 PM the chanters from Fr. George's parish had sneaked back into the room. There were now seven singers there, including a master of Byzantine chant. With an angelic voice he began to intone Psalm 1, "Blessed is the Man," in Romanian. One witness recorded:

"Something then happened that I will not be able to adequately describe to you because I had never seen anything like it before and probably never will again. When we came to the refrain 'Alleluia,' Father's hand, though he was sleeping as far as I could tell, started to make the sign of the Cross over himself. However, this was the most awkward sign of the Cross that I had ever seen him make. It looked completely uncoordinated and involuntary.... People started weeping. We had not been sure if Father would even awaken again and now his body was making the sign of the Cross in response to the prayers that were being deeply offered to God.

"As we continued the hymn, Fr. George started to make the sign of the Cross more deliberately at each 'Alleluia.' Then he woke up and looked at us very deeply with otherworldly eyes. I cannot tell you how poor my words are right now to describe what we experienced. Those eyes, which had many times seen the Uncreated Light of Christ our God and whose gaze of love was able to melt right into you, were now looking for the last time upon so many that he loved with all his heart and all his blood. He looked at us, in pain, but with deep joy and gratitude as we chanted his favorite hymns in Romanian. In between hymns he would start to speak in Romanian, and the depth with which he spoke is something I am unworthy to communicate. He would say only simple words: 'Praise the Lord for everything,' or 'Everything is from God.'"

After they finished chanting, the Akathist to Great-martyr George was read, during which Fr. George remained awake. Shortly after the completion of the Akathist, Fr. George again fell asleep sometime around 11:00 PM.

At 4:00 AM the next morning, His Grace Irineu, Bishop of Dearborn Heights and Auxiliary Bishop of the Romanian Orthodox Episcopate of America (OCA), arrived from Michigan and went into Fr. George's room. Fr. George had a great love for this hierarch, who had been an abbot in Romania before being consecrated a bishop in America. The bishop spoke with Fr. George privately and heard his Confession. Afterward, the other visitors were allowed back in and the bishop read the prayer of forgiveness over Fr. George. He appeared to be sleeping as the bishop read the prayers "If he has been under the ban of a priest, under excommunication, under a curse ..." And truly some of these things had happened to Fr. George when he stood up against the Communist regime in Romania. When the bishop finished the prayer, Fr. George suddenly rose from his slumber

THE LAST YEARS AND REPOSE OF FR. GEORGE

and, in a loud voice, exclaimed in Romanian: "AMEN! LORD, HAVE MERCY!" With that Fr. George once again fell asleep.

It appeared that Fr. George would not repose immediately; he seemed to be holding on, waiting for something. Dr. Stoica continued to hold a vigil by his bedside. The hospital nurses acted as a legion of angels, coordinating with Dr. Stoica, responding to every request, and being completely tolerant of the large crowd coming through the oncology ward every day.

On Monday, November 20, Fr. George was assaulted with a new temptation. In his last testament, which he had written in the Romanian hospital before his return to America, he expressed the desire to be buried in Romania at the Petru Voda Archangels Monastery,[2] where Fr. George's friend and co-sufferer in Communist prisons Fr. Justin (Parvu) is the abbot. That afternoon, His Eminence Daniel,[3] Metropolitan of Moldavia and Bucovina, who has jurisdiction over Petru Voda, communicated the decision that he would not permit Fr. George to be buried at Petru Voda. Bishop Irineu went to Fr. George to tell him of the metropolitan's decision and to discuss options for his burial. Fr. George's only response to this new turn of events was "May God forgive them all." The situation was eventually rectified when Patriarch Teoctist stepped in to permit Fr. George's burial at Petru Voda.

Later that evening, Fr. George's parishioners and spiritual children once again held vigil around the bed of their beloved pastor. One of the evening's visitors remembers: "That evening, I was blessed by Christ to spend several hours with Father in his room—kissing his hand, looking into his face, and being with

---

[2] Petru Voda Monastery was established in 1992 and dedicated to the prison-martyrs of the Communist regime. It is now a thriving monastery with approximately seventy monks and is a pilgrimage site for the faithful from all over Romania.—ED.

[3] On September 12, 2007, not long after the death of Patriarch Teoctist, Metropolitan Daniel was elected Patriarch of the Romanian Orthodox Church.—ED.

those who loved him so much. The love in that room was so deep and heavenly that it brings joyful tears to my eyes. Father at this point was looking rather peaceful.... At one point, his skin needed to be rubbed down to stay moist, and they asked me to do this. I remember how warm his flesh was. Then Dr. Stoica told me something that blew my mind. She said that since the previous night, his blood cell count had dropped below what a dead person's would be. He should have been dead but he was very much alive. What a sight to behold, a man in Christ stronger than death!"

Tuesday morning dawned. It was November 21, the feast of the Entry of the Theotokos into the Temple (new style). It became clear that Fr. George had been holding on for this feast of the Mother of God. Preoteasa Adriana, Fr. George's son, Andrei, and his family, along with a few other spiritual children, were gathered around his bed. Around 1:10 PM, just as Liturgy was finishing at his church, Fr. George gave his last breath. As Elder Justin of Petru Voda expressed at his funeral, Fr. George finally gave up his spirit to the angels and was carried by the Mother of our Lord in the sweetest embrace of her arms into the heavenly temple of the Savior.

Immediately after Fr. George's repose, Dr. Stoica walked outside the room and collapsed asleep in a chair—it was her first sleep in six days. A few moments later she had a vision of Fr. George walking out of the room vested in a radiant light that allowed her only to see his face. He told her to wake up because he had to go. Just then she felt the hands of the nurse shaking her, telling her that it was time to prepare Fr. George's body for the mortuary.

Three days later, on Friday, an All-night Vigil was served in the Holy Cross Church in Alexandria, Virginia. Bishop Irineu served the Vigil, assisted by twelve priests. In the center of the church was Fr. George's open coffin. The next morning, November 25, His Eminence Nathaniel, Archbishop of Detroit and the

THE LAST YEARS AND REPOSE OF FR. GEORGE

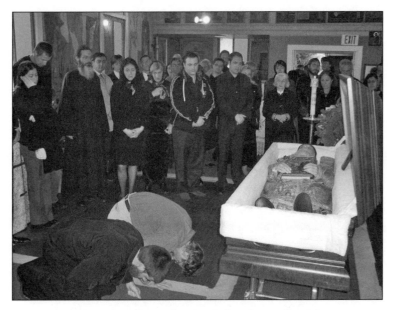

Mourners in front of Fr. George's casket at the Holy
Cross Church in Alexandria, Virginia.

Romanian Orthodox Episcopate of America, served Fr. George's funeral, assisted by the above-mentioned clergy. The funeral was served outside to accommodate the hundreds of the faithful who came to bid farewell to their pastor and spiritual father. After the service, Fr. George's final words to his flock were read aloud: "Love one another as Jesus loved us, so that it will be revealed that we are sons of Jesus Christ our Savior. Sacrifice yourselves! Pray and be merciful to those in need! May the blessing of our Lord Jesus Christ, the love of God the Father, and the communion of the Holy Spirit be upon all of you. Amen."

Fr. George's body was then sent to Romania. It arrived on November 30, the feast of the Apostle Andrew (new style)— one of Fr. George's favorite feasts—and was taken to the Radu Voda Church at the Bucharest Seminary, where Fr. George had taught and served until his arrest in the late 1970s. On Saturday,

Petru Voda Monastery on the day of Fr. George's funeral.

Fr. George's funeral procession at Petru Voda Monastery.

December 2, Patriarch Teoctist served a second funeral for Fr. George, attended by almost a thousand people.

After the funeral, Fr. George's body was taken on its final voyage to Petru Voda Archangels Monastery. That night, hundreds of people began arriving at the monastery during the All-night Vigil. By the following morning the crowd had grown to between fifteen hundred and two thousand people. Following the Divine Liturgy, a third funeral was served by Abbot Justin and thirty-three other priests. Many clergy and monastics, especially from northern Moldavia, came to bid farewell and give the final kiss to their beloved confessor of the Faith.

As he lay in an open coffin, Fr. George's face bore no marks of the pain and torture he had suffered during his imprisonment. Rather, he appeared to be merely in a peaceful slumber. On his chest lay a carved icon of the Mother of God, a gift of Patriarch Teoctist. In his right hand Fr. George held a cross and a prayer rope given by the nuns of Diaconesti Monastery.

According to Fr. George's wishes, he was buried at a double grave site, the second space being reserved for his beloved wife, Adriana, when she passes on to eternity. In his testament he wrote: "As I lived in life, so I will also be in death with my wife, Adriana."

Today the world grieves over having lost a righteous one from our midst, but rejoices that a new saint has joined God's choir of the elect. In Fr. Justin's funeral address, he urged the mourners not to sorrow: "The Church and our Romanian nation have today lost one of the most powerful consciences, an eternal living icon of an apostle, a great voice in the wilderness of indifference and compromise. After a life of martyrdom for God and his nation, Fr. Calciu has entered into the world of the saints. We have in heaven a father protector. Christ grant you rest in the Paradise of the living, Fr. Calciu."

Fr. George with children from the Holy Cross Church, Alexandria, Virginia.

PART TWO

AN INTERVIEW WITH FR. GEORGE

Fr. George with the interviewer, Nun Nina, in 1996.

INTRODUCTION TO THE INTERVIEW

by Nun Nina

I FIRST READ Fr. George Calciu's sermons in *The Orthodox Word*. Fr. Seraphim Rose, the co-founder of our St. Herman of Alaska Brotherhood, was deeply moved by the boldness and courage of Fr. George. Besides publishing his sermons, he spoke about him with great fervor in his lecture, "Living the Orthodox Worldview."[1] This was to be the last pastoral lecture of Fr. Seraphim's life. He ended his talk by quoting the powerful words of Fr. Calciu, and within three weeks he reposed.

Ever since reading Fr. Calciu's sermons, I had a prayer in my heart to meet him. So, in the summer of 1996 I heard that he was going to be at the dedication of a new church in Hayward, California, and God gave me the opportunity I had prayed for. I really did not know much about him, except that he was a confessor of Christ and had spent some years in prison for his witness of the Christian Faith. I had no idea that his years in prison totaled almost twenty-two years!

Fr. Calciu is short in stature, now in his early seventies. He greeted me with warmth and love. I could see the fire of his zeal and love for Christ in his smiling and sparkling eyes. I asked him if he had written an autobiography or if anyone had recorded his experiences. When he said no, a desperate sense of loss seized me. I knew in my heart that his life was one that must be made

---

[1] Fr. Seraphim Rose, *Living the Orthodox Worldview* (Platina, Calif: St. Herman of Alaska Brotherhood, 2007), compact disc.

known, especially to the youth of today. I let my strong feelings be known. Then, in October 1996, I received a telephone call from Fr. Calciu's friend, Mr. Nicolae Popa, who informed me that Fr. Calciu was coming to California for a visit and who invited me to his home to conduct an interview.

When I began the interview, I had no idea what depths of agony and suffering Fr. Calciu had reached. I did not know that he had passed through the diabolic experiment at Pitesti Prison, which attempted to eradicate from the human soul any trace of love, devotion, integrity, virtue, and goodness. As the interview progressed, my love and respect for him increased.

Fr. Calciu did not merely report to me cold facts of the past, but, rather, with such humility and ever so nobly, he opened his soul to me. The most intense part was when he told me how he was able to survive another moment, another day, of the hellish torture and deep despair in Pitesti by saying, "God, forgive me!" I could see that those feelings were being relived in his soul by the tears that flowed down his cheeks. He was willing for our sakes to go through it again. I am deeply grateful to him.

May Fr. George's example inspire us to be fearless confessors of Christ and to reach out with all our strength to the lost souls who, if only they knew the reality of Jesus Christ and His Kingdom, would also follow Him. Amen.

Nun Nina
April 23/May 6, 1997

AN INTERVIEW WITH FR. GEORGE

*This interview was conducted and recorded by Nun Nina on November 6, 1996, in Los Angeles, California.—*Ed.

1. Youth

I WAS BORN INTO a peasant family, a family of farmers. There were eleven children, and I was the youngest. My mother was very pious. She was an ordinary woman, without many years of education—only four years of elementary classes; but she possessed an extraordinary wisdom and knowledge of the Divine truth. We went to a church that was small. There were thirteen of us, including my father and mother. We children were very little, and it was very difficult for us to stand for two to three hours in church, so we tried to move around. There were no chairs or pews in church. After church, when we came back home, Mother used to say to us, "Don't you know that this is your prayer to God, just standing there until your feet hurt? This is a child's prayer to God."

I would like to tell you a story: There was a tavern in a village, and the men were in the tavern drinking and speaking evil against God. In every tavern there is only one devil, just one demon. This demon was sitting there on the counter, not needing to do anything because the men were doing all base deeds. On the other side of the village was a house where a widow lived with seven children, who prayed every night before going to sleep. This house was surrounded by an army of devils. So, where God is powerfully present in people's hearts, there the attack of Satan is greater. But if you do not have God, the devil knows that you belong to him and he has no interest in you anymore.

This is how we grew up in our family. Among all eleven children, I was the only one who went to school. The rest remained in the village as farmers. I never forgot my faith which my mother put into my heart. When we came back for the holidays, we would always go to church together and sing in the choir. The peasant tradition was very powerful and healthy. Communism had not yet come to distort all these things.

Then I went to medical school, where I studied for two years. I belonged to the group of Christian students who went to gatherings and lectures of the "Burning Bush." This was in Bucharest. When the Communists started to replace religion in schools with Marxist philosophy, we were even forced to study it in medical school, and I became one of the people who protested. Therefore, I was arrested and sentenced to prison.

I was sentenced in 1948. Communism took over in 1944.

Mother Nina: So, it took four years before they started sending everyone to prison?

Yes, because the opposition was still very strong. In 1947, the king was obliged to leave Romania, and the Communists took over everything. They began to create the same situation that was in Russia. The majority of the political councillors and Securitate were Russian. They had come from Russia to transmit their experience to the young Romanian Communists.

2. Pitesti Prison

After entering prison I experienced great difficulties, but I kept my hearty faith untouched until I came to Pitesti Prison. All the students ended up there. There in Pitesti I went through very difficult situations. I think you have heard about what went on in Pitesti. It was an experiment, a diabolical experiment.

AN INTERVIEW WITH FR. GEORGE

Fr. George (on far left) with family members, in the early 1970s.

Namely, some prisoners with sadistic behavior were selected from among us. They were defectors from the Communist Party or Communist Youth Union who had joined the Peasant Party or the Iron Guard Legion, but had now become Communists again. Nevertheless, the Party did not forgive them. They arrested them and put them into prison and instructed them to become our interrogators. So, you were no longer summoned to an office to be beaten and interrogated, afterwards returning to your cell for some peace; now these people were permanently with us—twenty-four hours a day they were with us. This experience altered our souls and hearts, and little by little, one by one, we fell. Namely, we came to deny God and to sever ourselves from our families. We came to forget all that was good in our hearts. Fortunately, this experiment lasted only about three years.

How could you have possibly survived this experience without betraying God or your brother?

The majority of us betrayed God and father and mother

and everything. But in time, this satanic experience came to an end. We went into normal prisons, and there we met the priests, because after this they started to arrest the priests.

So you weren't a priest yet?

No, I was a medical student. The priests came then, and they were better prepared for suffering than we were. I was only twenty-two years old. There were students in high school fifteen years old, fourteen years old. I later met a young student in Jilava Prison who was only twelve years old.

Now, the priests were better prepared than we were. They knew what suffering was. They were prepared for it. They came with consolation for our hearts; they came with forgiveness. They brought forgiveness for us, so to speak. And in this way, little by little, our hearts healed and our souls and our faith came back to us. Eventually we were stronger than before. This experience badly hurt our hearts, but in the end when we came back to God, we were stronger. I decided to dedicate to God the remaining years of my life and to become a priest, because when those priests came into the prison, they had comforted us, forgiven us, and confessed us. Some had with them Holy Communion secretly sewn into the pleats of their garment. They were prepared for this and gave us a crumb of Holy Communion. It was then when I understood the words of our Savior: *Ye are the salt of the earth.... Ye are the light of the world* ... (Matt. 5:13–14). Because, really, these priests were the salt of the earth, the light of the world.

3. THE THEOLOGICAL INSTITUTE

I married in 1965 and taught French to elementary school children. I went to the patriarch, Justinian Marina, and told him everything I had to tell him, and he answered, "Good." He gave me a note (a letter) to the Theological Institute stating that I had already graduated from the university and therefore it was

George and Adriana Calciu
with their son, Andrei.

not necessary for me to go to seminary. He gave me this note so that I could be admitted to the school, without being obligated to attend all the classes. I was to come when I could because I was also a teacher. He did not report that I was attending this school. He was required to report to the Department of Cults, a Communist department controlling every theology student, every priest, and every church. There was no freedom; everything was strictly controlled. But he did not report to the Department of Cults that I was a student in theology.

So I was like an underground student—I studied theology underground. Patriarch Justinian was amazing. He died in 1977. The patriarch in 1948 was Nicodemus, followed by Justinian, then Justin Moisescu, and then the present patriarch.[1] But Justinian was amazing. In the beginning he was not so sure about his path. But later he was very strong in his stand against the political

---

[1] In 1996 this was Patriarch Teoctist (1986–2007).—ED.

administration—very strong.² And he helped us—the people, the priests who had been in prison and were now coming out of it. He helped us very much. He made it possible for some of us to study theology.³

I studied theology for four years. In the fourth year, when I was finishing and preparing my thesis for my diploma, the Securitate discovered that I was a student, and they kicked me

---

² Fr. George later noted: "When the Gheorghiu-Dej regime decided to oust the monks and nuns under the age of forty from the monasteries, Patriarch Justinian was the only bishop not to apply the decree in his diocese (only the monasteries in Ungro-Vlachia were under his jurisdiction).

"When I was a professor at the Orthodox seminary, I visited the monastery of Pasarea, in the neighborhood of Bucharest. I had some twenty students with me. The monastery had many nuns, it was looking very prosperous, and I asked the abbess for some explanation of this. She told me that they had no problem with the Gheorghiu-Dej decree. When the decree was issued, Patriarch Justinian went from monastery to monastery, accompanied by the chief of the Department of Cults, some members of the Political Bureau and other officials. The abbess told me that the nuns were very afraid; they knew that, in other monasteries in Romania, the Securitate obliged the nuns and monks to leave the monasteries. Many of them found refuge in the forest, but in wintertime they had to come back during the night. The Securitate would be waiting to arrest them and send them to different factories to work for the 'glorious future of humanity': Communism. With the arrival at Pasarea of the patriarch, the nuns assumed that their time was at hand.

"The patriarch, however, when he told them about the governmental decree, added: 'I do not believe that any of you want to leave the monastery and go into the world. I do not believe that any of you came here because of some delusion or for any other reason than faith. I assure you that no one can force you to leave the monastery against your will. I am here to tell you this and to beseech you to believe what I say.' The abbess told us that the patriarch cried when he told them this. In His Holiness' monasteries, no one was obliged to go into the world."—ED.

³ Fr. George: "When I left prison and desired to fulfill the promise I made to God to become His servant, Patriarch Justinian helped me very much. He accepted me as a regular student. From the autobiography I wrote for my application, he told me to take out the section in which I said I had been imprisoned; and so I was accepted into the school of theology."—ED.

AN INTERVIEW WITH FR. GEORGE

Fr. George teaching French after his release from prison.

out of the school because I was not allowed to be a teacher.[4] But Patriarch Justinian Marina appointed me as professor of French and the New Testament at the seminary. I started this work, being in close contact with the young students. I realized how confused they were. They didn't know anything, because

---

[4] Fr. George: "Patriarch Justinian was in Belgium at the time, and the Department of Cults took advantage of the situation. There were a dozen other students who shared a similar fate. Upon his return, the patriarch was upset by what had happened and did everything he could to resolve the problem. He succeeded in obtaining permission for us to graduate.

"After that, the Securitate forced the minister of education to expel me from my position. (I was teaching French in a public school.) The patriarch then appointed me as a teacher of French in the Orthodox seminary in Bucharest, saving me and my family from poverty. Likewise, after the general amnesty of 1964, all the priests who had been in prison were appointed to similar or better positions by Patriarch Justinian. By doing this, great professors, such as Fr. Dumitru Staniloae, entered the theological school, teaching and forming a new generation of priests and monks."—Ed.

Patriarch Justinian ordaining Fr. George in 1972.

the Communists had instituted Marxist classes even at the Theological Institute and seminary, and the young people were so puzzled that they did not know where to go! They came with very pure souls from their parents—in other words, they were formed in a simple faith as I was myself at that age. But at school they came in contact with things that were not Christian at all, from the interference of the Securitate. The Securitate was always present in the schools.

I became very close to the students. I talked with them; I shared with them my experience in prison, yet I did not share too much because I did not want to. I knew that every step I took was watched. I would speak to them especially about my spiritual experiences, not about the torture—not those things—but about how we were converted in prison, how those who were not believers converted to the Faith, and how strong we were through faith. We had nothing and we could have been killed in a twinkling of an eye, but God saved each of us and gave us the opportunity to accomplish what we had promised Him.

I taught French and the New Testament, and slowly a group of young students formed around me with whom I created a prayer group. We had a beautiful church. Radu Voda is the name. In the evenings we would go there and pray. We read the Holy Scriptures, and if God gave the word to anybody to speak, we spoke. If not, we prayed, meditated, and departed without saying anything. I was their spiritual father in the shadows, behind the scenes. That is, I allowed the students to decide themselves if they would speak—if God gave them the word to speak. The same applied to me—if God gave me the word to speak, I would speak, but not everything was clear to me. The Securitate would come and take some boys and threaten them and question them about what we discussed there. When we prayed in the evenings we would not turn on the lights—we would use candles. There was a very profound atmosphere of prayer. It was like that from 1972 to 1977. The group grew to over one hundred young people. Many friends of the theology students came from the university—engineering students, philosophy students—they came from everywhere and we prayed together. It was spreading, and this growth of faith alarmed the Securitate even more. They started to demand the cessation of prayers. They forbade us to use the church and ordered us to pray in the hall, but we continued. This continued until Ceausescu began to destroy the churches.

Then Ceausescu demolished the first church, Enea Church, a very old church from the fourteenth century. It was a historical church and the church of the university. It was the church for the students. It reminded the people of God, and the students attended it, which is why he destroyed it.

4. The "Seven Homilies to the Youth"

When I saw that the youth were very, very confused, I decided to deliver some sermons addressed to them. Many of them wanted to know about the Church, about Christ, about the Faith. Some had religious education from their families, but they had lost it in the university and in high school. Yet the remembrance of their first education was still in their minds and hearts. I decided to address special sermons to them.

It was during Lent. I began delivering sermons every Wednesday at seven o'clock in the evening. It was very interesting. On Tuesday I had no idea what I was going to say to the students.

But every time—during the day or the night before—God would put something into my mind. Thus, I gave seven sermons during the seven weeks of the Fast: a sermon every week. Because I knew there were Securitate agents present, I would not just speak, but I would write my sermons down and give copies of them to my students. For I knew that there would be a time when I would be arrested and judged, and they would say that I said more than I actually did. What I said in those sermons was very well said; I spoke against Communism. I declared Communism, together with Marxism and materialism, to be a religion, a philosophy of hopelessness, because a regime that demolishes churches to build taverns is a regime that has lost the notion of its true mission. I actually attacked like that. I asked God and prayed beforehand, together with my students, that God would give me the word to speak each of these seven weeks. And God gave me the word. God gave me the words, the ideas, the inspiration of the Holy Spirit, Who told me what to say. More students started to come. This was in the Brincoveanu Church.

During this time, the Department of State and the Securitate, as well as my hierarchs, all called me to judgment and told me to stop. I said, "I cannot stop because ... who should I obey? Men or God? God says that I should speak, and this is the mission of the Church." After four weeks, the church was locked, so I spoke in the courtyard of the church. In the fifth week they closed the gates. The seminary was surrounded by a very high wall. They locked the gates and put guards around, but the students climbed over the walls.

How many were there?

Three hundred, four hundred, five hundred, sometimes. They [the authorities] were very scared by them.

I was standing alone against the Securitate!

No one stood with you?

No one! Not one of the professors. They were very scared. I was judged in the council of the professors. The representative of the Department of Cults, the bishop, and the director of the seminary, asked the professors to kick me out of the seminary. One of the professors (he was not a priest—the priests said nothing) said, "We cannot see Fr. Calciu leave. If you want to put him out the door you can do it, but do not oblige us to do it." So God protected me, and they did not kick me out.

5. Persecutions

After the seven weeks, when I had finished, the Paschal holidays began. During this holiday period, I received threatening telephone calls and letters from Securitate agents saying they would kill me and my child. My child was twelve years old at that time. When he went to school he was watched by the Securitate, and when he came home he was also watched. It was the same for my wife. They threatened to kill my son and my wife and to put me in prison; they said they would burn me on the street, trying in any way to scare me. So, after Pascha, when we started school again, I announced to the students that I would deliver one more sermon. God had already given me the opportunity to deliver seven sermons; now I wanted to begin a new series in order to explain what had happened to me during the holiday period. So, after Pascha I intended to begin this new series entitled "The Culture and Christianity." However, it was clear that God was saying to me, "You asked for seven sermons, seven weeks, and I gave this to you. There is no need to explain and defend yourself. These sermons were not for the purpose of

Fr. George at the time of his second arrest, in 1979.

defending yourself, but to bring My word to the students and to worship God."

And on the day when I was to deliver the eighth sermon, I was expelled from the seminary and the church. This is how I began my civilian life. I could no longer wear priestly clothing; I could not serve.

How did your wife feel about all this during this time? Did she support you?

She was with me all the time.

When no one would stand with you, she was right there?

Yes, absolutely!

Did she tell you to go out there and preach?

Yes, she was very courageous. I was not the one answering the provocations—she was. She would say, "Let us alone. He did nothing wrong. He just preached the word of God because he is a priest."

This was in the month of May. During the period from May until January, I was constantly under persecution and receiving threats. I was not allowed to go to church. When I went there, the priests were so scared that they avoided me, they did not speak to me. The priests were very scared when I entered the church because there would be seven or eight agents of the Securitate with me. The priests were absolutely scared. They hadn't the courage to say a single word to me or to invite me into the altar to take Communion. Only one priest invited me in every time. I avoided going to the same church all the time because it could cause trouble for that church. Every Sunday I would go to a different church. But one priest from Bucharest accepted me into the altar. He would say, "Father, come into the altar," and he would allow me to receive Communion—not to serve, only to receive. This was a big consolation for me.

6. The Second Prison Term

In March I was arrested. I was arrested and accused of being an agent of a foreign country—America, of course. I knew no one from America and had no connections with Americans. They accused me of giving information regarding the security of the state. They sentenced me under an article for capital punishment because when I was delivering my sermons, other people would attend besides. These people had recorded my sermons, and the first cassette reached Jerusalem. From Jerusalem it was disseminated throughout the world. In Germany my "Seven Homilies to the Youth" were printed.

So this is how I became renowned. Religious associations (Catholic, Orthodox, Protestant) all defended me. This scared the judge, so he changed my sentence from the death penalty to ten years in prison. During the time I was in prison, I did not see my wife and child. Only when some important personage from Europe or America, like Bush or Giscard d'Estaing, visited our country was I allowed to see my wife. Usually I was brought from prison to the Securitate headquarters, where I would meet her.

What year did you go into prison?

In 1979. In prison I had many experiences. Ceausescu was very angry with me. I never spoke against him, I never even pronounced his name. I was speaking out against the regime, against the terror and against the forbidding of knowledge to young people. I told the youth: "You are young people gifted by God with wisdom and you have the right to know. You have the right to know about materialism, but also to know Christianity. And you have the right to make a choice. As long as you know only what the government is offering you, you are not free; you are slaves. And spiritual slavery is worse than material slavery. The slavery of ideas is worse than the slavery of the body. No government has a right to institute this slavery of ideas, of faith. Knowing nothing other than Communism and materialism, you have no option. You are not free. You have no responsibility. You are like slaves, like animals. By knowing the good and the bad and making a decision, a choice, you become responsible for your choice. You become like God. This is what it is to be like Christ—to know what is good and what is bad and to make a decision for the good." I talked to them [the students] about love, dignity, the Church, friendship, faith, the Last Judgment.

When I was in prison, Ceausescu was very angry with me, and he wanted to kill me in prison. He could not sentence me to death because my case was known all over the world, so he ordered that I be put in a cell with sadistic criminals. Therefore, I was put in a cell with two sadistic criminals. One of them killed his own mother. He did not just kill her; he tortured her—days and days, cutting her fingers and her body. The other one killed two young men in the same sadistic manner. I was forced to work with them in the cell. I had refused to work—I had told the director of the prison that I refused to work for a government that kills the people, that persecutes the people, that destroys the souls of human beings. I told him, "I do not want to work for you, the prison. I want to work for Jesus Christ. I am ready to preach but not to work for your progress." So the director told these men to force me to work. If I refused, they had the right to kill me. Right away they began to persecute me, but not so badly. There was something human in them, you know. I noticed that all these people without anything in their soul—criminals and thieves and so on—they had something very, very dear and even very holy in them. The majority of them had a mother they loved, a wife or a child, so they were not completely lost. They had something very sensible. I noticed this and tried to reach them through this. I began to tell them about love, about Jesus Christ; to tell them that Jesus Christ loved them. At first they laughed. "How can Jesus Christ love me? I killed my mother! I killed two young men. How can He even allow me to live?" I said, "He can! And He really loves you." Then I began to talk to them.

Before I was arrested, I had learned the Holy Liturgy by heart, because I knew that I would be arrested. It was very difficult for me not to be able to celebrate at least once a week, so I learned everything by heart. I was prepared for death, and I knew that I had to be tortured before I would be killed. Every Sunday I recited the Holy Liturgy. In the beginning I recited the Holy Liturgy mentally, just sitting. But later when I was alone in prison, I actually celebrated the Holy Liturgy. I said to myself that if I have only the bread and not the wine—because Jesus Christ transformed the water into wine—I cannot stop reciting the Liturgy because I have only the bread. So I really celebrated the Liturgy. I remembered that during persecution, the tombs of the martyrs were the altars in the early catacombs. I had no tomb there, but I said to myself, "I, myself, am a martyr because I am suffering for Jesus Christ. The first time I entered prison I was not a priest. But now I am a priest. I have a duty to celebrate the Holy Liturgy." After I came out of prison, some priests disagreed with me about this. But many of them agreed with me that my Liturgy was a true Liturgy. I am convinced because, I tell you, something happened.

7. Transformations in Christ

Every day these two men were called by the administration. I think they were scolded because they did nothing to me. They were working. I was not working; I was praying all the time. I think that they asked them to kill me. One day, after three months, they were called again to the administration. They were very upset when they came back. Two times a week we were allowed to go outside into a small courtyard, smaller than this room, fifteen by twenty feet. We went outside and they said to me, "Stay there." They went into the other corner and they talked together. I was sure it was time for me to be killed. I stood there facing the wall. I was praying, making my confession to God for my sins. After ten minutes—we had only ten minutes to walk—they came to me and said, "Father"—this was the first time that they called me Father—"Father, we decided not to kill you. Let the guards kill you." I started to cry. I had thought for sure I was going to die. We came into the cell and now we talked together. I told them about myself and everything. They told me about their experience, and that they now noticed that I was a good man. The next day I got their permission to celebrate the Holy Liturgy there. They stopped working; they refused to work.

This wasn't the first time you had served, was it?

No. But living with them, I was not allowed by them to serve the Holy Liturgy. Now, after a three-month interruption, I began to serve again. Sure, perhaps it was because they were never in a church before, or because what happens in the altar was mysterious for people, but they were behind me when I started to do the prayers, reciting all the prayers in a low voice. The guards would come and look in at us. I forgot where I was, but sometimes, you know, the priest has to turn around and say, "Peace be unto you." When I turned to them, they were kneeling! They were praying with me! I was so happy. From then on, we were really brothers. All three of us. One of them killed his mother; the other killed two boys. Really, it was for them faith and love.[5] After a few weeks we were separated. Then my new life began.

They isolated me in a special cell. I got a piece of bread in the morning, and on the third day I got some other food, in solitary confinement.

How long were you in solitary confinement?

Seven months. I began to forget my Romanian. Every third day I had no bread. But from one day to another I kept a small piece of bread in order to serve the Liturgy every Sunday. One Saturday, the day when I received the bread, they did a search in my cell and found a small piece of bread. They confiscated it, so the next Sunday I had no bread to celebrate the Liturgy. I could not celebrate the Liturgy without bread because I needed to have the Body of Jesus Christ.

The guard was a very bad man, an extremely bad man. He was the secretary of the Communist organization in Aiud Prison.

This was Aiud that you were in in 1979?

Yes. I hesitated to ask him for bread because I knew he would insult me, and so on. He was a very bad man. I think he was possessed by the devil. He was a simple man—a very simple man—but he could find just the word to hurt you. He would always find the exact word to hurt me. I think the devil was in him. This Sunday, on the one hand, I wanted to have a quiet day, a happy day, but, on the other hand, I wanted to celebrate the Liturgy. Now I did not know whether to be quiet—not to talk or ask for the bread—or to be possibly insulted and even beaten. Perhaps it was an angel of God that pushed me to knock on the door. You know, if you knock on the door in prison, the guards let you wait at least half an hour. During this time, your mind begins to work: What happened? Will he come to beat me? So the terror was increasing in my soul. During this half hour, I

---

[5] Fr. George spoke in greater detail about this incident in his lecture series "Divine Light in the Devil's Lair." See pp. 252–56 and 274–75 below.—Ed.

imagined that he would come ... and I would have destroyed my Sunday, God's day. I thought, "He will come to beat me or insult me." And I became more and more scared.

After a half hour, he came and opened the small window and asked me what I wanted. I said, "Sir, I would like to have a small piece of bread to celebrate the Liturgy." He was amazed! His jaw dropped, because every inmate asks for bread, but to eat, not to celebrate the Liturgy. He was absolutely crazy, acting like a crazy man. He slammed the window. But after two hours he came with a small piece of bread. He opened the door, and he gave me the piece of bread without saying anything! I was amazed! This was impossible! How could it be that this bad man is bringing me the Body of Jesus Christ Himself—because that is what it would be. It was the most mystical Liturgy that I ever celebrated in my whole life, because it was a miracle. And in prison it was completely quiet—this guard usually went from cell-to-cell insulting and beating people. This time when I celebrated the Holy Liturgy, there was no noise in the prison. Peace and quiet. I served the Liturgy, and I was so happy. I thanked God for this. After one hour he came again, opened the door and said, "Father, do not tell anybody I gave you the bread. If they discover it, I will be fired." I said, "How could I ever say anything? You brought to my cell the Body of Jesus Christ. You concelebrated with me! By your act, you concelebrated with me. You are now the son of God." He said nothing, but then he never insulted me again. So, many miracles happened in my life in prison. I had the feeling that an angel of God was always with me; that the protection of Jesus was in the cell with me.

Before I was arrested my mother died. I was completely isolated in the cell. I knew nothing about my family. I knew nothing about what happened [outside]. I was surrounded only by the hatred of the guards. Little by little, in my soul, I started to ask myself, is there no love for me in this world? Nobody loves me? The Securitate had come and said, "Your wife divorced you.

AN INTERVIEW WITH FR. GEORGE

Your son has forgotten about you. Your students say that you are a crook and that you tried to betray them—to enter into conflict with the priests and the hierarchs and the state. Everybody hates you." And so I was asking myself, "Isn't there anyone to love me in this world?" I had the love of Jesus Christ—I knew that. And I started to have this conversation with my mother. I asked her, "Mom, will you come to protect me, to tell me something?" Soon, after fourteen weeks, I saw my mother. I think it was when I was asleep. I think so, but perhaps not. I am not sure. She was very angry, and she said, "How can you imagine that I have forgotten you? My love is with you. Be strong and be faithful. Believe in God. Believe in me." Perhaps it was something in my imagination, but it was very real. The next morning I awoke with a good state in my soul. And after three days, for the first time my wife was allowed to come to see me. I am sure that my mother protected me and prayed for me. Then I was very sorry about my feelings and thoughts, and so on. From that time I never had bad thoughts about my wife or other people. I understood that everybody loved me. Even some inmates knocked on my door and said, "Father, be strong, be strong!" They did not even know me! They were perhaps even criminals, and they encouraged me.

I remember, it was 1979, at Pascha. It was during the night and there was a guard, a young man, a very nice-looking man, very handsome. He had a face like an angel. He was a peasant, but he was very bad. Every day he had to beat at least three or four prisoners. He was so bad that I could not associate in my mind his beautiful face and his beautiful eyes with the cruelty of his actions. He was very elegant, very proper, and I could not understand. It was Pascha. In the morning I heard the bells announcing the Resurrection of Jesus Christ. I sang, "Hristos a Inviat" [Christ is Risen] in my cell. I did not celebrate the Liturgy because I wanted to be attuned to everyone celebrating Pascha outside. In the morning this guard was on duty. A young man, a beautiful man, with the face of an angel—but so cruel.

I prayed to God: "O God, give us a quiet day; the day of Thy Resurrection."

In the morning at seven o'clock the new guard came and entered the cell. There were eight sections in the prison, and for every section there was a guard. When the shift was changed, all eight guards would come, and one would remain at each section. The other seven then went on to the next sections. When the guard entered the cell to inspect it, the inmates had to stand facing the wall so that they could not see him. If he spoke to you, he did so in a loud voice in order to be heard by his comrades. And if he asked us something, we had to answer in a loud voice, as well. Thus, everyone [all the other guards] heard the discussion between the inmate and the guard.

This particular morning, I did not face the wall; I faced him. And I said, "Christ is Risen!" He looked at me and then turned his head and looked at the guards, because I spoke in a loud voice. After a moment of hesitation, he answered, "In Truth He is Risen!" And that day he did not beat anyone.[6]

Around eleven or twelve o'clock, the chief of the prison came into my cell. Sure, the guard had to report to him all my actions, as the guards had to report every day on the behavior of the inmates. The colonel came into my cell because he knew that I had said, "Christ is Risen." He was sure that I would say the same words to him. I heard his voice. I heard his steps in the corridor, and I knew what he wanted to tell me [FG laughs], and he knew what I had to tell him—it was like a play. He entered the cell. I did not face the wall. I faced him directly and I said, "Christ is Risen!" and he said, "Did you see Him?" [FG laughs.] "No, I did not see Him. I did not see Him, but I believe what the apostles and the martyrs say. Did you see the North Pole? Did you see Stalin or Marx? But you believe in them by the authority of those who wrote about them. Because of the authority of the

---

[6] Following this incident, Fr. George was granted the experience of seeing the Uncreated Light. See pp. 272–73 below.—Ed.

apostles, of the priests, of the martyrs, I believe in Jesus Christ. And I know that He really did rise from the dead." He had no response, but he left me alone. So this day of the Resurrection of Jesus Christ was a very quiet, holy day for me. I did not celebrate the Liturgy because I knew that Jesus Christ had come into my cell and changed the minds of these guards. He closed the mouth of the colonel, and he gave me the words—not big words—but just what I needed to say. So it was a wonderful day for me.

8. Solitary Confinement

During the seven months that I was alone in that cell, I had no right to talk to the guards. I was only supposed to execute their orders, you know. Sometimes I would try to talk to somebody, even to the walls. It was impossible. I started to forget my Romanian. My wife was allowed to visit me, perhaps because George Bush, who was then vice president, had come to Romania after a number of organizations outside the country began to protest on my behalf. Everyone then who came to Romania would ask about me. Because he came to Romania, my wife was allowed to come visit me with my son. But I was unable to talk to them! I had lost the ability to speak, having been alone in my cell for seven months. I had so many things to tell them that my tongue could not express everything. She could not understand anything I said. She said, "Be quiet. Keep your silence. Try to explain to me what you want to say."

How long did you have together?

Half an hour. After she left, I went back to my cell. I had a fly in my cell, and I put some bread out to feed her. I decided to talk to this fly, to make her a spiritual friend. [FG laughs.] But her commotion exhausted me. I also had a spider. I tried to talk to the spider and he paid no attention to me. Absolutely none! Not to my words, not to my presence—he was not impressed by me. [Laughs.] I was very tired. But from time to time, there was a big cockroach that came into my cell, which I tried to domesticate. I put out some bread. He did not trust me. If I made a movement, he disappeared. Have you ever read *The Little Prince*? Well, I remembered that when the little prince arrived on the earth, he met a fox. He tried to approach the fox, and the fox said, "Do not approach me. You have to domesticate me. You have to institute a ritual. You must approach me each day, one step at a time. By this ritual we will become friends, and when we leave the country, I will see your blond hair blowing in the wind." Well, I remembered this, and I began to do the same. He started to eat the bread. When I moved, he disappeared. As I was lying on my bed near the piece of bread, the cockroach, little by little, came closer and started to eat it. I watched his every movement. He was amazing, like a monster. If you look at him from up close, he is like a monster. Little by little I began to talk to him, and he actually came to visit me for weeks, until my isolation came to an end. I was saved in my ability to remember my language by this cockroach. It was amazing for me. You know, God sent all kinds of beings in order that we would not be alone. I am sure that in every movement, every insect, every conflict with the guards—it was the hand of God that tried to save me, to help me, to make me sure that I was on the right path. Because, you know, in such a situation, doubts come, but God ...

9. The Battle Between Good and Evil in Pitesti

That's a good point, for earlier you talked about how when you were sent to Pitesti Prison as a student, your soul was confused and you were not prepared at all.

No, one is not prepared for it. We are only prepared theoretically. We lived a normal life. We had no experience that would have prepared us to be arrested the first time. We were unfamiliar with what happened in Russia. Oh, we heard about it, but as history, like a novel. So, we were not prepared for the worst. But in Pitesti there was a fight between the spirit of good and the spirit of evil. It was not just the persecution of a regime against some people, you know. It was really the battle between God and the devil. In relation to this, I said in my sermons that the whole history of humanity is a fight between God and the devil, and that our heart is the battleground. But it is not dead ground; it is living ground, and it can decide the victory—whether God or the devil will reign in our hearts. We are responsible for this. Fr. Nicolae Steinhardt accepted my words.[7] Later, we understood it is not just the hatred of men against men, or the violence of the strong against the weak, but a spiritual fight between good spirits and evil spirits. And we failed on the field of battle; we failed, many of us, because it was beyond our ability to resist. Only the students who died were saved—they did not fail. However, some of us died after failing. I think the limit of the human soul's resistance was tried there by the devil.

---

7 In his book *Journal of Blessedness* [in Romanian] (Cluj-Napoca: Editura Dacia, 1991,), Fr. Nicolae Steinhardt wrote: "The only chance of survival for Eastern Christianity is that of a war within the Word. Our solution is that of [Fr. George] Calciu-Dumitreasa ..." (p. 417). As Fr. George explains: "The idea of this war between good an evil on the battlefield of our hearts was confirmed by Monk Nicolae of Rohia."

Fr. George tells us about Fr. Nicolae Steinhardt: "Nicolae Steinhardt was a Jew who was arrested and sent to prison, where he met the Iron Guard [Legionnaires]. They made a very big impression on him and convinced him to become a Christian. He was baptized in the Jilava Prison. His godfather was a professor, a foreign minister during the government before Communism, called Vidrashcu. Later, when he left the prison, he became a monk in a monastery called Rohia. For this reason he is called 'Nicolae de la Rohia.' He wrote many books. The most important is *Journal of Blessedness*, in which he describes his experience in prison. He wanted to say that since suffering in prison had such a spiritual result in his soul, he called this time—and the events in his diary—a *Journal of Blessedness*. He also wrote another book called *If You Give, You Receive*. It is a very interesting book. He died four or five years ago as a monk with a very, very spiritual life."—ED.

Fr. Nicolae Steinhardt (1912–89).

How did you survive it? What went on inside you?

I, myself, I tried to commit suicide. Many of us committed suicide. I tried, but I was saved at the last moment. I was on a big staircase, three stories high. The moment I tried to climb over it to throw myself down, a friend of mine caught me and saved me. I was cruelly beaten for this because you were not allowed to kill yourself. But, anyway, I was saved, and I am grateful to my friend. He died after the Revolution. I am grateful to him. Otherwise, I could have been lost.

So, only by God's grace you survived, for it was beyond you.

Absolutely. You can imagine. Even the second time I was in prison. I was alone. Without anything, no protection. Ceausescu was the supreme chief of Romania, of all the security, the guards, even the inmates—the two murderers. They had to kill me. They could have killed me any time, like a fly. Nevertheless, God saved me. Who protected me? Who put me under their protection? It was God.

You were speaking of the heart as the battleground. As Orthodox

Christians, how should we live now? You learn to forgive and you learn to not hold grudges. What is important now in our hearts if those times of testing come? How do you look at your torturers? How do you see them? What do you do if someone is beating you, or forces you to take off all your clothes? One of our young sisters asked me to ask you how you retain any human dignity in that situation?

I think before human dignity is Christian dignity. Many times I forgot my human dignity. I was humiliated. I was insulted. But beyond this is Christian dignity: forgiveness and prayer for the other one. I remember when that one colonel came into my cell on Pascha, he was very angry with me, and he said, "I know that you are praying for me!" I said, "Yes, I do pray for you. I pray that God will forgive you. I pray that God will give you the light of His Resurrection." He was very angry. When I told him this he became even more angry with me, because the devil in him wanted him to deny in his soul and mind that Jesus Christ *really* is resurrected. Many times it was a split between human dignity and Christian dignity. According to human dignity—as a human being or as a good man—it is very difficult to forgive. But it is not so very difficult for us, as Christians, to forgive. I do not deny human dignity, but I say that before it comes Christian dignity.

Following the commandments.

Absolutely. Sometimes when my human dignity failed, I became very angry with them. I was ready to ask God to punish them. I said, "God, they are Your enemies, not only mine. They are Yours, too." But as a Christian, I said, "Oh, God, forgive them. Give them the light of Your Resurrection."

Did you ever see any of your torturers converted?

Many of them, yes. The guard who gave me the bread of God. Afterward he stopped insulting me, and I had the most quiet time during his time on duty. Before, he would come to the door when I was praying and insult me and blaspheme God. But after the incident with the bread, he stopped. I am sure he was converted. I never met him again. Also, those criminals: I saw them in front of me praying, kneeling, and even crying. There were many others. God worked miracles in the prisons—many, many people were converted.

Afterwards I was put in prison with a young man. He was a thief. It was very interesting. I will tell you this because I remember how Fr. Dumitru Staniloae said that at the Last Judgment, we will answer before God, not only for our deeds, or for our faith, or for our sins, but for all the people whom our attitude influenced. So, this young man, he was a thief. Did you hear about Tudor Arghezi? He was a famous poet after the Second World War. He was a monk, but he left monasticism because he felt he was too big of a poet, a genius. He felt that as a monk he was not allowed to express himself as a poet. In the beginning he retained his dignity, but in time he began to collaborate with Communism. He wrote a book of poems entitled *1907*, which was when there was the peasant revolution in Romania. This book is full of hate, absolutely like the Communists. Some of his poems, the worst ones, the most criminal in intention and in word, were put into the students' elementary and high school textbooks. This young man [the thief] had tortured an old couple. He did not kill them, but he tortured them so that they would tell him where they kept their money, their jewels. He was arrested. I met him in prison, and I liked to talk to him about Jesus Christ. He was very reluctant. He said, "I am not a thief." He was only sixteen or seventeen years old. He said, "I was a man of justice because I took money and so on from rich people, not from poor people."

I asked, "Why did you torture them?" "Because they refused to tell me where the money and the jewels were. They started to cry out and I told them not to cry. But they cried continuously. For this I tortured them." And I asked him, "Who gave you the right to torture those people?" "I learned this in school." And he recited that poem of Tudor Arghezi, who said, "Take the rich man, torture him, kill him; take everything from him." "I listened to what Tudor Arghezi said, and I know that I did the right thing." I thought of this young man being at the Last Judgment, saying, "God, I learned to torture people from Tudor Arghezi." I told him that Tudor was a sinner. "He denied his first vocation as a monk. He denied his human dignity because he collaborated with Communism. And besides that, he made a criminal out of you! You knew nothing about this. You learned in school from the poem of Tudor Arghezi that you have the right to kill everybody, to steal, and so on. It is not right." I talked to him about Jesus Christ. We were together for two months in Aiud Prison.

This young man asked me, when he saw that I was praying, "Father, can you teach me a prayer?" "I can!" I taught him the "Our Father." This he began to pray. Soon afterwards we were separated. But after this, his soul was changed. He was not completely converted, you know. Perhaps he lost it after entering the company of thieves and criminals. But, anyway, in hell he will keep this [ray of goodness]. He was praying and he would say, "Father, I do not feel big things in my soul when I pray, but it is good for me."

What was his name?
Symeon.
We will pray for Symeon.
I was amazed, because he was a young man, only sixteen years old. He was completely corrupted by somebody. He was in a bad group, you know. He was a very nice guy, a very young man. He had beautiful eyes—there was even some innocence in them. Then, I understood what Fr. Staniloae had said. It is a big responsibility to know that your words, your poems, your novel or articles caused someone to become a criminal.

I've heard it said that the most serious kind of neglect lies in the passivity of Orthodox pastors—the silence and passivity of Orthodox pastors who are not reaching out to those who are hungering and thirsting for the Truth.

In the Orthodox Church often the priesthood is merely a

profession. I tried not to fall into this attitude. I tried to make my priesthood a living action, a vocation. There was a priest in my village when I was a child. He would never touch money. He never took a coin into his hand. And if he had to go somewhere, he took someone else to pay. He would never touch money. I could not understand then and everyone was very amazed by this, but later I understood: by touching money, you start to love it. And, loving it, it becomes your treasure. It is better to have one's treasure in heaven and not here, because the heart has the inclination toward corruption. It requires great struggle to keep the heart pure. The devil attacks every time.

10. Release from Prison

The majority of the students I had in seminary are good priests. I remember when I was set free, I had forty agents of the Securitate watching my apartment. The apartments were surrounded by the Securitate. There were forty-two, in three shifts, you know. Night and day; night and day. One of my students who was a priest came, and the Securitate stopped him. The priest said, "I want to see Fr. Calciu, because he was my teacher in seminary." This was in 1984. I was under house arrest. I was freed in 1984 while under house arrest with my wife and my son, and then expelled [from the country] in 1985. This priest came—he was young—and he said, "I want to see Fr. Calciu." They said, "You have no right to see him. Fr. Calciu is under house arrest, and no one is allowed to see him except his family." So he sat on the steps of the stairs and said, "I will stay here until Fr. Calciu goes out or you let me go into his house." And he stayed there perhaps seven hours. Finally, the Securitate called me to talk to him. It is an expression of love, you know.

How did you support yourself? What did you eat? (Fr. Calciu thought I was asking about his prison years, so his response takes us back to the prison.)

AN INTERVIEW WITH FR. GEORGE

During the seven months [in solitary confinement] I ate bread for two days, and the third day I had hot food. For seven months. But I made a vow to Jesus Christ, and on Monday, Wednesday, and Friday, I ate nothing. But I was not hungry, I was fasting for God. During my first arrest, there was a nun from Vladimiresti. She was arrested and died in prison. Her name was Mother Michaila. I did not know her, but for three months in prison she ate nothing. She only received Holy Communion. She did not eat anything during her three months in prison, and she survived. I think it was the same for me. I heard about her later—at that time I did not know about her. I think that having Liturgy every Sunday and receiving Communion was quite sufficient for me. I was never hungry, nor was I obsessed with food. During the first time of arrest, I was obsessed by this, as were the others. Perhaps because we were not so resolved to give everything to God. Now I was resolved from the beginning, because I never thought that I would survive. I was sure that I would be killed by Ceausescu and his agents. So, if I came out of prison, I knew that these days, these years of living, after being in prison, were a gift from God. I knew I had to be killed in prison. They had decided that. But God had other ideas. I think that these days, these years, are given to me by God as a gift; and I pay nothing for this gift. I pay no interest on these years of living. Therefore, I am praying to God and preaching Him according to my powers and possibilities.

What happened after your seven months in solitary confinement?

After that, I was with different people. They kept moving me around to different prisons. I was in Galati, for instance, with some thieves, and in Jilava with some crazy people. Yes, they put me in the section of crazy people. I do not know why, but I think they wanted to declare me crazy. Perhaps, under the pressure of organizations and governments, they wanted to let me go free. I suspect that they wanted to let me go free but not to let people know that they did this under pressure. They wanted to declare me crazy and then put me back into society.

There was a woman doctor in this section. She was very hard on me. I remember, there were three crazy people [in the cell with me]. They were simulating. You know, they were not really mad people.

You mean they were not really crazy—they were pretending?

Yes. This doctor.... One day I was praying and the guard cried from the door, "Stop praying!" I paid no attention, and continued to pray. He entered the cell and started hitting my hands with a club. It was interesting; I felt nothing. I was not able to separate my hands, but I wanted to. I did not want to make him angry with me. I was in prayer. God does not want to make him crazy.... But I was not able to separate my hands. Because he wanted me to separate my hands and I was not able to, he hit me and my hands started to bleed. Then this lady doctor came, and she said, "What happened to you, Father?" She said, "I do not want to hear anything about it. Tell me about your liver." I did not have anything wrong with my liver. I was really angry with her. But when I came out of prison, I found out that this doctor came to my wife once a month to tell her about me. Can you imagine this? She was very harsh with me, but in secret she was coming to my wife. My wife was working in a medical institute; she was a biologist. Because it was a medical institute, this doctor could come [without arousing suspicion]. Looking from floor to floor, room to room, she succeeded in reaching my wife and telling her about me.

How did your wife endure all those years of your being in prison and not knowing what had happened to you?

She was very courageous; she was very strong. Generally, she was a shy woman, but God gave her the right words—there were a lot of people supporting her, talking to her. There were also priests who helped her. Different people, the faithful, would send her money or oil. Oil was hard to get.

AN INTERVIEW WITH FR. GEORGE

I was told that during the years that you were out of prison, it was the young people who helped you. Can you tell us more about that?

During the time I delivered my sermons to the youth, the students of theology were obliged to stay on the campus. They were not allowed to leave. I finished my speeches and discussions with the students around midnight. What was very interesting is that the majority of the students who came to listen to me were not in theology school but were engineering students. I think their souls yearned to learn about other things that matter. Their souls wanted to know more. Leaving the seminary and going to my house, I had to walk about seven kilometers, which is about four miles. During the night, at midnight, with the Securitate on my heels, these students accompanied me to my house to protect me. Many times the Securitate tried to attack me, not as the Securitate, but as though they were drunk, or thieves, or under the guise of someone who wanted to insult me because I was wearing my priest's robe. But the students protected me. They were very courageous; they were with me all the time. One student of the School of Engineering said something to me that was shocking and, how do I say, very spiritual. He said, "Truth before justice." It was a very deep thing. Afterwards I started thinking about it and I understood that, really, before justice is Truth. I experienced this during my trial, you know. I told the truth before justice and I did not ask for justice. I only asked that they respect my truth. I said that I had nothing to do with espionage or foreign powers; I had dealings with only one Power, which is not foreign to anybody—the Power of God. It is not a foreign power; it is a Power which is intimate to everybody. I said, "I am a simple priest. Why are you so scared of me? I am a simple teacher in the seminary. I have no army. I have no power with me. Absolutely, me and God. Why are you so scared of me? Do not make me a martyr; let me be a simple priest." They sentenced me to ten years.

When I came out of prison, many young people knew about me. These young people, who were then about sixteen years old, had been only eleven years old when I was preaching my sermons. (I was in prison five and a half years.) So they had not heard anything about me, but, by word of mouth, from one of the faithful to another, I was known by these young people. For example, when I went to the market with my wife and my son, I would be surrounded by these young people. They would say, "It's Fr. Calciu, it's Fr. Calciu!"

You were a hero to them.

And later, this fame was increased by the presence of the Securitate around my house. Everyone was asking themselves— Why? Why is Fr. Calciu being watched by forty agents?

Would they bring you food and money?

Yes, through my son. They would come to school and give him money. There was a young man who came from the countryside, not from Bucharest. I do not think he knew I was being watched by the Securitate. He entered the apartments, the main door, and was surrounded by six Securitate agents. Everybody was interrogated. "Who are you? Where are you going now?" In the hall there were mailboxes with everybody's name on them. He read a name there, of someone on the fourth or fifth floor, and he said, "I am going to see this lady." They let him go there but accompanied him to the apartment. He knocked on the door; the lady opened the door. She saw the young man and understood instantly what was going on. She said, "Oh, come inside, come inside! [FG laughs.]

She did not even know him.

She supposed, because she did not know him, that he was coming to see me. So he entered her apartment, and after half an hour or an hour he left. During the night, the lady came to us and gave us food that he had brought for us. She said, "Do not tell anybody that I brought this food to you. I did it because I love you and I love Jesus Christ."

AN INTERVIEW WITH FR. GEORGE

So, it seems that people served God in various ways. Maybe there were even some servants of God in the Securitate; would that be possible?

Yes, sure. I was a priest before I was arrested. I very much liked to visit the monasteries, and I would go from monastery to monastery, sometimes with my friends and sometimes with my family. Once I was in Lainici Monastery. There was a Securitate officer there with his wife. Securitate officers came to the monasteries to watch, or whatever, not to pray. We were together there for one week. I was with my wife, and he was with his wife and child. One day he came to me and said, "Father, I do not believe in God, but my wife is a believer. We were not married in the Church, and my wife feels that without the blessing of the Church, our life will be very bad. Can you be my sponsor, my godfather?" "Yes, why not?!" And I was the sponsor of this Securitate agent. My wife was very cautious. She said, "Be attentive, this man is trying to put you into a bad situation. He will denounce you, saying you agreed to be his sponsor." But I felt it was God's will, so my wife and I became his sponsors, and the hieromonk married them. Any time after that when he saw me on the street in Bucharest, he would say, "How are you, godfather?" Perhaps he was a believer. He denied belief in God to me. "My wife," he said, "is a believer and she wants to get married in the Church." Many of them would also come to the monasteries to baptize their children. But, officially, they were against Jesus Christ, and they could kill you in prison or even during the trial. But in their hearts, many of them were believers. I think God works in many ways. To me, He gave the words and the courage to speak out in front of the people without fear. To others, He gave the courage to work underground with the Army of the Lord or with people. There were the young monks and nuns who, as you recall, were forced to leave the monasteries.

What year was that?

Nineteen fifty-nine. Many of them had to leave. At first the monks and nuns refused to go into the world. They would hide in the forests and would come into the monasteries secretly.

So when they had to leave, they would all go off into the forests?

Yes. But in time, the Securitate discovered it, and they had to enter the world. But even in the world they had their groups. I had a friend, a colleague from my school in the village. She had been in a monastery but had been forced to leave. She became an employee somewhere, but she immediately founded a group of young girls and other people who gathered to pray in her house. It was like a monastery, except that they could not wear monastic clothing. It was forbidden. God works in different ways, you know. These nuns, now dressed like ordinary people, were openly preaching the word, calling people to Jesus Christ. On the other hand, the old monks and nuns could stay in the monasteries, and they became a center of spirituality. Those over forty years of age could stay in the monasteries. And the monasteries were a center of attraction for people. Those in authority in society tried to instill a materialistic philosophy into the most simple man—to make him accept that there is nothing other than the material. They [the people] wanted something else and would come to the monasteries. Every summer, I would go from monastery to monastery with my students.

This was after your first time in prison?

Yes. For example, one year I would visit the monasteries in Moldavia. The next year I would visit the monasteries in Transylvania, the next year Oltenia, Muntenia, and so on. And every time, I saw hundreds and hundreds of people visit the monasteries.

The Securitate didn't try to stop that?

They tried to stop it, but it was impossible. They couldn't. There is a monastery in Transylvania called Nicula. This monastery is dedicated to the Mother of God. There is a miracle-working

AN INTERVIEW WITH FR. GEORGE

Neamts Monastery in the region of Moldavia, where Fr. George would travel with his students.

icon of the Mother of God there. Before I was arrested—in 1975 I think—every summer, for the Dormition of the Mother of God, I would go there; and that summer there were sixty thousand people! They came, walking—not by train—but walking, a week ahead, with priests; walking and coming for the feast of Mary, singing all the time. In villages, in front of the *troitsa*,[8] they would sing songs dedicated to the Mother of God. And when they arrived at the monastery, they would walk on their knees three times around the church. Three times around the church! As you can imagine, the Securitate was there, but nobody cared about them, for the Securitate had not the courage to stop sixty thousand people.

Why was the ground ripe in 1944–45 for Communism to come into Romania?

It was not ripe. Communism came because the Russian army was in the country. Terror was installed between 1944 and 1945. In 1947, the Russian army forced the king to leave the country.

---

[8] *Troitsa:* wooden shrine-crosses found throughout Romania.—ED.

St. John of Kronstadt in Russia, who died in 1908, prophesied the coming of Communism to Russia. He saw it coming because people did not treasure what they had. They were not treasuring and teaching. It sounds like your faith was passed on from your parents, in your villages.

Yes, in my country the Faith was very strong; it was very strong. The intellectuals—they betrayed the Church. They were attracted to this American freedom, to the liberty of sexual freedom, Freemasonry, and so on. But the people—the peasants and the workers—were very good and very faithful. The Army of the Lord did a very good thing: it traveled through the villages preaching, singing, and preventing the spread of sectarianism, for the sects were coming with songs as well. The people, the simple people, wanted to take part in the singing. So they would sing Orthodox songs. The Protestants were also coming with songs. Fr. Joseph Trifa started this movement. It began after the First World War. The Army of the Lord was strong in Transylvania.

It was controversial, wasn't it?

It was controversial because, during the Church hierarchs' collaboration with Communism, the Army of the Lord split and went in two directions. Some broke off and went toward Protestantism and the others stayed in the Church.

11. The "Reeducation" Experiment at Pitesti

This may be more difficult for you to talk about—I know a little bit about what happened in Pitesti Prison in Romania, but most Americans have never heard of Pitesti and what happened there and the whole experiment of reeducation that took place. Can you tell us about what happened?[9]

Pitesti was a copy of Makarenko's experiment. Makarenko

---

[9] On what took place in Pitesti, see also Dumitru Bacu, *The Anti-Humans: Student Reeducation in Romanian Prisons* (Englewood, Colo.: Soldiers of the Cross, 1971).—ED.

AN INTERVIEW WITH FR. GEORGE

was a Communist educator who reeducated children and young people who had infractions against the Communist world. In his book called *Pedagogical Poem*, he describes in very pink colors what happened there. But if you are very attentive, you can see that it was a real terror. The Communists extended this experiment of Makarenko to Romania's students—the young generation.

How old were the students?

Eighteen to twenty-five. Communism wanted to make a gap between the generations. The most dangerous category for them was the students, the young people. We had inherited a Christian education, family values, and basic Christian principles. The older generation was a generation that had to die, but this generation had to be transformed. So they tried this experiment in a very concentrated medium. They wanted to break the people, the whole country. Romania was not a primitive country. We were connected to European culture. We are a Latin nation, not a Slavic one. We believed in Christian values. Therefore, they wanted to do this experiment with the young people, to create a gap between the children and the older generation, and make this generation of students a Communist one. They wanted to build a new world—a Communist world, a new man—the Communist man, and so on. So they arrested the young people—the students—and put them in a special prison, in Pitesti, for this very experiment. But you have to understand that it was not just a fight between two political principles. It was a fight between God and the devil.

They took very distinct steps. The first step was to destroy the personality of the youth. For example, the guards would come, together with a group of young prisoners who had converted to Communism, into a cell where there were perhaps twenty young students, and would try to intimidate them. They would beat them without mercy. They could even kill somebody. Generally, they would kill one of them—the one who opposed them the most; the most important one. Generally, he was a leader. They would beat him and even kill him. Thus, the terror began.

After that, they began to "unmask."

What does that mean?

They wanted to force you to say, "I lied when I said, 'I believe in God.' I lied when I said, 'I love my mother and my father.' I lied when I said, 'I love my country.'" So everyone was to deny every principle, every feeling he had. That is what it means to be "unmasked." It was done in order to prove that we were the products of the bourgeois, and the bourgeois are liars. We lie when we say we are virgin, we are Christian, and when we try to preserve our bodies pure for marriage.

They were against that?

Sure. They tried to say that I was a prostitute, a young man who had connections with all the girls; or that in the Legionnaires or the Peasant Party there were perversions. We would be tortured until we denied everything we believed before. So, that is what it means to be "unmasked." It was done in order to prove that Christian principles were not principles, that we lied when we said we loved Jesus Christ, we loved God, mother, father, and so on. It was to show that I lied when I said that I was a chaste man, when I held an ideal of nation and family. Everything had to be destroyed in our souls! This is the second step.

After this came a declaration against everybody who was in touch with us, everybody who believed as we believed. I was to make a declaration against everybody who knew about my organization or my actions, to denounce everybody—even father, mother, sister. We were to sever completely any Christian connection and moral principle.

The final step was to affirm that we had given up all the principles of our Faith and any connection we had with it. With this we began to be "the new man," "the Communist man," ready to torture, to embrace Communism, to denounce everybody, ready to give information, and ready to blaspheme against God. This is the most difficult part, for under terror and torture one can say, "yes, yes, yes." But now, to have to act? It was very difficult.

It was during this third part that the majority of us tried to kill ourselves.

That is when you tried to commit suicide?

Yes, this was the most difficult part. Thus was a new category of man built by Communism. And we were forced to go with some of our own former torturers into another cell and to start doing the same thing. It was very difficult. It was a very devilish directive.

At this time we could not understand the mystical implication of this action. We were political prisoners and the Communists wanted to learn everything about us—about our friends, our families—because the majority of the people were against them. They wanted to terrorize my father and mother, for example, by saying to them, "I know that you were going to church," or, "I know that you gave some food to some people who tried to escape the Securitate." They wanted to strike terror in them and in the country. It was like a political fight.

Only later did we understand that there were mystical implications. All these people were just instruments of the devil.

How long did it take you to realize that?

After the actions stopped, some of us understood. But, we were too involved in the political fight before we were in prison. Even if I and others protested against the introduction of materialism into the schools and the forbidding of the students to go to church, I think the majority of our effort was being involved in the political fight. However, little by little, under the terror, the torture, and suffering, we understood that this political implication was just the surface. In fact, it was a fight between good and evil, between God and the devil. It was the devil who had taken Russia, Romania, and other countries into his possession.

When we understood that, we started praying even more than before. God sent us illumination. We understood it and we were aware of the nature of this fight. We understood that it was not [a name] who was our enemy—it was the devil. He tried to destroy our soul. It was not just a political fight or someone's struggle for power. They wanted to destroy our soul, our faith, our spiritual connection with our families. We understood this, and we tried to resist.

Was the reeducation over a long period of time?

For some, it lasted three years. Happily, I was among the last ones. But for others, it was for three years: After they had passed through all of these steps, it was discovered, let's say, after one year that one of them did not say everything—he had kept some secret in his mind. They would then put him back into the same situation as in the beginning. He passed again through all the steps of torture. It was impossible to resist.

How long did you pass through this?

One year.

So there were four steps: the installation of terror, the unmasking, the denouncement of other people, and, afterwards, the changing of our souls. These four steps were strictly thought out and planned. It could not be only images in the mind. They had had long experience of this in Russia and were now bringing this experience to Romania.

I do not know if you want to go into this. But did they do different kinds of tortures? I remember someone saying that they were extremely humiliating tortures.

There was no torture, moral or physical, that was not used.

Do you have nightmares from that now?

No, now I am free, but for years and years I had nightmares. The others also cried out during the night, trying to escape the agony. It is too humiliating and absolutely inhuman to tell you every torture. Too humiliating. You cannot imagine, to be completely naked and to be beaten and forced to submerge your head in a bucket of excrement. You cannot imagine. We never imagined that it is possible, you know. Only the devil could give images like that.

But you can pass through the tortures. The problem for us was the moral problem. To deny the Faith, to deny everything, to say that all my life was only lies: that I did not believe in God, I did not love my parents, I did not respect my parents, or that I did not respect the Church. To deny every Truth, real Truth you believed in before. To say now it was not true, it was a lie. This was the problem for many, for we can pass through the tortures—or we can die. But, to survive, and to deny everything you believed before, everything that was the cornerstone of your soul. This was our difficulty.

It was not the torture that was the most difficult problem, because they could torture you today, but tomorrow they had to torture someone else, so you had one or two days to rest. But you were always watched and forced to say bad things, blasphemy. They did not have time to beat you every day, from morning until night. But they could force you to say something against your friend, something against God every day. When you were tortured, after one or two hours of suffering, the pain would not be so strong, but after denying God and knowing yourself to be a blasphemer—that was the pain that lasted. Spiritual pain is more difficult to bear than bodily pain.

It is difficult now to remember exactly the physical torture. You cannot remember now if you have eaten something good, or, to imagine, to remember, exactly what it means to be hungry. The ability to remember this is very weak. But the regret in remembering spiritual denial is the same all the time. It never diminishes in intensity.

Were there moments when you thought you were going to lose your mind, go insane?

Yes.

What do you do? What if it happens to me; what would you say?

Only prayer. Only prayer. Without prayer, you cannot survive.

How did you even pray during those moments?

One cannot pray during those moments. But during the night, when everyone goes to bed, you gain your strength and you find your repentance. You pray for this. It is not complicated. You say, "God, forgive me!" It is enough! Just to say, "God, forgive me!" It is enough for your soul to regain its strength and to resist one day more ... and one day more ... and one day more. Not to die. Not to go crazy. Many of us went mad. But just to say, "God, forgive me," was like a shield. Just to say, "Forgive me, God." You knew very well that the next day you would again say something against God. But a few moments in the night, when you started to cry and pray to God to forgive you and help you, were very good.

You just washed away all that anguish.

Yes.

So, in the moment itself, when you thought you would go insane, you relied upon those prayers of the night before? There was not much you could do during those very moments?

Perhaps not every night, but maybe once or twice a week, during the night, you had these moments of repentance. Many times we were quite angry with God—if You exist, why did You allow all this? But, there was one moment when the mercy of God would come upon you and you could say, "God forgive me; God help me." It was enough to help you. For another day, another day, another day.

It is incredible, you know. It is very difficult for us to call back into our memory what happened there. Not the torture or the torturers—we forgive the torturers. But it is very difficult to forgive ourselves.

Because of this, I was very well prepared for the second imprisonment, you know. Because I accepted prison and I fortified my soul with Liturgy, with prayers, with songs. I was very protected. I consider this second time in prison to be an expiation.

Well, you are heroes to us. One of our nuns said to me, "When you talk to Fr. Calciu, tell him we are warriors that have never been in direct battle before. We realize there is an unseen war going on, a battleground in our own hearts." Some people think we are morbid in being interested in what happened to you and what happened in Russia....

It is not morbid. Perhaps it is morbid to recall every physical torture or physical humiliation; it can be morbid. But to recall what happened in the spiritual plane is very important, even for me. But for you, more so. Because God helped me to pass through the second imprisonment, and He gave me the strength to resist. There was a collaboration between me and Jesus Christ before I went into prison. I prepared for it. I accepted it. I knew I had to enter prison, and I wanted to enter prison.

During my second time in prison I had a very strong desire to become a martyr. I wanted to die in prison. I was completely isolated from the world, even from my family. I loved them; I did not stop loving them, but it was like an exaltation. I wanted to become a martyr for Jesus Christ. He decided otherwise.

You are a living martyr. You survived so that you could tell us all of this.

Perhaps, yes.

I never denied the hierarchy, even in my sermons. Every time I told the hierarchs they are the framework of the Church. They are the ones who give the Church the strength, the verticality, and so on. We had to expose the hierarchs, but most of the time we had to support them and tell them to have a Christian attitude, not an attitude of political power.

The bishop is supposed to be as the Apostles, feeding the flock.

Absolutely, yes. I said in one of my sermons that I am a simple priest. My voice cannot be heard. But a bishop's voice is strong; if he took action, he would be heard. Or the patriarch.... Who could stop the voice of the patriarch from being heard by the whole world?! But they did not have the courage.

I was very fortunate in that God opened my spiritual eyes to understand the importance of material things and the importance of spiritual things. What is most important for me is that I understood this fight between good and evil, between God and the enemy of God—the devil. Nothing in this world just happens in a mirror. All of these visible phenomena are only a reflection of what happens on the spiritual level, you know.

You probably really saw that with all the veils removed.

Absolutely, yes. If every priest, monk, nun, hierarch—and all Christians—could understand this, we would have the key to victory against the devil.

Unseen warfare must be conducted in the heart.

Most of us are prisoners of matter, prisoners of physical things, and we are not able to make this connection.

This experiment went on for three years at Pitesti, after which it was stopped?

They stopped it because people heard about it in the West. But the torture continued—I mean forced labor, hunger, beatings, and so on. But not with the same intensity as in Pitesti. It was carried out only by the guards and administration.

They did not bring in students to beat other students anymore?

No. For instance, because we were very weak, skinny, and did not have the strength to work and to meet the norm that they asked of us, they would beat us. They would put us in isolation. They would not give us food to eat. After not eating for three days or a week, or having only a piece of bread and water, we would come back to the shops to work completely exhausted; and then we would work less than before, you know. Those who were not so resistant died or became very ill with tuberculosis, and so on. The persecution and torture continued, but not with the same intensity. I mean, you were sure that there would be no torturer with you in the cell. It was difficult, sure; they would beat you, they would not give you food to eat; they would force you to work more than you are able to work. Many of them became very ill.

You were not allowed to work in Pitesti?

No, we had no right to work. They had no interest in our body. Our body was just an instrument through which to reach our soul. They were interested in our faith, in the destruction of our souls.

Was it just young men at Pitesti?

Yes.

Did they do the same thing somewhere else to young women?

No, only the men. The experiment was conducted not only in Pitesti, but also in Gherla, as well as in all the other camps. The adults were also subjected to it, not just the youth. But the first experiment was with us.

I was very, very opposed to the Communist regime. We were fighters—very strong, courageous, and faithful. We were praying. I remember at Pitesti, before they started this experiment, we had a month of continuous prayer in the cell. I would pray, let's say, half of the night until midnight. At midnight, I would knock on the wall to the cell next door, and they would continue the prayers. And so, night and day, we never stopped the prayers. The authorities knew this.

How long were you in Pitesti before they started this diabolical experiment?

One year, during which we made these continuous prayers. We were connected, we were strong, we were optimistic.

So, when the tortures started like that and you had such a strong brotherhood among yourselves, were you able to sustain some of that? For example, your friend saved you from killing yourself—so you did not all turn against each other.

I was very good friends with this young man and they knew that. So, after beating me and torturing him, they forced him to torture me and me to torture him—to destroy any connection between us, to isolate us. This is the tactic of the devil—to isolate everyone. God intended man to be in a spiritual community of prayer. Therefore, they isolated everybody; they made everyone to be alone. We can be one in Jesus Christ, but this was oneness in the devil. Everyone was completely isolated; no one believed in anyone; no one trusted anyone. Thus everyone was isolated and the resistance was annulled.

I cannot tell you how grateful I am. These are deep things you are telling me. As hard as they are, it is really what we need to know.

You know, in ancient icons they represented the devils as single—one, but the angels in twos. It has very deep significance, because the devil was alone, but the angels were in twos. They were not alone; everyone was with someone else. After Pitesti, I understood the iconography of the ancient icons, because we were put in this diabolical situation when we trusted no one, loved no one, were not in connection with anyone—we were absolutely alone. Around us it was like a desert. No cornerstone. No indication—we did not know where we were going. At this, the spiritual terror was complete.

After you had to torture those to whom you were closest and they tortured you, and then the reeducation stopped, were you able to rebuild?

Little by little. It took years.

Can you tell us how you did it?

I started to pray, first of all. I reinvented prayer.

Reinvented?

It was a special prayer. It was a prayer I made myself. I did not have the courage to repeat the prayers I knew [the prayers of the Church]. I did not want to defile them.

Because you felt that you were defiled and you did not want to defile those prayers?

Yes, so I made my own prayers. In the beginning, I was still in conflict with God, reproaching Him about what had happened to us. And little by little I started to recognize that He is good, He is great. But it took months and months.

AN INTERVIEW WITH FR. GEORGE

12. Constantine Oprisan

I was very fortunate because I was among the sixteen people that the Securitate took to Jilava Prison, where my healing began. In Jilava they built a special cell in a half-cylindrical shape. It was like a cylinder cut in two. We were underground; Jilava is built underground. Above the cell were seven meters of earth. You cannot see Jilava—the whole prison is underground. In this cylinder they built four cells with no windows, only a door. We had an electric bulb, day and night. They put four of us in each cell. In each cell there would be either a very sick man or a mad man. In my cell, I had a man—Constantine [Costache] Oprisan— whose lungs were completely emaciated by tuberculosis. Twice a day he had to cough up fluid from his lungs. We would help him by giving him a hat or something, and he would cough and bring up all the discharge from his lungs—blood and everything. It was horrible to see him. On the first day I entered this cell, with me were Constantine Oprisan, my friend who saved me from suicide, and another student younger than us. Constantine began to cough up the fluid in his lungs. I was leaning against the door, surprised because I had never seen anything like that. The man was suffocating. Perhaps a whole liter of phlegm and blood came up, and my stomach became upset. I was ready to vomit. Constantine Oprisan noticed this and said to me, "Forgive me." I was so ashamed! Since I was a student in medicine, I decided then to take care of him.

So I decided to take care of him and told the others that I would take care of Constantine Oprisan. He was not able to move, and I did everything for him. I put him on the bucket to urinate. I washed his body. I fed him. We had a bowl for food. I took this bowl and put it in front of his mouth.

He was like a saint. It was the first time that I was in contact with such a man. He was in this condition because he had been tortured in Pitesti for three years. They had beaten him on his

Fr. George's cell in Jilava Prison.

chest, on his back, and had destroyed his lungs. But he prayed the whole day. He never said anything bad against his torturer, and he spoke to us about Jesus Christ. All the while, we did not realize how important Constantine Oprisan was for us. He was the justification of our life in this cell. Over the course of a year, he became weaker and weaker. We felt that he had finished his time here and would die.

Once a week we were obliged to shave. I was watching Constantine Oprisan, and my friends were shaving. Afterwards, I began to shave and one of the others was watching Constantine Oprisan, because we watched him day and night. When anything happened, they would tell me to go to Constantine Oprisan, because I had told them that I should be the only one to take care of him, since I had hurt him that first day. I was sure that I had hurt him, and I felt very, very guilty. While I was shaving, Marcel, the student who was younger than us, saw that Constantine was ready to die. He said, "Go and see Constantine Oprisan; he is dying." I looked at him. His face was completely emaciated. He eyes were open, but I saw that over his eyes there seemed to be a curtain of mist. His eyes turned inside himself. I was so scared, so afraid. I felt that he would die and I would be alone in his cell. I put my hand on his and said, "Constantine, don't die; don't die! Come back; come back!" I cried with a great voice! Immediately he came back. His eyes became clear. He looked at me. I was right in front of his eyes, you know, bent over him. I don't know what happened in his soul, but I saw an immense terror in his face. His eyes were full of terror and he started to cry. I had the feeling that he had been ready to enter the spiritual world, and I had asked him to come back to the cell. This was a great terror, and so he started to cry. Tears were flowing out of his eyes. His face became the face of a child, a newborn child. He was crying like a newborn child coming out of the womb of his mother. Constantine Oprisan cried because I forced him to come back. In a couple of minutes he died.

How long were you with him in that cell?

One year.

After he died, everyone of us felt that something in us had died. We understood that, sick as he was and in our care like a child, he had been the pillar of our life in the cell. Then we were alone without Constantine Oprisan.

We took a towel and washed his body to prepare it properly to be buried in the earth. Then we knocked at the door and told the guards that Constantine Oprisan had died. They came after three hours. We had never before left that cell, which had neither light nor windows. The water was seeping into the walls; the straw mattresses were putrid under our bodies. So, after two hours, for the first time, the guard commanded me and my friend to take the body of Constantine Oprisan and go outside.

Outside it was so beautiful. Flowers and trees and blue sky. As long as we were in the cell, we forgot about the beautiful world. When we went out, we saw that the world had not changed. This vegetation, these flowers—hurt us. It was like an insult to us, because we were suffering, dying ... but the universe did not care about us! The sun was going down and there was a golden light. Everybody was shining like gold. We put Constantine Oprisan on the ground. He was completely naked because we had to give his prison clothes back. His body was completely emaciated. We could not believe that he was a human being. He was completely emaciated; only bones, only bones. And I think that the bile at the moment of death must have entered the bloodstream, because he was completely yellow. My friend took a flower and put it on his chest—a blue flower. The guard started to cry out to us and forced us to go back into the cell. Before we went into the cell, we turned around and looked at Constantine Oprisan—his yellow body and this blue flower. This is the image that I have kept in my memory—the body of Constantine Oprisan completely emaciated and the blue flower on his chest. He was nothing but bones and skin—no muscle. Nothing else ... his body lying on the ground with a blue flower.

Afterwards, it was very difficult. I may have sinned because Constantine Oprisan, before he died, said, "I will die, but after death, I will pray to God for you. All my prayers will be for you, because I do not want you to die in this cell." And I am sure he prayed for us, because all three of us succeeded in leaving this prison to go to Aiud [Prison]. I am sure that Constantine Oprisan was praying to God for us. The sin I committed was that all the time I was thinking and invoking the soul of Constantine Oprisan to come and give us light. He never came, though for months I asked him to come and give us light. I think this was a sin I committed, for perhaps it gave him some unrest. I am sure he was very grateful to me that I took care of him. I am sure he loved me very much. He loved everybody. But I think for me he had a special love because I had a special love for him.

Was he older than you?

Yes, he was about six or seven years older. And I never had a repulsion for him after that first time. I took care of him with

Constantine Oprisan.

love and respect. He was like a child in my hands. I had to put him on the toilet, to wash him—to do everything for him. I was thinking that for this love through which we were connected, he had to come to me to give us the light of God.

I am sure he prays for you. You probably pray for him now all the time.

Yes, all the time. At every Liturgy, I remember him and all the people who died in prison. But for him I have special prayers.

I named this cell the ship of death, because, really, everybody in this cell was destined to die. In the cell at our right, two men died. In our cell, one died. In the cell at our left, three died. In another cell, one died. Thus, out of sixteen people, seven died during one year because of the bad conditions. We had no medical assistance, no food, no air; the water was seeping in through the walls; the mattresses were putrid. We stayed in Jilava, and then after two years in this cell, we went to Aiud. I stayed at Aiud for four years, after which I was freed and kept under house arrest in Beragan. Beragan is a very vast plain north of the Danube that served for the Communist government as Siberia did for prisoners in Russia. It was a village created only for former political prisoners. I stayed there one more year—in 1963/1964.

And then they let you out. What happened in 1964 that everyone was let out of prison?

Romania was accepted into the United Nations under the condition that all the political prisoners be set free. When I came out of prison in 1964, I tried to go back to my school of medicine, but they did not accept me.

What did you go through interiorly? All of a sudden you are free, or somewhat free, after all these years.

When I was in Aiud I refused to work, so I ended up in isolation. I remained in isolation for two years. It was a special section, but it was not solitary confinement. We had no right to read anything, to get newspapers, or to go outside. We would just stay in the cell, day and night. There were four people in each cell.

AN INTERVIEW WITH FR. GEORGE

We had a very spiritual life there, because in this special section were special people. Some priests were there. There was a priest in that prison who had been there since 1941.
So he must have been a Legionnaire.
Yes, he was a Legionnaire. There was also a student of theology there. There were also some writers and ministers from Antonescu's[10] regime, who were very faithful, intelligent, and cultured people. We were, therefore, very busy all the time with edifying and educational conversations, as well as prayers. We began to teach each other and to learn new things—foreign languages and so on. We were very busy! There was one professor, Manu, who was a physicist. Before he was arrested, he had worked with Madame Curie in France. He told us about the atom and its properties, for at the time we entered prison these discoveries about the atom and its properties were only beginning. We knew about the explosion of the atom bomb in Japan, but very few knew what occurred to make this happen. He described it to us, and we understood the structure of matter. There was also a writer who had written many books before he was arrested. There were also priests, and everyone had his moment to say something about himself. Then we would have prayers. The priest who had been in prison since 1941, Fr. Grabenea, celebrated the Liturgy with our bread.

I remember the night of the Resurrection of Jesus Christ. The guards made a search in the cell—a fire drill. And they came in the cells with a machine and sprayed. We had started the Liturgy of the Resurrection of Jesus Christ right at midnight. They then announced the alarm and everybody was forced to lie on their bellies. For three hours we stayed on our bellies. They entered the cell and sprayed everywhere, leaving the cell full of whatever it was they sprayed—a white chemical. For three hours we were

---

[10] Ion Antonescu (1882–1946) was prime minister and *conducator* (leader) of Romania from 1940 to 1944. He was executed in 1946 by the Communist government as a war criminal.—ED.

forced to lie on our bellies—three hours. Fr. Grabenea recited the Liturgy of the Resurrection, and we sang "Christ is Risen from the dead...." It was so beautiful to celebrate the Holy Liturgy under pressure, lying on the ground. When he finished the Liturgy of the Resurrection we sang "Hristos a Inviat [Christ is Risen]" all the time.

There were special people in this section. I felt they were special because I was still wounded in my heart and my soul, and Fr. Grabenea and others took care of me. They healed my heart, and when I left the prison I was very strong.

So he was a real pastor, a real father to you.

Yes. I think he died during my second imprisonment. But he was like a saint, you know.

In a certain way, he reminded me of Constantine Oprisan from Jilava. He had a very, very illumined face. He never got angry with anyone. He was like Christ in the midst of us, you know.

Why did he go to prison?

He was a Legionnaire, but they put him in prison because he was a priest. He had done nothing wrong. He was very helpful to us. I was the only student there. There was a professor, a doctor, and the priest. I was the youngest, so they treated me like a child. They also knew my history, for I had told them the history of Pitesti. I told them about Jilava and what happened to us there. They were very affected by this, and so they were very kind to me. They healed the wounds of my soul.

So, when I left, my decision was made. I learned from Fr. Grabenea many things about theology, about the priesthood, and so on. I knew of the priesthood, but I idolized it too much. Fr. Grabenea told me about the difficulties of the priesthood, the temptations. I left prison before them. I finished my punishment in 1963, left prison, and went to this village under house arrest. They left the prison in 1964. But I was decided! I talked to Fr. Grabenea about the priesthood—what it means to be a priest and what difficulties a priest has to face, especially in a Communist country. He warned me about the possibility of being sent back to prison, so he prepared me for everything.

Thus, after I was released I wanted to study theology, but the doors of the theology school were closed for us. Therefore, I started studying French, but I never gave up. Being a professor, I was able to arrange my classes to be in the afternoon, so that in the morning I could study theology. I was surprised to see that Patriarch Justinian Marina was so understanding with us. He helped me a lot. In fact, I studied theology underground. Nobody knew about me.

So you were not even registered in the school?

I was registered, but nobody told the Department of State that a former prisoner was enrolled in theology school. It was great, like a plot. The students were young and did not know about me. But the professors covered for me all the time. As I told you, in the final year, when I had yet to receive my diploma, the Securitate discovered me and threw me out of theology school. They took advantage of the fact that the patriarch was not in Romania at the time; he was in Belgium. They threw me out of the school while he was gone. But when the patriarch returned, I asked him for an appointment. He received me immediately without any opposition. He said, "Do not worry. I will arrange everything for you," and he appointed me as a professor in the seminary. He was very courageous!

You said that at first he was not very courageous.

No, at first he collaborated with the regime. But, little by little, I think he understood his responsibility. And so he accepted all the priests back who had been in prison. He put them back in their parishes. Professor Staniloae was also appointed a professor in the theology school. It was a very important move. Thus, I was able to get a diploma as a professor of theology. One year later, in 1973, he said that I had been accepted as a candidate to the priesthood. I did not ask to become a priest, because I did not consider myself to be worthy—I had passed through Pitesti; I had denied Jesus Christ. But God decided otherwise. He said, "Be a priest." And on Sunday, the patriarch ordained me a deacon, then on Thursday he immediately made me a priest. It happened very quickly. I had asked for a delay between the diaconate and the priesthood. I was ordained a priest in January 1973, on the day of the Three Hierarchs. They were the patrons of the seminary. Thus, I was made a priest on the day of the patron saints of the seminary. I think it was a decision of God.

This gave me more courage and more spiritual understanding, and forced me to take care of the students, to learn about the lives of young people. Therefore, I made a strong connection with the youth in the seminary and universities and decided to give them direction.

You became a father to them.

I decided to give them direction, to make them understand what Christian dignity is, what human dignity is—to open their eyes to another world beyond the material world. The spiritual world is more important than the material world.

Do you have any words of wisdom for the youth of today in America?

You have to make them understand that this world means nothing. Justice or injustice, riches or poverty—it's all nothing, because the soul is above everything. It is also true that this world can destroy the soul. But they have something that is very precious—their souls. The body can get sick, it can grow old, disappear; but the soul is the most special thing we have. This is our crown.

I read in the newspapers just a few days ago that the pope [John Paul II] made a statement—did you read it?

That he believes in the theory of evolution.

Yes. He tried to justify his statement by saying that only the soul of man is made by God. But until the appearance of man—what did God do—did He sleep? When did He start to

AN INTERVIEW WITH FR. GEORGE

Fr. George serving in the early 1970s.

make the soul of a man, and why? If you accept that the body of man and the body of animals are not created by God, that they are the result of evolution, then why did God begin to make the soul of man?

I loved this pope. When I was in prison in Aiud, I heard about the election of this pope from Poland, and I asked the administration of the prison to let me write a letter to the pope. I composed my letter in my mind. Every sentence, you know, I had it all in my mind. Sure, they thought I was a crazy man, but I insisted. I refused to eat; I declared a hunger strike because I wanted to write this letter. I knew that the letter would never reach the pope, but I wanted to write it anyway, because the Securitate were obligated to give me a piece of paper and to put the paper in my file. So after ten days of not eating, the chief of the prison came to me and asked, "Do you think that we will let this letter reach the pope?" I wanted to make an historical act of writing this letter to the pope from the prison. Did you read my letter? I will give you a copy. I wrote: "Sanatate [Health]. It is a great joy to us to hear that a bishop from one of the Communist countries was elected as the chief of the Catholic Church. We think that it is a manifestation of the Providence of God. We want the people from the West to know what happened in the Communist countries. God called you to a big responsibility. Do not forget the Churches in the Communist countries. We are living in persecution. We are denigrated by the Communists. We have no right to catechize, and so on. Do not forget that we are the Church of Jesus Christ." Something like this. I wrote this letter and stopped the hunger strike. Time passed and I was freed. During my house arrest, I succeeded in rewriting the letter, for I had kept it in my memory. I sent the letter to the West with somebody. It reached the pope, was transmitted by Radio Free Europe, and was printed. I wanted to say to you that I loved this pope. I was sure that he was a man under suffering with his church and that he would understand and would keep the Christian tradition. So now I am very disappointed.

Maybe you need to write another letter.

This pope made many mistakes. I remember, I think it was in January when the pope celebrated the family. Do you remember this? I watched it on television. It took place at the Sts. Peter and Paul Cathedral, and the people brought some special families. There was, for instance, a family from Spain—mother, father, and twelve children. They were Catholics. They had raised their children in the faith, and one of the children was a priest. Anyway, it was a very Christian family. They presented some Catholic families from other countries. The atmosphere was very pious, and the pope always kept his eyes down. I thought he was a man of God. But from time to time, someone would cry out from the crowd, "Viva Papa." All the people started crying, "Viva Papa," and the pope waved his hands like a political man! I was very disappointed. It was a very mystical atmosphere, and it was during the war in Bosnia and Serbia. The atmosphere in the beginning was indeed very mystical. I expected the pope to say, "Everybody kneel and pray for peace in Bosnia, Herzegovina, Serbia. Pray to God to put an end to this war." I was sure that all these people, the majority of whom were Christians, could do that. They never pushed anyone to cry, "Viva Papa," but every fifteen minutes the crowd was crying, "Viva Papa." He was like God. They forgot they were there to celebrate God, not Papa....

And now he is speaking about evolution—limiting God to a being that could only make a soul from time to time....

There was a professor of apologetics at the seminary. He said that now is the time for science to be in accord with theology—not theology with science. And that is right! We have discovered many things, and all these things induce us to accept that energy comes before matter—spirit before matter. And the pope says that God has no role in the creation of the world? That matter created itself, without having any brain to organize the laws of the universe? And now human beings, who do have brains, are unable to discover the laws of the universe made by matter without a brain? And God only created the soul of a man? If we accepted the theory of evolution as the pope said we should, it would mean accepting that in the beginning was a cell, and only afterwards a man. When, then, did God decide to give man a soul? To Neanderthal man or to modern man? Thus it is absolutely stupid for a pope to say a thing like that.

Well, there are even many Catholics and other Christians who are "pro-choice"—who are supporting the slaughter of unborn babies. They just do not see this fight between God and the devil that you have spoken of.

What is surprising to me is that more and more the churches side with the devil in this fight. If the pope supports the devil, what will happen to the souls of the millions of Catholics? Until now, some [Roman Catholic] bishops have supported evolution, but there had been no decision within the synaxis of bishops saying: yes, evolution is right. But the pope has said it.... He is very inclined toward the Catholic worldly empire; he travels often. He tries to make the church stronger, but he completely forgets the spiritual life.

13. Contemporary Problems of the Church

Fr. Seraphim Rose did not support the ecumenical movement, because it attempts to unite the churches outwardly, but it is not being true and faithful to the Orthodox Faith, the Creed, the Seven Councils, and the whole tradition of the Holy Fathers of the Church. By remaining true to the Holy Fathers and drinking at that wellspring, we can still love our brothers. This does not imply hatred for Catholics or Protestants, but unity cannot be achieved by celebrating the Eucharist with them. Fr. Seraphim was concerned about the spirit of ecumenism that was entering into the Orthodox Church. When I was in Romania, I noticed most people were very interested in ecumenism. But I think I understood why. After being closed off for so long from the rest of the world, perhaps it was not possible to think about it properly. I might be wrong. I am just telling you some of my thoughts.

Because I was in prison for sixteen years, I knew nothing about ecumenism. When I came to study theology, I saw that the professors were for ecumenism and I could not understand this. In the beginning I was caught by them, but then I began to see what it really meant. For instance, I was kicked out of the Church and the school. There was a conference on ecumenism in Bucharest; the Secretary of Ecumenism (World Council of Churches) associated with Switzerland came to Romania. Because my case was already known, he asked Patriarch Justin (Moisescu), "What happened to Fr. Calciu?" It was not so easy for him to give an answer. He knew something about me, but not much. So Bishop Anthony Plamadeala said to the patriarch, "Let me explain to him." The Secretary of Ecumenism had asked the patriarch this after the banquet was over, so that he would not disrupt [the event] and thus miss it. Bishop Anthony said that Fr. Calciu was a rebel. He said that he rebelled against the Church hierarchy; he did not respect the rule of submission to the hierarch. Furthermore, he introduced elements of neo-Nazism in his sermons. He taught our students about neo-Nazism. Now, I am sure that this man from the World Council of Churches knew the content of my sermons, but he was very

AN INTERVIEW WITH FR. GEORGE

Fr. George with Elder Cleopa (Ilie) (at left) and
Fr. Ioanichie (Balan) during his 1998 visit to Romania.

satisfied with Bishop Anthony's answers without even calling me. I had not yet been arrested. It was January and I was not arrested until March. He did not call to ask me about this. He accused me, saying, "You are a neo-Nazi." He did not call to ask me what happened, for he was very satisfied with this answer. Thus, I began to lose my faith in ecumenism. I had been intoxicated by my professor: "Ecumenism is very good. Ecumenism is the future of the religions, you know. We have to make one single church." I heard later that at the ecumenical conferences they could not pronounce the name of Jesus Christ in order not to offend anyone. What kind of religion is this? Now I see that it is a great heresy of the twentieth century. Every conference of ecumenism has meant concessions made by Orthodoxy. The Protestants grow stronger and stronger—they begin to build, to provide priests opportunities to go outside the country, to have opulent banquets and eat very well. Is this serving God? They spend a lot of money. This is not serving God—going to the most beautiful resorts on the Black Sea, in the mountains, going on excursions, attending banquets, and so on. How can this be serving God? They are only interested in worldly comforts.

Tell me about the women who went to prison in Romania?

I met some women in prison when I was transported from prison to prison. I can say that the women were often more courageous than the men and very resistant to torture. I heard the Securitate beating one woman who was very courageous. All the time she would say, "You are criminals!" I had no courage to say something like that. She was saying, "Why are you torturing me?" protesting and crying. She was very courageous. I never learned who she was. It was in the prison in Bucharest—during the inquiries, the first time.

Later, I met a woman who was in prison in Mislea. They had a very spiritual life there. This prison is not far from Bucharest. They told me about their spiritual life—their life of prayer. I think they are more courageous than the men.

You mentioned this Mother Michaila.

Yes, she was a nun from Vladimiresti. She was the secretary of the monastery. When the monastery was destroyed by the Communists, by the Securitate, Mother Michaila and other nuns were arrested. She was very spiritual.

Did you know her?

No. In prison she lived for three months only on Holy Communion. I think the Securitate had something against her, because she was severely tortured, very persecuted, and isolated. She died after a few years in prison. She was not an old woman; she was a young woman. I think she was around forty years old at this time. In Vladimiresti, all the nuns were virgins. This was a cause of conflict with other monasteries. The nuns from other monasteries accused them of being too proud. Now Vladimiresti has been rebuilt. All the nuns that survived have returned, and many other young girls are joining it.

AN INTERVIEW WITH FR. GEORGE

Do you have any desire to go back and visit?
Yes. A lot depends on this election on November 17. If this election will be in the hands of the opposition, I will not go there.

When I was in Romania the first time [in 1990], I wanted to go to the Patriarchate to meet the patriarch and the bishops. I had no intention of insulting them, but I wanted to tell them something about my experience. I wanted to entreat them to be more active, to spend more time among the people, to renew the image of Jesus Christ. I was at the Patriarchate, but all the bishops had left—I was the only one there. They left; they avoided meeting me. Some went to the monasteries or elsewhere.

So they knew you were coming?
Yes, they knew because I had told them. I asked them to allow me to come to them.

Maybe you need to go back and do something. They will probably be unable to reach their young people unless they sincerely account for what has happened and repent. "We are sorry that it happened because of our human failings and our human weaknesses." They would have to face themselves as you did. If the Church representatives don't do that, they will have no moral authority in the lives of the young people, many of whom will turn to Eastern religions.

I think the sin of the hierarchs and the theologians in Romania is intellectualism. They pass everything through their minds. They forget the soul and the heart. They are very cultivated people; they speak very well and so on, but everything is dry. I think that is why the youth came to me.

Because you were alive.
They came to me, and they loved me.

You know, during these sermons I delivered, there were moments when I was ready to give up. Many of my colleagues and priests came to me and said, "Father, stop it, or they will destroy the seminary. The Communists are waiting and looking for motives to close the seminary. Can you understand what will happen if the seminary is closed?" And sometimes they convinced me to stop. But I would talk to the students and would tell them what the priests and professors said—that the Communists could close the seminary—and ask them what they thought about it. "Father, go ahead [and preach]," they would say. "We are with you! It is too late to go back now. We are with you. If they throw you out of the seminary, we are going with you." Thus the students, the young people, would not let me stop my preaching. For this reason, I knew that it was an inspiration of God. And God took measures to protect me in a miraculous manner, because, as I told you, the whole Department of State, the patriarch, the bishops, the professors and everyone were against me, yet they did not throw me out before I had finished the sermons to the youth. Can you imagine this? It's incredible! It's incredible! Everybody was against me, but they did not have the courage to stop me. They closed the door of the church, but they did not throw me out. I had asked God to let me deliver these seven sermons, and He said, "I will let you." When that was finished, I asked God to let me deliver the eighth sermon to justify myself, but He said, "You do not need to justify yourself, because I am justified."

Amen to that.

That brings up another question. Fr. Justin[11] *told me the Romanian people made many compromises with the Communists in order to prevent the churches and monasteries from being closed and destroyed. He said that he did not know if that was God-pleasing. What do you think about that? You may have answered this question by recalling how the priests had said that the Communists would*

---

[11] Fr. Justin (Parvu) is a beloved spiritual father in Romania today, to whom many come for spiritual counsel. He is the founder and abbot of Petru Voda Monastery. As a hieromonk, Fr. Justin was in Communist prisons from 1948 to 1964. See *The Orthodox Word*, no. 174 (1994), which contains three interviews with Fr. Justin.—ED.

AN INTERVIEW WITH FR. GEORGE

destroy the seminary if you kept preaching, but you kept preaching anyway. But if you were responsible for a whole parish, and they were going to destroy your parish, what would you do?

I have thought very deeply about this. Fr. Roman Braga has said that the compromises saved the churches and the monasteries.[12] I do not believe it. I think every compromise is wrong. Jesus Christ did not make any compromises. Why?

Because it would water down the Truth?

Absolutely. He did not give us any right to make compromises. I think the devil is the winner in any compromise. This compromise made by the churches saved nothing! Perhaps it saved the walls, but it did not save the souls. There were bishops who went from monastery to monastery forcing the monks and the nuns to leave. They were sent as messengers of the Communist regime to force out the monks and the nuns, because the monastics refused to leave their monasteries. The bishops told them, "Go outside. Go into the world. Become honest citizens." They forced the monks and nuns to go outside and help build Communism. They lost, I am sure, a lot of souls, because monks and nuns who have left their monasteries and their faith—and the majority did, as I have said—could be a stumbling block. That is, they could cause another person to turn away from God. And the priests were speaking for the Communist regime. In every letter that the patriarch wrote at Christmas, he never forgot to praise the Communist regime, Ceausescu, and so on. All of this lost many people. There were compromises! The Church in Romania has no moral authority, no power, because the priests and the bishops made compromises. And now they have not the courage to speak out and to say, "We made compromises! We made mistakes! Now we are ready to stand firmly against atheism."

---

[12] See Archimandrite Roman Braga, *Exploring the Inner Universe* (Rives Junction, Mich.: Holy Dormition Monastery Press, 1996), pp. 65–66.—ED.

14. Mission to the Youth

What can you and others do now for those lost youth in Romania?

I think there are now in Romania many monks, nuns, and priests who talk to the youth. Your mission is here in America. God will protect Romania and Russia and the Orthodox countries against modernism, against the immorality of the West—but here in America nothing protects the youth. Only you. Your mission is here.

Is there anything that you can do? You have a moral authority in Romania, because of all that you have suffered and all that you have done, and your voice is known. You could go into the universities in Bucharest, where many of the intellectuals have turned away from Orthodoxy, and reach out to them, showing them that the fullness of Truth is their inheritance in Orthodoxy, that Christ and His Kingdom are worth dying for. This needs to be passed on to the youth there.

I tempted God three times. I wanted to do something, and I did not know if God agreed with me or not.

I thought I had the right to try three times, and if I did not succeed the third time, I would give up. Now I have tried three times in Romania. The first time I had to leave in five days because I was watched by the Securitate. My students came to me—perhaps you do not know this. When I was in Romania in February 1990, I announced that I would serve a memorial service in University Square. [This was right after the overthrow of the Communist dictatorship in 1989.] I did not have access to the radio or television; I only told someone. But through word of mouth, ten thousand people heard of it and gathered there in University Square for this memorial service. The dean of the theology [school] issued a statement saying: "We are against Fr. Calciu. We warn the students not to go to University Square because Fr. Calciu has the intention of making a new revolution

AN INTERVIEW WITH FR. GEORGE

against the government. So, do not go to University Square. Stay on your campus, and let Fr. Calciu do whatever he wants. He is responsible for the trouble he makes." I had no intention of doing such a thing! The students came anyway—students that had never met me—and we celebrated the memorial service. I went to every cross, said a prayer for those who had died, and sprinkled holy water on it. The students were very sad about the statement of the dean of theology. They [the dean and other authorities] did not want me to be there. Afterwards I spoke on Radio Free Europe. Twice a month I delivered sermons and addressed the youth. The last time, they stopped me from preaching....

Now I am not as strong as I was ten years ago. Now I let God decide. I am still needed here in America. Even the Romanian youth in America are exposed to all the temptations. I am sure in Romania there are priests and monks who will speak to the youth.

It seems that most of the immigrant churches in America are losing their youth. They have no interest in the Faith of their forefathers, and, if they do, it is usually only to stay connected with the culture. There seems to be little awareness of Orthodoxy as a rich wellspring that, if put into practice, imparts the fullness of Truth. Most children of Orthodox parents from the old country are blending into the godless, modern American society.

I have this experience in my church, too. It comes from the parents. Many of the parents had no religious education in Romania. They came here and considered the church to be a place to meet other Romanians. Their children do not speak Romanian and have no Romanian culture. Their parents want them to be integrated in America, because they have lost.... I have tried to approach the young people in the church, and I have a very good group of young people helping me. They have little connection with the Church in Romania, but they are connected with me. I have succeeded in teaching them to sing Psaltica [Byzantine Church music]. I am very connected with them.

On the other hand, I do feel this impulse to go to Romania. Maybe next year.

Even though you have been rejected? Perhaps you could reach some members of the hierarchy and make them see the need to go through the suffering of facing the sin of cowardice in not confessing the Faith and standing up against atheism. If just one bishop would take responsibility in his own soul for what happened in Romania, for those who suffered and died there, and would bring that before the people—would bear the pain of that responsibility—this could bring about a healing and reconciliation of many souls with the Church.

There is a pious story in our country about John the Apostle. He was praying a long time for a thief who lived somewhere in Asia, very far from him. He had heard about him. There was a thief who was robbing the caravans, and he felt very guilty about this. So he started to pray for him, because he said that every neighbor of mine who commits sins in crime is a part of me. Thus he decided to pray for him. Through his prayers this thief was converted. He did not know that John was praying for him, but the prayer worked. There are no bars for prayer.

In my cell, from time to time, other inmates would pass under my window and cry, "People know you; people are praying for you." Sometimes I had moments of great spiritual joy in prison. There is no explanation for this, you know. I was tortured, I was isolated, I was alone, I had no connection with the world. I felt sometimes completely lost in prison. I had no prospect of liberation. The only prospect for me was to die in prison. But I had some moments of spiritual joy. I did not laugh—it was something in me—a happiness in me. Not all the time, but from time to time. Afterwards I heard that groups were praying for me all over the world, and I am sure that this joy was a moment of communion in prayer with these people, for there are no bars, no guards, to stop prayer. Thus I had these moments of spiritual joy.

AN INTERVIEW WITH FR. GEORGE

Fr. George with Marcel Petrisor: they shared a cell with Constantine Oprisan in Jilava Prison. Photograph taken in 2006.

Everyone I have ever talked to who has been in prison has said the same thing.

It is impossible for people outside of prison to understand. We were freed and we were very happy to be free, but we had a kind of nostalgia about the prison. And we could not explain it to others. They said we were crazy. How could you miss prison? Because in prison we had the most spiritual life. We reached levels that we are not able to reach in this world. Isolated, anchored in Jesus Christ, we had joys and illuminations that this world cannot offer us. There are no words to express exactly the feeling we had there. Those who have not had our spiritual experience cannot understand that we could be happy in prison. Many times we were not happy at all, but there were moments of happiness there. When I took care of Constantine Oprisan in the cell, I was very happy. I was very happy because I felt his spirituality penetrating my soul. I learned from him to be good, to forgive, not to curse your torturer, not to consider anything of this world to be a treasure for you. In fact, he was living on another level.

Only his body was with us—and his love. Can you imagine: we were in a cell without windows, without air, humid, filthy—yet we had moments of happiness that we never reached in freedom. I cannot explain it.

Everything is stripped away, and God becomes real. He is not a theoretical God anymore.

A living God.

How did you keep from cursing your torturers in prison?

I did curse them. [FG laughs.] The fight is very difficult, because we have to fight against the devil, and we have to fight against his servants, and we have to fight against ourselves.

If you had known what you were going to pass through at Pitesti before you went to prison, how would you have lived differently?

I don't know. Now, because I have passed through this and because I have explained it to you, you can make a judgment about it. But we could not imagine something like that. Knowing, even the first time, that we would have to be arrested—our generation was not able to think about this in these dimensions. Now I am able to imagine everything. I know that the human being can be a devil or an angel. But really a devil, not like a literary expression, you know. I know that man can be a devil. And I know that I can be a devil. So I have to be very, very cautious with myself. I have to watch myself, to stop every small inclination towards evil, because this small plant of evil can invade your soul. From the beginning, cut off your hand.... [E.g., an evil thought or an evil wish towards someone.] The devil is very subtle, you know. Jesus said to cut off your hand or your leg or take out your eye [cf. Matt. 5:29–30]. That means to cut off this inclination from the very beginning, the very first impulse of sin.

So that is what we can learn from this.

You have to. Especially the youth, because they are full of passion. Many times they have movements of the body more than older people, and they have to be very attentive to this. You must also dedicate every action to Jesus Christ. Even if you do not pray a lot, at least say, "I offer this action to Jesus Christ." "O God, I did it for you." This will create a kind of rhythm in your life. It is very important.

15. THE LEGIONNAIRES

Can you tell me anything about the Legionnaires?

It was not meant to be a political organization. It was spiritual. They were focused on the virtues, on prayer, honesty, etc. They were dedicated to the Christian formation and education of young people in the "Legionary Movement." And they succeeded. They taught a whole generation, and all the big cultural personalities in Romania entered this movement. There was the great philosopher Nae Ionescu; there were poets, men of science. The most beautiful generation between the ages of twenty and thirty-three entered this movement because they felt they needed to protect the Romanian nation against the influence of Russian Communism. But they were persecuted from the beginning.

Why?

The king of Romania, Carol II, was a very bad man. He wanted to be the king of a totalitarian government—to be the chief. He forbade even the other political parties: the Peasants' Party, the Liberal Party. He started a new organization called—I forgot (I was fourteen years old). But he failed, and in 1940–41 he was forced to abdicate under the pressure of the people, led by the Legionary Movement.

It was like a brotherhood, wasn't it?

Yes, it was. They had an organization for youth called the "Brotherhood of the Cross." They inculcated in the character of the youth the Christian Faith, honesty, a certain discipline, respect for the nation and for the people. I was in this organization for six months. But in January 1941 it ended. It was very interesting, really. It was very Christian. As I said, it was not a political movement; it was a spiritual movement. But I do not know why they entered into politics in 1940, and I think that this was their mistake.[13] The majority of the youth who entered prison in 1948 were arrested on a Legionnaire basis. They were former Legionnaires, former members of the "Brotherhood of the Cross." Even in prison they continued the same spiritual life.

What was the spiritual life they learned in the "Brotherhood of the Cross?"

There were some exercises. I do not remember exactly, but every student was obliged to keep daily a kind of journal of what he did—if he did good things or bad things that day, to examine if he was upright with others, if he prayed every morning and night. In school they were expected to be first. They learned discipline. One was sometimes ordered by the chief of the group to do something—to go from here to there, to give something to somebody. So, there was obedience. It succeeded in inculcating these values. The people who succeeded in passing through Pitesti, and in surviving and regaining their balance, were Legionnaires.

Later, it became political....

The intention was not to make a political man but to make an honest citizen. No matter what politics he practiced, he was to be a man of conscience and a man of justice and a man of faith. This was destroyed in a short time.

---

[13] In 1940, following the death of Corneliu Codreanu and the ascendancy of Horia Simi as the leader of the Legionnaires, the movement took not only a more political but also a more violent turn. Fr. George chooses to pass over this darker side of the history of the Legionary movement. Although his portrayal of the Legionnaires may be said to be one-sided, it can serve to counterbalance the unreservedly negative portrayal commonly found in modern Western sources. From the testimony of Fr. George and others who survived the Communist prisons in Romania, we know that, for many of the early Legionnaires who were incarcerated, the movement was primarily a spiritual one. Purified of sin in the crucible of suffering, these God-centered members of the movement attained a level of sanctity which transformed the hearts and lives of their fellow inmates.—ED.

It hardly had time to get off the ground. It was persecuted almost before it even started.

I want to tell you that Constantine Oprisan was a Legionnaire. He was the chief of the youth after the Second World War. He was the chief of the youth of the "Brotherhood of the Cross," and was educated in the Legionary Movement. He learned the spirituality of the Faith, and he was very penetrated by Christian principles. I remember in prison there was a young man called Valeriu Gafencu.[14] He was put in prison in 1941 by Antonescu. At that time he was twenty years old. When I met him he was twenty-seven or twenty-eight. He died in prison. He was really a saint. A real saint. He was like Constantine Oprisan. After the Revolution, the Legionnaires wrote his biography and asked the patriarch to canonize him. That was three years ago, but they did not get any answer. I am sure that the Patriarchate, the hierarchs, were scared because Gafencu was a Legionnaire. They were afraid to declare him a saint.

Can you tell us more about Constantine Oprisan? How he taught and strengthened you?

He did not talk much. He talked to us everyday for about one or two hours because he was not able to talk very much. But every word which came out of his mouth was a holy word—only about Christ, only about love, only about forgiveness. He said his prayers; and [what a deep impact it had on us] hearing him say those prayers, knowing how much he was suffering! It was not so easy. Out of his gentleness of soul, he wanted to protect us, not to cough too much to spread the germs in the atmosphere. He was like a saint in the cell with us. We felt the presence of the Holy Spirit around him; we felt it. Even during his last days when he was no longer able to talk, he never lost his kindness toward us. We could read in his eyes the spiritual light and the love. It was like a flood of love in his face.

---

[14] See his Life in *The Orthodox Word*, nos. 224–25 (2002), pp. 109–55.—ED.

Did he tell you stories about when he was head of the "Brotherhood of the Cross"?

Yes, he did. He told us about how he worked with the youth. I am sure he loved the youth and that he was loved by them. He was completely dedicated to mankind. He was a very clever man—amazingly clever. He was so kind with us. He did not talk much about himself. He talked about faith, about love, about prayer. He was praying all the time. It was not so easy to be in the cell all the time with the same people, you know. When there arose some conflict between us, he prayed. And his prayer was very effective. We were ashamed, just because he was praying, and we knew it. He was not praying in a loud voice, but his face was completely transformed. We understood that he was praying for us and we stopped [arguing].

And what about Valeriu Gafencu. You knew him?

Yes. He died in Targu-Ocna. He became sick with tuberculosis and was therefore transferred out of Pitesti before the reeducation began. He died in 1952. God protected him. I met him only two or three times. All the inmates living with him in the cell were separated by categories; I mean: forced labor, jail with a special regime, and correctional. He was in the forced labor [category]. So we met sometimes at the doctor before they started the reeducation, because he was very sick. He was transported by the fellows from his cell. It was enough just to see him and to pass by him, to immediately feel the influence of Gafencu. We men who were freed from prison were moved many times. So he might have spent time with four hundred different people as they moved through his cell. The moment they were in the cell with Gafencu, they completely forgot any bad thought, any rebellion against Jesus Christ. A church was established there in the cell. There were young people, rebellions, conflicts and so on, but he changed their soul and their mind. Therefore his memory is greatly revered, and the people who stayed with him in the same room still pray to him as to a saint.

AN INTERVIEW WITH FR. GEORGE

Valeriu Gafencu.

Did he know Cornel Codreanu,[15] or would he have been too young?

I think he knew him. Cornel Codreanu was killed in 1939. Gafencu entered the prison in 1941. It is possible because Codreanu organized the camps of young people. I am not sure because I did not talk to him, but he probably did, because he was very dedicated to Cornel Codreanu, to the Legionary Movement. He kept the spirituality of the movement.

There was a group of about twenty to twenty-one young men who had been in prison since 1941. This entire group was completely dedicated to Jesus Christ. They lived together during the Antonescu regime. They were not separated as was done under Communism. They were living in different cells, but during the day they were together. They could organize,

---

[15] Cornel Codreanu was the founder of the Legionary Movement in Romania.—ED.

they could pray together, they could read books, and so on. This whole group was under the influence of Gafencu. Really, they were amazingly faithful. We learned from them many things regarding the Faith. Everyone was like a monk, praying. Under their influence we established this continuous prayer in the prison. They initiated it.

So you could say that you gained your spiritual foundation in prison from the Legionnaires?

Yes, in a sense. I had received a spiritual education from my mother, but I learned from the Legionnaires how to use this spirituality, how to practice it and to become strong. It is interesting, but these old prisoners were dying. They had a very bad period before we came.[16]

The Legionnaires were put into prison by the regime before the Communists. When Russia invaded Romania, all of the political prisoners were set free except the Legionnaires. And I remember a moving event: In Bessarabia, in the city of Chisanau, there was a prison for young boys. There were perhaps sixty or eighty young men between fourteen and twenty years of age there, and when Russia took over Bessarabia, the director of the prison told the boys that they had to make a decision. They would not be allowed to immigrate from Bessarabia to Romania, so there were only two possibilities: to let them stay there and be killed by the Russians, or to give the director their word that they would promise to go from the prison directly to Aiud Prison [in Romania]. The director knew that the Legionnaires were men of honor. Each one of them gave their word. They went by many different ways: by train, by

---

[16] Fr. George explains further: "In 1940 the Legionnaires took power in Romania with General Ion Antonescu. I do not know what happened between them because the explanations of the Legionnaire Party differ from those of other parties, but they had a conflict and Antonescu put them all in prison. Those who were adults were sent to the front during the war and the majority of them died. Those who were too young to be sent to war were put in prison."—ED.

AN INTERVIEW WITH FR. GEORGE

Fr. George holding an iconagraphic-style painting of Valeriu Gafencu.

cart, however they could. And every single one of these boys, without exception, went straight to Aiud without even going to see their parents, because they had given their word. They were children! This was 1944. They were in prison from 1941 to 1948. When we came in 1948, we found them already there. By then they were twenty and twenty-one years old. Because they had passed so many years in prison in suffering, they did not survive. They all died in prison except for two or three of them. At the time I did not consider Communism to be the devil's organization. I considered them to be men, bad men who tried to kill us and so on—but not the servants of the devil in the spiritual sense. They [these Legionnaires] considered them to be the soldiers of the devil, and they were right. So, later, when I began to review what happened, I remembered what they told me and then I realized that the Communists were members of the army of Satan.

I remember another Legionnaire. He was not an old man—I was twenty-one and he was perhaps twenty-five, twenty-six years old. He was a professor of philosophy, and he told us in Jilava before he was sentenced that these were the times of the Apocalypse. He said that we have to build an apocalyptic conscience in order to resist Communism to the death, because the Communists are the servants of the devil. I did not pay too much attention then, but later I remembered it and knew it to be a reality. These men, especially the Legionnaires, realized that the fight between Communism and nationalism was not just a political fight, it was a spiritual fight.

You said something earlier about that certain moment when you decided to give all your life to Christ—where prison became easier and you had nothing to lose....

Yes, my life changed completely. It was after the experience of Pitesti. I told you that I met a priest in prison in Aiud. He taught us about Jesus Christ. We knew, but now we heard it in a new manner of understanding. Our understanding was enlarged. We could understand Jesus Christ. We could understand His suffering. It was perhaps pride to compare our suffering with the suffering of Jesus Christ, from one point of view. But we felt we were fellows of Jesus Christ.

16. On the Priesthood

This gave us a new understanding of Christianity. We also came to understand the importance of the priest. I told you before that I understood what Jesus Christ said about the salt of the earth, the light of the world. I then made a vow to Jesus Christ to become a priest—to become, myself, the salt of the earth and the light of the world, not to put the light under a bushel.

I tried to respect my own vow. No one forced me to make it. I made it in my own soul. I think that God put some obstacles in my way before I entered theology school. He wanted to test me and to see whether I would persevere in my decision. I was a teacher of the French language. I talked to students in high school. I made some trips with them to the monasteries in order to teach them in a hidden way what Christianity is. But I felt I was missing something. I missed my promise to Jesus Christ, and I never had peace in my heart. This was in 1968, after I was released.

You did not have peace because you were not yet a priest?

I had no peace because I wanted to be a priest and I wasn't. I did everything to fulfill my duty as a Christian professor, but I did not have the courage to be open and to risk being arrested again. Yet, I wanted to be a priest and God helped me. It was amazing to go to the Patriarchate. From the very first moment the patriarch said, "You are accepted into theology [school]," I understood that I was under the protection of God. And when the Securitate discovered me and kicked me out, I was not scared. I trusted God. The patriarch came back from Belgium, and he called me and appointed me a professor in the seminary.

Who ordained you?

The patriarch ordained me.

Is there still an underground church in Romania, since the Communists are still in power?[17]

I don't think so. For instance, the Army of the Lord is now out in the open. The conflict between the Protestant faction and the Orthodox faction [within the Army of the Lord] is very bad now. On the other hand, there are some priests who accept the Army of the Lord in the Church, while other priests do not accept them. Therefore, this group has split from the Church. They have their meetings outside the Church. I remember, in my sermons I said the Church has to open her doors to the Army of the Lord, because people are working for Jesus Christ and they are spreading the true Orthodox Faith all over Romania.

---

[17] This was before the November 1996 elections, which removed the Communist president.—ED.

If you do not embrace them and use that energy, you are going to lose them.

I was with them. I participated in their meetings many times. I counseled my students to go to the meetings of the Army of the Lord. While traveling from monastery to monastery in the summer by train, we would even sing the songs of the Army of the Lord, and the singing would spread many times from our car to others. Many people would come from the other train cars to sing with us. It was very, very spiritual and good for us and for the others. I really loved the Army of the Lord, and I really suffered with them when the others split off and became Protestants. I suffered with them.

When did that happen?

It happened after the hierarchs started to collaborate with the Communists. The Army of the Lord was forbidden then, and they went to prison. They were very faithful, and they suffered much. Many of them were killed in prison. Coming out of prison, I tried to meet some of them and reestablish a connection with them. I counseled my students to go into the midst of the Army of the Lord and tell them about the Truth of Jesus Christ. If someone was inclined to become a Protestant, they were to tell him that the Truth of true Orthodoxy has nothing to do with the [particular] hierarchs, priests, and so on. The Church is holy, without any wrinkles.

You have been in America since 1985?

Yes. I still have connection with them; I send them letters and my bulletin.

How can we prepare ourselves?...

I do not really believe that what happened in Romania can be repeated. I think America is under a big threat from a religious point of view, but it will be easier for a Christian to resist here than in Romania, because the people are still accustomed to a certain freedom. It would be very difficult for a regime to come in and take away that freedom. There are millions of people;

AN INTERVIEW WITH FR. GEORGE

Fr. George baptizing a baby in the United States.

they would have to put too many in prison. On the other hand, I know that Americans have had a very good life and they are not prepared for shortages of food and everything, you know. I am sure that if something like that should come, they would be ready to collaborate with Satan without any hesitation. For this, you have to prepare the young people for difficult times as Christians. We have to accept, you know, that bad times will come to us. But those who are good, by the mercy of God, will be able to resist. God will shorten the times for this. People must be made to understand that spiritual resistance is more important than anything else. The body must submit to the spirit.

The scariest thing is that children in our culture are actually being taught to torture through television, movies, and music—which is very demonic. Performers kill chickens and suck their blood on stage, doing horrible things. Many of our young people have a fascination with that. So it seems that being fed on that, they could turn around and torture and gain enjoyment out of it.

Yes, I saw it. I was in Canada and a Romanian woman came to me. She had four children. She had a sixteen-year-old and an eighteen-year-old: good children. The others were ten and twelve years old, and these younger ones were in a satanic cult. The mother said, "Father, pray for my sons to come back to Jesus Christ." What was amazing to me was that when I tried to make the sign of the Cross on them, they became furious with me. The mother was very unhappy. Small children, and already they belong to a satanic cult! It is very rare in the Romanian community for somebody to be in a satanic cult.

Did you know any of the monks and nuns who were forced to leave their monasteries in the 1950s?

Yes, I met a lot of them. During the persecution, many of them, nuns especially, did not want to go into the world. They would go to the men's monasteries and would serve as cooks, and so on, but they were living like nuns there.[18] I met some monks during my pilgrimages with the students, and many of them preferred to become priests in a parish. And they did a big, big job there. These monks who were parish priests succeeded in filling the church with people by their example of Christian life, by their love, by their care for the poor, the sick, and so on. You know, the other priests—the married priests—they had a lot of problems with their families. They had to take care of their children; it was a difficult time. So even if they felt their obligation as a priest, they were not able to fulfill it. The monks

---

[18] Fr. George later gave more information: "Generally, the nuns and monks hid in the forests (the majority of the monasteries are in the forest), and during the night they came in order to pray and to get food. For monastics whose monastery was near a village or town, it was easier. They could find shelter in the houses of the people, or even work. Many of them lived together in apartments and continued their monastic life. For the others it was more difficult, especially in winter when they were obliged to sleep in the attics of the monastery or of their families' houses. Sometimes the Securitate came to the monasteries, searched everywhere and arrested the monastics. All the nuns and monks I knew did not interrupt their monastic life."—ED.

did it. I was amazed by this one monk in a village. He sent ten children who lived in this small village to the seminary to become priests. I was surprised to see every year one or two children from the same village. I asked them, "Who told you to come to seminary?" "My family and the priest." "Who is the priest?..." I went there to see the priest, the monk. He told me he had been in a monastery. He was still a young man—perhaps forty years old. He had dedicated all of his life to Jesus Christ. I said in my sermons in the universities and the schools: Perhaps one million young people every year enter the world, and they are lost in their professions. But if every year one thousand students would leave the seminary and become good priests, I think in three years the face of the country would change.

What is a good priest? How would you train your priests?

I train my priests to be really faithful, to practice prayer; to love everyone, not to hate anyone, not even the Communists. They are not to hate. They were coming with resentment against the Communists because they were children of peasant families, and these peasants had lost everything: animals, land, everything. Many parents of the students were coming to me for Confession because the children talked to them about me. On the other hand, perhaps they were ashamed to go to their priests or perhaps they did not trust them. Everyone confessed—not great sins, but that they stole something from the land, such as grains or chickens. I said, "But it is forbidden by Jesus Christ. How can you steal such things?" And they said, "Father, they took everything from me. They took my cart, they took my plow, they took my animals—my horses and cows. They took my land, my garden, my orchard. They took everything from me. And you tell me that I sinned to take a small piece of my own property?" I was very embarrassed, you know.

What did you say?

I said, "Stop sinning, stop sinning, because it is not ours, but Jesus Christ's." "But it is my property." They could not understand,

and it was very difficult for me to convince them. I, myself, passed through the same thing. All of my family's things were taken away. My father died because of it. He was not able to survive losing everything. All his life was to be a farmer, to have his animals. Because of this, my father became ill and refused to go to the hospital. I understood this peasant's Confession to me, but I knew I had to tell him it was against the commandments of Jesus Christ. I told him this, but my heart was aching.

The priests were subjected to the same situation—having children, being forbidden to preach, or to catechize their children, and so on. I can understand that it was a sacrifice on their part. Nevertheless, to stand and to pray and to convince people to come to church.... I understand that they were torn between their family and their obligations. But the monks did not have these problems; they were completely devoted to Jesus Christ. Because of this, they did a very important job as priests. When the situation called, they went back to the monasteries. I remember, after the Revolution I got a letter from one of these monks. He said, "Father, I left my parish and am now in a monastery. I have to tell you that the whole parish cried when I left the village. Everyone accompanied me to the railroad station; and the children, the women, and the men were crying, and I was crying with them. But I felt it was my duty to go back to the monastery."

What monastery?

Cernica.

17. Preserving the Moral Integrity of the Soul

Would you recommend learning prayers by heart? You said you only said your own prayers for a long time because you did not feel worthy. But, for example, reading the Psalms.... You probably learned prayers at home, but our young people ...

I do recommend that they learn prayers by heart: the prayer

Fr. George writing in the guest book of a Romanian monastery in 2006.

to the Holy Trinity—the Father and the Son and the Holy Spirit. "O Heavenly King" is the prayer to the Holy Spirit; it must be learned by heart. The "Our Father," and prayers to the Mother of God. The Morning and Evening Prayers—let them learn them by heart. I learned these prayers when I was a child, and when I was in prison I would recite these prayers before God in my mind and in my imagination. I felt that my mother, my father, my brothers, my sisters, the whole Church, and my friends were praying with me, because I knew that they were praying the same prayers at the same time. I felt that in my prayers I was not alone in prison. Afterwards, I also had my own prayers. But these prayers make a communion between me and other Christians. I knew, for instance, that at a certain time in the morning these same prayers were recited in the whole Church in Romania. Everybody was repeating the same prayer. I was in a communion of prayer with them. It is very important not to be alone; to be two angels, and not one. For this reason, it is very necessary to learn the prayers by heart.

What about Akathists and Canons?

You can. I met monks in prison who knew four, five, or six Akathists by heart, and they were able to recite them. They were strengthened by this. I learned the Holy Liturgy, and it was very good. It was the same feeling of community. We felt in communion with the whole Church. Praying, "O God, I am in this situation, save me," is a very personal prayer. But praying the "Our Father," "O Heavenly King," or the Fiftieth Psalm puts us in communion with the whole Church. It is very important to learn them. I think it is your duty to have catechumens and those who come to your church learn the Creed by heart. You could be in a difficult situation, or imprisoned, or arrested. One has to pray the common prayers; afterwards comes personal prayer. But before everything, we are in the community of prayer with others. If you say, "O Heavenly King," or the "Our Father," you know you are in a communion of prayer. This feeling of community is very important.

AN INTERVIEW WITH FR. GEORGE

I am happy because I had this opportunity to tell you these things and to tell this to the young people. They have to be prepared—not for physical torture, not for hunger, or something like that, but they have to preserve the moral integrity of their soul and the image of God within them. They have to trust God and trust themselves, because Jesus is in their heart. I have tried to make them partakers of my experience. As long as I had Jesus Christ in my heart, I resisted. Whenever I forgot Jesus Christ, I was lost. People who completely lost their faith and trust in Jesus Christ became very weak and died. In such a situation, only faith in prayer is able to save them. These are not just words. I do not say only words; I speak the Truth, because I lived it. I am not an intellectual or a poet or a writer, speaking words just to make a beautiful sentence. I say this from the depth of my heart. I lived it. I understood it. I know it. And I am speaking the Truth, not beautiful words. God bless you.

Fr. George speaking in Kodiak, Alaska, in 2004.

PART THREE

HOMILIES TO THE YOUTH

INTRODUCTION TO THE SEVEN HOMILIES

by Hieromonk Seraphim Rose

In 1982, when Fr. George Calciu was still imprisoned in Romania, Fr. Seraphim Rose began to serialize Fr. George's "Seven Homilies to the Youth" in the English-language journal he co-founded and edited, The Orthodox Word. *He wrote the following as an introduction to the first installment, which was featured in issue no. 102: the last issue of the journal published during his lifetime. In addition to publishing Fr. George's homilies, he often spoke to brothers and pilgrims of his monastery (the St. Herman of Alaska Monastery in Platina, California) about Fr. George's heroic witness of the Orthodox Christian Faith, seeing in Fr. George's words a key message for our times (see p. 61 above).*—ED.

THE LENTEN SERMONS of Fr. George Calciu, originally addressed to Orthodox seminarians and students in Romania, are just as appropriate to the young people of America and the Western world in general. His words will strike a responsive chord in the heart of any young person who is awake or ready to awaken to the call of Christ to this corrupt generation of mankind.

In the Communist-dominated countries of the East this call is jammed by the atheist control of education, the press, and all the means of public expression. In the West there is little of such open persecution of faith in God, but the spiritual atmosphere is not as different from that of the East as it might seem. The same unbelief and unremitting worldliness are pounded into the heads and hearts of young people in the West in almost every public

An archival photograph of the Radu Voda Church at the Bucharest Theological Institute, where Fr. George delivered his "Homilies to the Youth."

institution and medium; the same violence and rebellion disturb young souls that know no other way to express their need and frustration; and religion, although outwardly free, has become a private and subjective matter that does not move society as a whole and is generally seen by young people to have no particular power or significance in their lives. The name of Christ—unlike the situation in the East—can be freely pronounced, but most often it is associated with a religion of dead formalism or, at best, of subjective revivalism, and at worst of a self-centered exploitation of religious feeling.

The Christ of Fr. George Calciu is quite different. He calls to the suffering, longing, but unfulfilled hearts of young people who would believe in the whole Christ of Orthodox faith if only they dared, or if only someone would dare to preach Him to them, together with the call to Christian commitment and acceptance of the path to salvation which He has given us in His Church.

The voice of Fr. George is not for Romania only. What young man whose heart is burning with the love of Christ and His True Church in America—or any other land where Orthodoxy has taken root and begun to grow—will not be moved for his own people when he hears Fr. George say, "Our people are like a ripe harvest, waiting to be gathered in for Christ.... But where are the worthy harvesters?... Be harvesters! Be pastors! And above all, pray to God to give this nation good harvesters who will not love parents and children more than Christ." "If, in a single year, we were to see one thousand priests graduate, full of the spirit of sacrifice, priests as Christ would have them to be, then in less than one year the spiritual face of our country would be changed."

One can only pray that the young Orthodox people of America, and all those whose hearts are ripe for genuine Orthodoxy, will pay heed to these messages from the suffering Orthodox soul under the atheist yoke and respond to them by shaking off the worldly enticements of these decadent times and at last *taking seriously* the Orthodox Faith which is given too easily to us here, thus making the beginning of the genuine, committed Christianity which this land so desperately needs.

May it be so!

EDITOR'S NOTE: *Footnotes from the Romanian edition of Fr. George's "Homilies to Youth," published in Bucharest in 1996, are signified by the abbreviation* ROM. ED. *All other footnotes are by the American editors.*

Fr. George with his students at the Theological Institute in Bucharest, class of 1976. This picture was smuggled out of Romania in 1985.

FIRST HOMILY
THE CALL

March 8, 1978

*The former treatise have I made, O Theophilus,
of all that Jesus began both to do and teach.*

Acts 1:1

THE TIME HAS come, young man, for you to hear a voice which has been calling you. It is a voice you have never heard before, or, perhaps, one you have heard but which you did not understand and to which you paid no heed. It is the voice of Jesus!

Do not shudder, do not be amazed and do not smile suspiciously, my young friend! The voice which calls you is not that of a dead man, but of One Who has risen from the dead. He does not call out merely from history, but from the depths of your own inner being. The words written and read today [from the New Testament] issue out of depths within you, yet they are unknown to you. Perhaps you have been ashamed or afraid to delve inside yourself and discover them. You believed that within you lay a wild beast, a sepulchre of instincts from which there would rise frightful spirits of passions. You did not see the face of an angel, and yet you are an angel. If this has never been told you before, Jesus is telling you now, and His testimony is true. No one has proved Him a liar.

What do you know of Christ, young man? If all you know is what they have taught you in atheism classes, you have been deprived, in bad faith, of a truth—of the only truth which can set you free.

What do you know of the Church of Christ? If all you know can be reduced to the concepts of Giordano Bruno,[1] about whom you have heard in classes of so-called scientific atheism, then you have been spitefully thwarted from experiencing the light of true culture and the brilliance of spirituality, which is the guarantee of human freedom.

Friend, where did you ever hear these words: *Love your enemies, bless those who curse you,... and pray for those who despitefully use you and persecute you* (Matt. 5:44)? If you have never heard these words, my friend, who hindered you, and with what right? Who prohibited you from knowing that there exists a better way, more just and simple than that on which you now wander blindly? Who has pulled the veil over your eyes so that you would not see the most wonderful light of the love proclaimed and lived by Jesus unto the final end?

I have seen you on the street, my friend, young and handsome; and suddenly everything changes in you: your face is disfigured, your instincts break loose, ravishing your being in elemental fury, and you become violent. Where did you learn such violence, young man? From whom? I have seen your mother meek and tearful and your father with his face stunned by pain, and I knew that you did not learn it from them. From where, then?

Lend your ears and listen to the call of Jesus, the call of His Church. Outside of her, your reckless violence will lead you to judgment and imprisonment, where your soul may be irrevocably destroyed. I have seen you in pain before the magistrates, where your actions have assumed horrible dimensions. I have seen you afraid, cynical, and full of bravado. All these attitudes showed me how near you are to the edge of destruction. And I ask myself once more: who bears the guilt for your fall?

---

[1] Giordano Bruno (1548–1600) was an Italian philosopher whose enthusiasm for nature led him to hold an extreme form of pantheistic immanentism. Since the nineteenth century his name has been associated with anticlericalism.—ED.

Come to the Church of Christ! Here only will you find consolation for your ravished soul. Only in the Church will you find certainty, because only in the Church will you hear the voice of Jesus saying meekly to you: "Son, all your sins are forgiven. You have suffered much. Behold, I have made you whole; go and sin no more."

No one has ever said such words as these to you. Yet you hear them now. Rather, you have heard of class hatred, political hatred—always hatred. "Love" is a strange word to you, but now the Church of Christ shows you a better way, the way of love. Up until this moment you were a slave of your instincts; your body was a simple instrument through which your instincts expressed themselves. But now you hear the words of Jesus, through His Apostle, pleading with you: *Know ye not that ye are the temple of God, and that the Spirit of God dwelleth in you?* (I Cor. 3:16).

You have been told that you descend from the apes, that you are a beast which must be trained; but now you discover an astonishing thing: that you are the temple of God and in you dwells the Spirit of God. You are being called, young friend, back to your dignity as a metaphysical being; you are raised up from the low place in which false education has sunk you to the sacred office of being the temple in which God dwells.

We call you to purity. If you have not forgotten the meaning of the word "innocence," if there is still an area within you of undefiled childhood, you will not resist this call.

Come to the Church of Christ—to learn what innocence and purity are, what meekness is and what love is. You will find your place in life and the purpose of your existence. To your astonishment you will discover that our life does not end in death, but in resurrection; that our existence centers on Christ, and that this world is not a mere empty moment in which non-being prevails.

You will receive hope, and this hope will make you strong.
You will receive faith, and this faith will save you.

You will receive love, and this love will make you good.

This, my young friend, is the first word which Jesus addresses to you in the midst of the turmoil of this world, through the thicket of your passions, with which no one has taught you to fight, and out of the transparent dreams of innocence which still haunt you from time to time.

Jesus is seeking you; Jesus has found you!

Radu Voda Church
Wednesday of Cheese-fare Week[2]
March 8, 1978

---

[2] The last Wednesday before the beginning of Great Lent.—ROM. ED.

SECOND HOMILY
LET US BUILD CHURCHES

March 15, 1978

And I say also unto thee, That thou art Peter, and upon this rock I will build My Church; and the gates of hell shall not prevail against it.

Matt. 16:18

DO YOU REMEMBER, young friend, how I told you last time that a new voice is calling and that this is the voice of Jesus? But to where and to what does He call you? What alluring promise to assuage your thirst for knowledge and truth does the Savior make?

The voice of Jesus calls you to His Church.

You live within a family, within a society, within a world. You are bound to your family by the unbreakable bond of blood, which you cannot deny and which seeks vengeance, if ever you betray it through your suffering. You live in the midst of your nation, which you feel to be one metaphysical entity—not a group of isolated individuals, but one immense and united soul in which you are the whole and in which the whole lives through you. And, finally, you exist in a world of suffering and joys, to which you respond because something in you unites and binds you inextricably to all your fellow human beings.

Where then is the Church of Christ to which you are called?

She is everywhere. She holds within her all human life, and, more, she contains all heavenly beings, too. For the Church knows no history; her history is the spiritual present. Family and society bear within them the tragic fate of their own limitations within the boundary of history. History is, by definition, the chronology of unhappiness, yet the road to salvation. But you, my young friend, are called to the Church of Christ, which was conceived in God's eternity and which bears within her perfection, just as the world bears within it its own limited nature. Society considers you simply a component part, one brick lined up alongside other bricks. Your freedom in it is to function as a brick, fixed for all time. This freedom is the freedom of constraint, and in this lies your tragedy. For your true freedom lies within you, but you know neither how to discover it in its true meaning, nor how to use it when at last you have found it. You have been told that you are not free, that freedom is the understanding of necessity, and that necessity is imposed upon you from the outside by factors entirely exterior to yourself, as in a lifeless construction.[1]

The Church of Christ is alive and free. In her we move and live through Christ, Who is her Head, and have full freedom, because we learn the Truth and the Truth makes us free (cf. John 8:32).

You are in Christ's Church whenever you uplift someone bent down in sorrow, when you help someone elderly walk more easily, or when you give alms to the poor and visit the sick. You are in Christ's Church when you cry out, "Lord, help me." You are in Christ's Church when you are patient and good, when you refuse to get angry with your brother, even if he has wounded your feelings. You are in Christ's Church when you pray, "Lord, forgive him." When you work honestly at your job, returning home weary in the evenings but with a smile upon your lips, bringing with you a warm and kind light; when you repay evil with love—you are in Christ's Church.

---

[1] The essence of political totalitarianism is underlined here. However, the problem is more general: true freedom does not come from outside, but from within us, its basis being not material but spiritual. Christ represents the supreme freedom which raises us above all worldly enslavement.—ROM. ED.

Do you not see, therefore, my young friend, how close the Church of Christ is? You are Peter and God is building His Church upon you. You are the rock of His Church against which no one and nothing can prevail, because you are a liberated rock—a soul that is fulfilled within His Church and not one condemned to stagnation.

Let us build churches, my friend. Let us build churches from the depths of our hearts ablaze with the light of the Sun of Righteousness, Who is Christ Himself, Who has told us that by faith we are free from sin. Let us build the churches of our faith which no human power can pull down, because the ultimate power of the Church is Christ Himself.

Feel for your brother at your side, ever present, and never ask, "Who is this man?" Rather say, "He is no stranger; he is my brother. He is the Church of Christ just as I am."

Look back, my friend, and be filled with awe; look forward and rejoice. History is a series of set events out of which arises from time to time living witnesses of princely faith, now embodied in our churches and monasteries. Treasures of the Romanian Christian soul, they represent the spirit which gives life to our national tradition. All which falls outside this spirituality is destined to perish. Mountains have been leveled, forests have burned, people have died, but churches have remained alive and monasteries continue offering the incense of continuous prayer to heaven. If we destroy the churches which express the national identity, we cannot affirm the continuity of a Romanian spirituality, nor can we maintain that we have preserved unaltered the tradition and soul of Romania. There are no references to Romanian princes destroying the foundation of churches, or of Michael the Brave[2] ordering the disappearance overnight of an

---

[2] Michael the Brave (1558–1601): Prince of Wallachia, Transylavania, and Moldavia. He is regarded as one of Romania's greatest national heroes for being the first ruler to unite the Romanian principalities.—ED.

Enea Church.[3] There is no wine cellar or *Dunarea* tavern,[4] old or new, to equal a single stone from the foundation of the Enea Church. Nor can any scientific atheism or scientific argument stop you, dear friend, from inquiring about the meaning of life and about God and salvation.

This search is the proof of your freedom in the face of any constraint and in the face of matter itself. It is your road to the Church, the gate through which you will enter. Do not waver on the doorstep, friend. Come in! How many years will you stand in the shadows of the Church without knowing her? How many years will you hear the voice of Jesus saying to you: *Him that cometh to Me, I will in no wise cast out* (John 6:37)?

The world will cast you aside; it oppresses and alienates you. Jesus receives you, comforts you, and returns you to yourself. Come and build churches with us. Let us reconstruct in our own souls an Enea Church—princely, Christ-centered, alive, and immortal—until we actually see her raised up again on her site, a steadfast witness to our Christian Faith and to our national identity.

Without churches or monasteries we are aliens. Whoever destroys churches, destroys the very substance of our material and spiritual endurance on this land given to us by God. Young man, you are no longer alone. You are in the Church of Christ.

Radu Voda Church
First Wednesday of Great Lent
March 15, 1978

---

[3] A church in Bucharest destroyed by the Romanian Communist government. See p. 71 above.—ED.

[4] A tavern was built on the site of the destroyed Enea Church. *Dunarea* is the Romanian name for the Danube River.—ED.

THIRD HOMILY
HEAVEN AND EARTH

March 22, 1978

We, according to His promise, look for new heavens and a new earth, wherein dwelleth righteousness.

II Peter 3:13

YOUNG MAN, I am addressing you again today because I have chosen you from all those to whom I could be speaking, for you are most ready to hear the word of Christ. You are noble and pure; atheist education has not yet managed to darken the heaven within you. You still look upward, you can still hear the summons from exalted realms. The soaring of your spirit heavenward has not yet been barred through arbitrary concepts. The desire for heaven still exists within you; materialism has not yet made you its prisoner.

Therefore, I call you, young man, seven times. Seven are the praises of the day to God, according to the Psalmist: *Seven times a day have I praised Thee for the judgments of Thy righteousness* (Ps. 118:164).

Today we will speak of heaven and earth.

I will not frighten you, my friend, with colorful descriptions of the end of the world. We stand before death daily. Its presence is more suffocating than life itself, more real than life. Death is our nightmare every moment. You live with death by your side, friend, and yet you have not grown accustomed to its presence because you are alive and authentic—more alive and authentic than you realize yourself.

Heaven and earth—the concepts remind me of a poem I

once heard recited by the poet himself on television. He held up his right arm as he spoke. His face was a picture of forced inspiration and his voice recited in a monotone, as he tried to induce some kind of trance among his hearers. Each verse was supported by a chorus of children chanting an artificial litany spontaneously prescribed: "Can you count us, heaven, one, two ... three ..." and so forth up to ten. It was a curse, a defiance, thrown up at heaven. The poem was essentially saying that heaven might be able to count the poet and his companions one, two, three ... well and good, but it could not vanquish them. That was the basic idea. He was an atheist poet, patterned for the materialists.

But to which "heaven" did he address himself? Was it to the vault made up of the successive strata of the atmosphere? If so, his monologue was senseless. The poet was obviously addressing someone who could hear and even count, at least that is what one surmises from the conviction with which he spoke. How strange! For it was not a matter of inventing a trivial personification for the sake of the poem's rhythm, but the poet himself actually believed in the depth of his being that his appeal or invocation was being heard and that it was an act of heroism. He addressed the metaphysical heaven which he was striving to diminish and to deny—by affirming it!

It is this heaven I want to talk to you about, my friend.

In the beginning God made the heaven and the earth (Gen. 1:1). He created a heaven and an earth, a transcendence and an immanence, an aspiration for perfection and a material manifestation; a spaceless, timeless existence, on the one hand, and a space subjected to time, on the other. From the moment of creation to the present we have kept within ourselves the nostalgic memory of our union with God's heaven. We have never forgotten that there is a place in heaven to which we, or rather, heaven within us, aspires.

Tell me, young man, how much have you believed the

statements which you have heard repeatedly to the point of obsession—at school, on the radio, on television, in the newspapers, and at young people's meetings—that you descend from apes? And how honored did this revelation make you feel?! Noam Chomsky[1] has said that the most stupid human beings can learn to speak, but the most intelligent ape has never reached such a height of achievement.

And now, behold, a voice from heaven addresses you: "You are My son!" And again, the voice confirms this for you, as it did before for Jesus when He lived in the world, *I have both glorified it, and will glorify it again* (John 12:28).[2]

You are heaven and earth; darkness and light; sin and grace. I know, friend, that you are tortured by questions concerning the meaning of your life in this world, and concerning the purpose of the world in general. Do the ready-made authoritarian statements in answer to your limited questions satisfy you: namely that "heaven is fiction, matter is everything, and it is matter speaking to you through your internal and external senses"? Matter organized its own structure and evolution by certain laws of great complexity before even the slightest rudiment of the human brain was formed. Thus, once the higher brain of man appeared—the only means by which matter recognizes itself—it could no longer recognize itself. And from that time until now human intelligence has been struggling in a sterile and vain effort to discover laws which heedless matter fixed in a period when there was nothing but darkness and unconsciousness!

What do you think of this game of non-intelligence which annuls all human intelligence, even the collective one? Do you

---

[1] Noam Chomsky (born 1928): a famous American linguist, the father of generative grammar.—ROM. ED.

[2] Every Christian, by virtue of the Mystery of Baptism, is a son of God, not by nature but by grace and adoption. In this context, "glorifying" has the meaning of theosis. "God became man so that man might become God." (St. Athanasius the Great, *On the Incarnation of the Word* 54.)—ROM. ED.

Photograph of Fr. George taken while he was under investigation, following the preaching of his Homilies to the Youth.

not see that the most elementary logic obliges you to admit the presence of an intelligence outside of this world?

But I call you to a much higher flight; to total abandonment; to an act of courage which defies reason. I call you to God. I call you to the One that transcends the world so that you might know an infinite heaven of spiritual joy, the heaven which you presently grope for in your personal hell and which you seek even while in a state of unplanned revolt.

This heaven, with its divine hierarchy and its divine light gradually descending only to return to its source which is God, does not count us in twos or fives or tens. For, my friend, in the eyes of heaven you are not a piece in a machine which drives you around; in the eyes of heaven you are a soul, a whole being, so free in your actions, so priceless in your worth, that God Himself, the Second Person of the Trinity, came into the world to be crucified for you.

How ridiculous it seems to you now—the curse of the poet who believed so much in heaven that he needed to have a chorus of children to hide behind as a shield! Do not believe, my friend, in the all-powerful nature of matter. This earth is finite. We can destroy matter in minutes through fission and achieve oblivion if we do not admit the presence of God. The absolute claims of materialism are supported on a limited premise. You realize that the attributes of matter—such as infinity, eternity, and self-creation—are purely spiritual notions. To deny the existence of heaven is to deny all existence which does not fall into the orbit of my feelings. To deny the spirit means to admit that, for those moments when I close my eyes or block my ears, the world becomes non-existent.

And now, my friend, I want to recite to you the most beautiful poem ever written about heaven and earth. It is the beginning of the Book of the Evangelist John: *In the beginning was the Word, and the Word was with God, and the Word was God. The same was in the beginning with God. All things were made by Him, and without Him was not anything made that was made. In Him was life; and the life was the light of men. And the light shineth in darkness; and the darkness comprehended it not* (John 1:1–5).

How can darkness confine light, or matter confine the spirit, or atheism destroy faith and annul freedom? The heavens count each of you, one by one; for each of you is a unique and unrepeatable creation, my friend, O man.

Radu Voda Church
Second Wednesday of Great Lent
March 22, 1978

FOURTH HOMILY
FAITH AND FRIENDSHIP
March 29, 1978

He that hateth Me hateth My Father also.

John 15:23

SO, MY DEAR friend, we are halfway along the road on which we started together that first Wednesday before the Lenten Fast, called "Cheese-fare Week." On that occasion the call of Jesus resounded for the first time in your ears, hungry for truth; and your soul, yearning for the absolute, followed it.

At that point I was alone, but I knew that my voice was not *one crying in the wilderness,* for the words were those of Jesus. I knew that the words with which I called you, *Prepare ye the way of the Lord; make his paths straight* into your hearts (Matt. 3:3), would penetrate your ears. And I was not mistaken. For look, how many we are today to confess, even if only within our hearts, faith in Christ and love for one another.

Why have I been calling you, my friend, and why have I put my soul into your hands, young one? Why have I believed in you to the point of implicating you in my actions of faith, and even to the point of placing my very life on the line for you?

Why? Because my spirit knew your soul even before you heard my words or even before we set eyes on each other. I knew of your disquiet and troubles, of your unhappiness and suffering. I understood long ago that your badness was but a shield against the world, and that your bravado was but a defense for your wounds. For you are my friend; we are bound together by a friendship which no one and nothing can destroy, because our freedom is guaranteed by Jesus Himself. And our love is founded upon the Resurrected One, Who says to us, *Henceforth I call you not servants, for the servant knoweth not what his lord doeth; but I have called you friends, for all things that I have heard of My Father I have made known unto you* (John 15:15).

Who has ever confessed such truths to you? On all sides you are surrounded by an atmosphere of secrecy, as within a conspiracy devised by the powerful of the day. A selective network prevents anything reaching you other than that which subjugates you to a certain idea or imposed concept. Where is your freedom to choose and where is the power of your word? Where is the exercise of that noble freedom given to you by God, based upon having the satisfaction of fulfilling your responsibility in history? Why then am I surprised that you do not know what this freedom is or how to use it? Why should I be amazed that you actually know nothing of friendship or love, or to whom to give them or how to preserve them?

Who in this world would be your true friend, or who would give his soul for you? In any social group to which you would belong, you are always excluded by the fundamental arguments themselves, which justify its existence as a social phenomenon.[1] Every exclusion based on these grounds puts you in the position of a slave. It is a social and philosophical secret which you are far from understanding. You are offered only the conclusion, authoritatively. Yet, if you were unfit to learn the road by which the conclusion came, how can you be fit to know the conclusion itself? And if you are fit to know the way, then why the mystery? Is someone afraid of your right to judge? or of your freedom? or of your friendship? Could religion or faith be an object of prohibition?

Slavery to ideas is as serious a form of slavery as any other. But

---

[1] The exact wording in the typed manuscript is unclear. It surely refers to the justification of the existence of various social groups. The attempt to avoid the Marxist terminology, "social class," is obvious.—ROM. ED.

Jesus offers you, through His Church, the deep mystery of His Divinity and His friendship. You are no longer called a slave but a friend, because you discover the mystery of Divine things.

You have avoided choosing Jesus as your friend for too long. Perhaps you were afraid of the ocean of spiritual freedom into which you would have to plunge. But Jesus has chosen you to hear His voice. He did so a long time ago: *Ye have not chosen Me, but I have chosen you, and ordained you, that ye should go and bring forth fruit, and that your fruit should remain* (John 15:16).

The choice was made long ago, for Jesus has always loved you, young friend, but now you have responded to His call. In responding you are ordained to go and bear fruit that will remain. To be a prophet of Christ in the world in which you live; to love your neighbor as yourself and to make each man your friend; to proclaim through your every action this unique and limitless love which has raised man from the level of a slave to that of a friend of God; to be the prophet of this liberating love which delivers you from all constraint, giving you back wholly to yourself so you can offer yourself freely to God.

The most humiliating bondage is that which forbids you any theological flight, any attempt to transcend the immanent and its captivity. "You are a slave of my will," it seems to say to you, "and my will forbids you to believe in anything other than what I direct you to believe."

Why are you forbidden the right to leave the space in which you are kept a prisoner of feelings and reason? Why is only that which belongs to this dimension imposed upon you as reality and the rest dismissed and decreed as fiction? And subsequently, why are you not allowed to penetrate this so-called fiction with your own knowledge and thus shatter it? Is it that there lies somewhere the fear that this "fiction" is more real than that which is imposed upon you as "reality"?

A philosophical or theological system, especially if it is a way of life, cannot be destroyed from outside. From this standpoint it remains unassailable to its besieger. Phrases like "religion is the opium of the people," or "religion was created by the exploiting classes," cannot even raise a smile today. They are purely and simply ignored.

Yet you, for you are young, are asked to take seriously the half-baked arguments of the atheist "bible" or the anti-catechism [column] from *Scinteia Tineretului*,[2] which hold fast only because of the prohibition preventing you from responding to them. In Christ freedom means liberation from sin and death, but on the social level—the struggle for ideas. In our country atheism takes a forced course, becoming more and more narrow. But life does not lie in the authority of the state. Faith, however, is on full wing, for it is a fact of life.

Authoritarianism creates bondage, faith gives freedom.

I read in *Contemporanul*[3] (November 11, 1977) an article entitled "With Atheists on Religion," which contained declarations of some young people in an interview carried out by the magazine reporter. Every investigation into religion is for us a source of disquiet and fear because, according to officialdom, to be a believer is tantamount to betrayal of one's country. Nevertheless, in this interview the young people, who were all Party members, replied according to their beliefs, and their faith made them free. I suggest that you all read this article in *Contemporanul*—the official literary organ of the materialist ideology of the Romanian Communist Party. You will see there that the young people interviewed set themselves free from the bondage of terror that would have made them hide their true Faith and declare formal statements about atheism. They overcame their instinct of self-preservation and affirmed publicly and courageously their Faith and the freedom to choose it. They openly chose Christ and

---

[2] *Scinteia Tineretului* (Young People's Spark) was the Romanian Communist Party youth paper.—ED.

[3] *Contemporanul* (The Contemporary) is a Romanian literary magazine.—ED.

His Church. All were young people like you, my friend, as good and generous as you, as brave as you. They were our friends. As a consequence, some of you wrote them precious words of encouragement, through which you wanted to tell them that they were not alone, that the best believe as they do, love as they do, and wish to express themselves as freely as they have done.

Friend, we are bound by the infinite love of Christ. Our faith in Him binds us together as One Body. Our common friendship binds us together, for we are all Christ's friends. Do not be afraid to affirm that you are His friend. Do not be afraid to reject an atheist ideology which has no other aim than to kill your soul as a metaphysical entity, or to cripple it within you. Do not be afraid to affirm that our nation has been Orthodox Christian since its inception, and that thirty years of enforced atheism and imposed [anti-Christian] propaganda cannot stop our people's aspiration towards the absolute.

Believe and love. Faith will make you free; love will unite you. You will be free in union with Jesus, and you will abide in His love.

See how high you have soared, my friend; you are now a friend of Christ! For this I love you, young one; for this I believe in you.

Radu Voda Church
Third Wednesday of Great Lent
March 29, 1978

FIFTH HOMILY
THE PRIESTHOOD AND HUMAN SUFFERING

April 5, 1978

> *Thou art a priest forever after the order of Melchizedek.*
>
> Hebrews 5:6

PERHAPS YOU HAVE been asking yourself, my young friend, why I have even been addressing you, and by what authority? What right do I have to give this message which is disturbing you and obliging you to face up to disquieting questions? Why have I come to confirm your own misunderstood fears and to open up to you perspectives which are so new and unexpected that they may break down your fragile balance of defenses?

Perhaps, by uncovering for you the purity and innocence which you did not recognize, I have made you even more vulnerable in this wicked world. I have made you more open to suffering, and it is natural that you should ask what is the purpose of suffering. Has it a finality or is it just a blind happening, a fate traced by the stars, or an endless ocean in which you swim without hope of reaching any shore?

I speak to you in the name of Christ and His Church, in the name of the priesthood to which Christ called me, because nothing in this world is an interplay of unconscious, arbitrary happenings. All things stem from a cause and hold fast towards an end which stands outside this world. The cause is God, the end is God. He is the Beginning and the End, the Alpha and the Omega (cf. Apoc. 1:8 and 22:13).

But what is the image of this world? What certainty does it offer us, what happiness awaits us at the unknown corners of life, what consolations in misfortune?

I will not begin with life or death, neither with the beginning nor the end; but with the given: that which happens to us every day.

Have you asked yourself, young person, what is your purpose in the world and whether everything is reduced simply to that? If we were born to be slaves of matter—even if only as a philosophical justification—then the end of your life is slavery.

If our freedom is reduced to need and logic, then our freedom is slavery.

If all our knowledge is reduced to a sterile and never-realized understanding of the laws of matter, then our knowledge is slavery.

If our love is reduced to the struggle for existence, and our sacrifice is for the perpetuating of the species, then these things too are but slavery.

And finally, if all our convictions spring from an imposed, official doctrine, then they cannot be but slavery.

And in all this series, young friend, where is the place for your soul?

You sense that there exists, away from all the materialism with which you have been intoxicated, and far from the atheism which has been imposed upon you like a violent ideology, something vaster, more authentic, and yet closer to you personally than all that which suffocates you in this materialist bath. Your spirit within you propels you towards that "something," as towards a world only envisioned and suspected. This world sees its own image, like the blue sky glistening in the sun, through the grid of prohibitions which this society imposes on you.

You must know, friend, that neither an atheist ideology, nor the materialist order, no matter how authoritatively it might be imposed upon you, is capable of raising up an absolutely impregnable wall between you and the spiritual world. The soul cannot be made prisoner. This is a law which the materialists refuse to recognize at their own peril. On the spiritual level there is no captivity without hope.

Your teachers speak to you of atheism and secretly go to church! Behold a crack through which the golden light of the spiritual dimension reaches you. Your ideological leaders thunder and hurl lightning against religion, uttering the most foul curses, yet at the moment of disaster they make the sign of the Cross, asking for God's help—as, for example, during the earthquake of March 4, 1977. Behold another crack through which the soul escapes the suffocating locker which the official ideology diligently built up for you.

In atheist meetings those obliged to speak condemn those who believe or who were caught in the criminal act of going to church. Yet away from the lying words, far from their false-toned platform proclamations, you discern their fear of being discovered as also having religious beliefs. The lie in which they so lamentably swim breaks down once more the wall of your incarceration, and you say as the sweet light breaks through, "Whence this unnatural light? It is a light foreign to our world."

I spoke to you about these things in my previous four sermons. I will continue to speak about them—for I am a priest of Christ. God has revealed to us through love the mysteries of His works. And Jesus has commanded me to make it known to you so that you will say no more, "I did not know it." I speak so that you might know that you can fly, and that only spiritual flight is truly exalted. The flight of materialism is flight with broken wings.

I speak openly to you about all these things because the Church of Christ has come out of the catacombs. She shines blindingly on the soil of this country which is highly esteemed in our hearts.

The Enea Church was destroyed—but who among us, Romanian and Christian, can forget it? A tavern, a symbol of a concept which considers the Church a plague, will be put in its place. A tavern—so once more the people will be happy!... Woe to the architect who builds there, binding his name forever with the destruction of something that was a demonstration of the Romanian genius of construction and faith. Woe to the officials who believe that they can win glory and power by the destruction of churches and the construction of bars. Woe to the concept that considers an Agapia Inn more valuable than the Agapia Monastery. Woe to those who consider that the Romanian Patriarchate is a piece of history which can be placed in a museum, and who have not understood that it has a real life which is always present. It is not a historical relic but a living soul. Woe to those who bow to force, allowing destruction which will never be accepted by history.

I have said all these things to you because I am a priest. And because we are priests we obey the command of God which says that a burning light cannot be hid under a bushel but must shine before all (cf. Matt. 5:15).

I have said all these things, young friends, that you might judge if it is right before God to listen to men rather than to God (cf. Acts 4:19). For He Who gave Himself upon the Cross for the salvation of the world commanded us not to hide the Divine Truth. I have said all these things to you that you might understand that through faith we shatter walls and break down the bonds of prejudice and abuse, even if we shall have tribulation in this world (cf. John 16:33).

There is a continual battle between good and evil, between right and wrong, between freedom and captivity of ideas, between purity and corruption. All these battles take place on only one field of combat—the heart of man. I, a priest of Christ, address this heart; for as Pascal has said, "The heart has its own way of thinking, which reason ignores."

What, then, does the priesthood mean? It means to be an enduring witness to human suffering and to take it upon your own shoulders. To be the one who warms the leper at his own breast and who gives life to the miserable through the breath from his own mouth. To be a strong comfort to every unfortunate one, even when you yourself are overwhelmed with weakness. To be a ray of shining light to unhappy hearts when your own eyes long ago ceased to see any light. To carry mountains of others' suffering on your shoulders, while your own being screams out with the weight of its own suffering.

Your flesh will rebel and say, "This heroism is absurd, impossible. Where is such a man, where is the priest you describe so that I may put my own suffering upon his shoulders?" Yet, nevertheless, he exists! From time to time there awakens within us the priest of Christ who, like the Good Samaritan, will kneel down by the side of the man fallen among thieves and, putting him upon his own donkey, will bring him to the Church of Christ for healing. And he will forget himself and comfort you, O man of suffering.

Who else could be moved by your suffering today? Who else would bear your burden, giving you words of comfort? From whom else would you hear today the words of Christ: *Come unto Me, all ye that labor and are heavy laden, and I will give you rest* (Matt. 11:28).

I have seen you, my young friend, bullied by your elders, mocked and insulted for the simple crime of being young. I spoke to you then as one in weakness and pain, as a sensitive and defenseless being. Then I saw you, to my horror and joy, bow and kiss my hand, that of a priest of Christ who brought you comfort.

Because you have overcome death, to which atheist doctrine had condemned you, because you have been exalted above the ruins of fallen materialism through your youth and faith, I speak to you the words which Jesus spoke through the Apostles to the Gentiles. They sound absurd to the prisoner of matter and materialism, to those who substitute taverns for churches and indecency for suffering. But to you they will resound full of spiritual meaning and truth:

The preaching of the Cross is to them that perish foolishness; but unto us who are being saved, it is the power of God. For it is written, I will destroy the wisdom of the wise, and will bring to nothing the understanding of the prudent. Where is the wise? where is the scribe? where is the disputer of this world? (I Cor. 1:18–20).

Where are all these men, my friends? There are none of them left. But you have remained here alive and whole in the Church of Christ, a holy people, won by God, a foundation stone on which the Orthodox spirit of the Romanian people is built. You are its only salvation and preservation through this age.

Radu Voda Church
Fourth Wednesday of Great Lent
April 5, 1978

SIXTH HOMILY
ABOUT DEATH AND RESURRECTION

April 12, 1978

> *Verily, verily I say unto you,*
> *If a man keep My saying,*
> *he shall never see death.*
>
> John 8:51

WE WILL TALK today, friends, about death and resurrection. What a strange and contradictory pairing for your ears which have heard only of death and life! You know nothing, my young friends, but the logical meaning of affirmation or of negation. Forcibly held by the materialist straitjacket, you know that water flows to the valleys, that fire burns and clouds contain electrical current. But this information is intended to make you sleep easy, with your ears bent to obedience and your understanding restricted to what is given to you. The universal remedy is offered to you like a message in a fortune cookie.

The deans of atheist ideologies have received "illumination" which has placed them in possession of absolute truth: the substitution of one glaring error for another only a little less flagrant. The only problem is that each new error is imposed on you as an absolute truth. The attempt to criticize such an ideological truth is considered a dangerous heresy. The officials of atheism begin at once to hunt the witch.

"The poles of our existence stretch between life and death," every materialist concept states. You, O man, are destined to be born and die by a caprice of nature, or by the simple play of passion. You have no destiny. You follow the law of necessity and quantity, which through some miracle becomes quality, and you must accept this as the only law governing your life and death.

This means that you are the most unfortunate being on earth, for neither plants nor animals have any consciousness of life and death, but you do. You know that you live, and you especially know that you will die. Your whole life unfolds under the somber perspective of death. If our modern world has not increased at all the chances for life, it has multiplied infinitely the possibilities for death. Civilization and Death, the tragic horsemen of the Apocalypse, have been ravaging our planet for centuries. And no angel of the Resurrection is evident on the horizon; no archangel flashes through the heavens with his thunderous voice, to the dreadful horsemen, "Stop! In the Name of the Lord, stop!"

In the material heaven of the atheist, there are written the dismal words: "Nothing exists but life and death." And after them, a striking prohibition: "It is forbidden to believe in the resurrection!"

Friend, what has atheism given you in exchange for its dispossessing you of faith in the Resurrection? What gift has it given you for taking away from you Jesus, the Risen One? To what serene celebration has it called you when it made you labor on Pascha and Christmas? What purification and spiritual rest has it outlined for you after the Christian celebrations were soiled with the dirt of denigration and violent verbal slogans?

At another time, men sought to live out the time of God, dimensions stretching out towards infinity; today, with our eyes on the clock, we boringly measure time by meetings, like a curse. At another time we reconciled ourselves at Pascha to our fellow men with the words of the Paschal hymn: "Let us embrace one another. Let us speak, brothers and sisters, also to those who hate us, and in the Resurrection let us forgive everything." Today on Pascha we are offered picnics, with alcoholic orgies which inevitably end up in violence.

You know, young ones, that an idea is valid, not through the fact that it exists, but through its positive effects. So judge for yourself, my friend; compare and appreciate. But above all, commit yourself. For you must choose between good and evil; between meekness and violence; between life and death.

But now I will take you with me onto another plane. To go on this unexpected flight you must renounce the materialistic prejudices which were planted in your mind. You must purify your heart of passions which your educators have cultivated within you since your childhood, calling them by shining and virtuous names. You must wipe out faithlessness and atheism, hatred and lack of respect for men, servility and violence, cowardice and arrogance. And thus purified, you must direct yourself toward the great festival of the Resurrection.

You must understand that the Resurrection of Christ is a renewal of the universe. Through your transformation the whole world is changed. At the Lord's Supper, when Jesus announced His approaching sufferings, these suffering words were to assume a mystical and saving value for the whole world. You must understand that suffering leads to death, but death leads to Resurrection. Yet if there be no Resurrection, if the only reality is death, then we are more unfortunate than stones. For in seeing things without faith, our life endures but from birth until death, which could be a day, or it could be seventy years; for "from the moment of your birth you are old enough to die." What sense, then, has this short interval in the face of the eternity of death? To die like an animal means, simply and purely, to die—like a stone loosened from its pile, or a calf struck by the axe of the butcher in the slaughterhouse. Such a death has nothing human in it. It is a nightmare, for beyond it there is no light, but only a terrible darkness. Human life appears as a tragedy because of such a death and the suffering which goes with it.

Whether a believer or not, no man can escape that ultimate judgment which momentarily precedes the agony of death and which is the tribunal of our own conscience. Who among us will feel totally innocent at that judgment?! Death with its somber absence of perspective terrifies us because our faith has weakened and because, in the general fear which rules the world, death appears no more as a liberation but as a supreme terror. For we have dehumanized death by denying the idea of God, and matter itself cannot dominate the spirit except by force.

The greatest and most rabid atheists of our century, who have not only made of matter a god, and of atheism a new mystical way, but have also used every means of persuasion to kill the true God in you, young friend, are all themselves afraid of their own disappearance, with an incurable, metaphysical fear. That is why they build grandiose tombs for themselves, attaching themselves to their earthly remains with a pitiable devotion. Tragically, they try to substitute their aspirations for eternity with these stones. The drama of their idolatrous lives ends in a more idolatrous death. They have lived in terror of suffering and have desired an instantaneous death, because death itself is nothing else than a useless and unbearable blind alley of suffering. They were not spared even this ultimate act of solidarity with mankind, namely death.

But Jesus has bestowed upon us a death without fear, a reconciliation between death and happiness, for He has brought to us the assurance that death is not the end, but a beginning: the beginning of eternal life—life through resurrection.

To love someone is to say, "You will not die," and to believe what you say. This inarguable faith is in fact the only fundamental truth which we feel in our genuine and profound love. I speak of all types of love. The mother, caressing her child, says to him with a faith that moves mountains, "You will not die." The lover, who whispers to the dear one words full of passion, says in effect with the same deep conviction, "You will not die."

Man's darkened history knows one moment of sunshine, which since then has been poured over humanity: I speak of the Sun of Righteousness, Christ Incarnate, the Son of God, Who came into the world to save it. What necessity could determine the Divine Perfection, Who knows no need, to become man? Nothing, save love. Only love [for man], since it is the only virtue which is both free and liberating. Not passionate love, but compassionate love. *For God so loved the world, that He gave His only begotten Son, that whosoever believeth in Him should not perish, but have everlasting life* (John 3:16).

Thus Jesus became Love incarnate, tangible Love, crucified Love. It was so hard for men to believe what they saw—for perfect Love stood before them in human form. They wanted to see Him on the Cross, pushed to the limit, which is suffering and death—to verify His authenticity as if through fire, to see if Love would preserve its identity to the end. And Jesus passed the examination to which mankind subjected Him.

Remember, friends, His words from the Cross: *Father, forgive them, for they know not what they do* (Luke 23:34). What greater proof of love could anyone give than this? And if you believe it when you tell your loved one, "You will not die," why do you not believe the words of supreme Love when He promises you eternal life? *Verily, verily, I say unto you, He that heareth My word, and believeth on Him that sent Me, hath everlasting life, and shall not come into condemnation, but is passed from death to life* (John 5:24).

But you believe, and you know that in truth you believe, as I also know it, even if what you believe is not very clear, my young friend. Yet to those who make room in your young conscience for the practice of their violent doctrines, and to those who incarcerate your soul in the narrow forms of atheism, your faith is a reality which frightens them more than anything else.

Ideas are preserved through their truth. An idea which is maintained through force and violence is deeply undermined by the falsehood within it. If materialists do not speak of death, it is because they are afraid of it and they pass over it in silence, just as they pass over all ideas which cannot be falsified.

Why was March 4 passed over in silence one year after the earthquake in 1977? Because death obliges you to think of God, of the life you have led and your moral responsibility. And they fear your capacity for intuiting metaphysical truth and your spiritual freedom, just as much as they fear death.

I speak to you about death as your single possibility to be victorious. For without resurrection both life and death become nonsense, absurd. The love of God, however, is the guarantee of our resurrection; and the Resurrection is the foundation of our faith in God and in Jesus Christ, His Son. It is the sublime and glorious occasion of a vital affirmation, an invitation to an amnesty of the past, as one French journalist has said; it is an invitation to a commitment in the future.

"Let us forgive all things because of the Resurrection." Any other attitude means death. He Who died has also risen, and those who saw Him testified to the fact because they sealed it with their own suffering and death. We cannot doubt the truth of their accounts.

In the end of the Sabbath, as it began to dawn toward the first day of the week ... behold, there was a great earthquake: for the angel of the Lord descended from heaven, and came and rolled back the stone from the door, and sat upon it. His countenance was like lightning, and his raiment white as snow (Matt. 28:1–3).

This is the majestic depiction of the Resurrection of the Lord, the One Who broke the bonds of death and brought to man the unexpected perspective of the universal resurrection.

From now on, young man, be not afraid of death. For Christ is risen, being the first fruits of the Resurrection (cf. I Cor. 15:20).

From the moment you discover this truth, your life has a new meaning. It will not end between four sides of a coffin and remain there—which would make our lives a useless mockery.

But passing through death, life issues forth to the glory of the resurrection.

Go, young man, and tell this news to all. Let the light of your angelic face shine in the light of the Resurrection—for today the angel in you, which I uncovered in my first address, has overcome the world in you. Tell those who until now have oppressed your divine soul: "I believe in the Resurrection," and you will see them coil in fear, for your faith has overcome them. They will fret and shout to you in despair: "This earth is your paradise and your instincts are your heaven."

Do not stop on your path, but go on, shining and pure, giving the light of that Resurrection on the first of Sabbaths to all. You, my friend, are the unique bearer of your deification in Jesus Christ, and with yourself you raise up the entire Romanian people to the height of its own resurrection. From death to life and from earth to heaven!

Radu Voda Church
Fifth Wednesday of Great Lent
April 12, 1978

SEVENTH HOMILY
FORGIVENESS
April 19, 1978

Wherefore I say unto thee, her sins, which are many, are forgiven; for she loved much: but to whom little is forgiven, the same loveth little.

Luke 7:47

WHEN I BEGAN this series of homilies, young friend, I did not know you. I only knew that you existed, that you were aspiring after something which the world could not give you, and I called to you as to my unknown brother, to show you a new road to walk.

I told you of Christ and His Church, of a new heaven and a new earth, of death and resurrection, and, above all, of the love of Jesus for you. Now I call you my brother, not just my neighbor; and I love you not with an abstract love which seeks after its object, but with a love which has found its object. For I know you and you are in my heart, as I am also in your heart. For if you have been coming here regularly to listen to me, you have done so because you have heard the voice of Jesus, that irresistible voice which has awakened you from your materialistic stupor and from the atheist lethargy into which you had sunk. You heard when Jesus said to you, "Come to Me!" and when you turned to Him, He put His ring upon your finger and new shoes upon your feet and the best robe around your shoulders (cf. Luke 15:22).[1]

This is because you came wounded and bleeding. You were

---

[1] From the Lord's parable of the Prodigal Son.—ROM. ED.

oppressed by all that you had learned about the deification of matter and by all the prohibitions, raised by the fetishes of atheism, against your inner searching. Before your eyes, blind until then, was lit a light more enchanting than any song of a Siren. You left behind you the ravenous land of unbelief and the "husks" which you had eaten up until then. You forgot your teachers who said that this was the only food, without which you would die. And you heard the word of Jesus saying to you: *Man shall not live by bread alone, but by every word that proceedeth out of the mouth of God* (Matt. 4:4).

Friend, when did you come to feed on the word of God, for this is what you are doing. For the word of God you have renounced your rest, your comfortable peace; you have overcome obstacles and prohibitions and have come here to be nourished on the word of Christ. Honor to you, my friend! God will give His word and His grace will be poured upon you in full. For it is written: *Everyone that asketh receiveth, and he that seeketh findeth, and to him that knocketh it shall be opened* (Matt. 7:8).

For your persistent asking, my courageous friend, Jesus will reward you. Because you had the courage to fight the habits and inertia which made you their prisoner; because you had the courage to break the restricting barriers which have been imposed upon you, like an uncrossable threshold, by the materialist ideology which believes that authoritarian demands do not need proof and that authoritarianism supplants faith; and, finally, because you had the courage to go forward, once released from slavery to their doctrines, towards that which emerged before you like a tangible love. And the further you advance, the better you understand that this infinite, crucified Love shines for you, O unique and unrepeatable man, as I called you elsewhere.

For your courage, you have received forgiveness. Do you not feel somehow in this spirit of love and quietness, which has now been placed within your soul, an assurance with which to walk on the new road of obedience to Christ? It is the grace of God which comes to you. At first this grace visits you softly, but when, as you pray, you feel a fiery moment of ineffable joy sweep through your heart, and when on your knees, you feel an inexplicable affection in your soul and an imperative need to weep, know then that the grace of Christ is visiting you. Persevere, my friend, and grace will come more and more often, until it lives in you permanently. You will then know a continuous state of grace, and the inner peace whose source is the forgiveness of Christ will transform itself into spiritual joy, which will invisibly radiate through every pore of your being. You will know the happiness of being forgiven and of forgiving.

Our life is hard as long as our earth and heaven are but matter, and our spirit remains blind as long as atheism is our religion. But if, nevertheless, there exists something that can save you, my friend, even during your call to Christ, before your soul is flooded with the light of faith, then it is the joy of forgiving and of being forgiven. The common life is hard. You must know how to forgive. You must know not only how to forgive—which can bring you the vain satisfaction of pharisaical goodness—but how to be forgiven, which produces in one an utter humility.

I remember telling you about Jesus and His Church as a holy institution, a spiritual reality whose threshold you found long ago. But only now have you succeeded in breaking the multitude of invisible cords of certain concepts which have dragged you back. I spoke to you of churches scattered throughout this land of ours on which we walk with joyful or sorrowful feet. I have also shown you that we have endured down the ages through our humility and glory, through our indestructible Orthodox Faith. That love of our land and the bond of blood and language have been expressed in our vivid and true history by the erecting of churches by princes and magistrates as living letters of stone which time can never wash away. And even now if we see a church demolished to make room for a tavern, we say, "Never," with all our agonizing soul, in opposition to those who believe that in

Radu Voda Church (the site of the "Seven Homilies").

destroying churches and forbidding the word of God in schools, in the press, and even in men's hearts, they have abolished the One by Whose mercy we live and survive.

I spoke to you about your freedom in Christ and how you should use it. I showed you that minerals do not know death or life except by analogies, but that they have only one state of being; that animals have an unconscious knowledge of life and death, but that you, my friend, know both life and death, and above all, resurrection—even though it is forbidden for you to believe in it. For Christ has called you to deification, not to the simple condition of survival, not even to your present state as man; but He has raised you above the human condition when He said, *Father, I will that they also, whom Thou hast given Me, be with Me where I am* (John 17:24).

These are the things that I have said to you, my young friend, and many similar things—all from the words of Christ. And for this my brethren hate me and have forbidden you to come and listen to me—you who were thirsty for the word of God and who wanted to know if you were totally condemned or if you had been chosen for a more exalted destiny, for resurrection. They closed the gates on you and erected walls of obstacles in front of you. You who wrote in one of your letters (for each letter I have received from one of you represents all of you) about your search for that which transcends matter and the immanent that is deified nowadays, about your whole hope to embark upon the road of truth and about the joy of catching a glimpse of the One Who is the Truth, the Way, and the Life—you wrote to me several days ago: "What joy to hear talks about God and about a world other than that of matter from a secular professor in a secular college the other day![2] It was like an unbelievable dream. And to understand that this layman was enlightened by a spirit of faith which he made known to us not only by his words but also by the light which radiated from his being. Thus I almost envy you theologians for knowing and living that which we do not know and yet towards which our whole being aspires."

Or you, young professor of thirty-three years of age, who said, "All these years of teaching I have spent driving students from the Church with a club. But now I have understood what led them there and why they returned to the Church, forgiving me. I understand now that if you, pupils in the first class in seminary, believe so strongly and know so much about the deep things of the human soul and about a world which I have forbidden to my students, then I ought to believe more than you."

Do these words not remind you of Paul on the road to Damascus? For if we admit with Albert Camus that every man passes at least once over the Mount of Olives, we ought also to admit that every one of us has experienced the road to Damascus also—when the voice of Jesus resounded out to us: *Saul, Saul,*

---

[2] He was speaking about the poet Ioan Alexandru and his classes. (Noted in the margin of the original manuscript.)—ROM. ED.

why persecutest thou Me?... It is hard for thee to kick against the pricks (Acts 9:4–5).

No man is exempt from suffering. If we suffer, let it be for Christ. If we forgive, let us forgive for Christ's sake. May truth stand before us always. "Truth before peace" is how one engineering student put it as he listened to these "Seven Homilies to the Youth." And this "peace" is not the peace of Christ in John 14:27, nor the peace between the two world wars as defined by Titulescu,[3] but that spiritual and material comfortableness for which we trample underfoot our principles and justice; that state of "tolerance" which helps us to go to bed each night with a compromise in our heart, only to wake up the next morning with a new compromise under our pillow.

And now I will read to you a statement by one of the students regarding the "Seven Homilies," since several statements have been taken at the Theological Institute, by forcing the students against their conscience to write them. We know what a written declaration means—what a source of fear and terror it releases, as is so often the case. I have chosen one statement from a number of declarations given to me because this one is clearer (not more correct; for all are equally correct).

"I declare that on Wednesday, April 12, at 9:00 PM, I listened to the 'Sixth Homily to Young People' given by Fr. George Calciu-Dumitreasa, in the Radu Voda Church, Bucharest. I had also listened to the Third, Fourth, and Fifth Homilies, but in other circumstances.... I declare that I met on this occasion, as well as during his other sermons, a large number of students from the Theological Institute, doctorate students in theology, students from other departments, people whom I had never seen before, as well as a great number of seminarians. The atmosphere in the church was always impressive, and I experienced genuine moments of spiritual exaltation and concentration. With respect

---

[3] Nicolae Titulescu (1882–1941) was a Romanian diplomat who was involved in the League of Nations.—ED.

to the content of these sermons, I declare that I am in total agreement with the ideas expressed by the Father Professor, who did nothing more than elucidate in a realistic way the problems which demand attention, while adhering strictly to the teachings of the Orthodox Church.

"Rev. Professor George Calciu was my teacher for a number of years at the Theological Seminary in Bucharest, from where I graduated, and he has contributed in the greatest measure to our formation as pupils and true servants of the Lord Christ and of the Church of the people."

Is it necessary to add anything? Except my homage to this student's courage, and to all of you who, trampling over instincts of survival, have placed "truth before peace" and have come here. Perhaps I should also add the joy that these declarations—both written and spoken—have brought me along with your presence in this church. Finally, I should also add my sense of submissiveness to you all, for you are good and you love Jesus more than me, for without being His servants you would not have been predisposed to sacrifice your comfort to come and express your love for God.

Let us pray for all our brethren who love or hate us, those who have done us harm or good, those who have forgiven us or have not forgiven us. Let us forgive everyone everything.

I will close, my young friend, this final "word" to you with a quotation from the homily of St. John Chrysostom which is read on the night of the Resurrection in every Orthodox church, for Pascha—the Day of Resurrection and our joy—is approaching. Then, you will know that Christ is risen and that we will be risen with Him. When I say that you will know, I mean that your heart and soul will discover this certainty of resurrection, which has been long within you and by virtue of which you are here.

"If any have labored from the first hour, let him receive today his rightful due. If any have arrived at the sixth hour, let him in no wise be in doubt, for on no wise shall he suffer loss. If any be delayed even until the ninth hour, let him draw near, doubting nothing, fearing nothing. If any have tarried even until the eleventh hour, let him not be fearful on account of his lateness; for the Master, Who is jealous of His honour, receiveth the last even as the first. He giveth rest to him that cometh at the eleventh hour, as well as to him that hath labored from the first hour.... Wherefore, then, enter ye all into the joy of your Lord; both the first and the last.... Christ is risen, and the angels rejoice! Christ is risen, and life flourisheth! Christ is risen, and there is none dead in the tombs!"

I have read these lines to you that you might know them. I have read this homily because Passion Week is before us, before which every mouth is dumb. I have read these words that you might find that, in the days which follow, we will live in spirit and in flesh the Calvary of Jesus. At the top of Golgotha there awaits us forgiveness and resurrection. I have read these truths to remind you that this Romanian people has always climbed the hill of history's Golgotha, ceaselessly re-creating in spirit the way of Jesus and anticipating in faith this Resurrection which you, my friend and brother, will bring forth as a torch burning in your heart.

Radu Voda Church
Sixth Wednesday of Great Lent
April 19, 1978

AN ADDITIONAL HOMILY TO THE YOUTH
A HOMILY TO THEOLOGIANS
May 17, 1978

This sermon was to be preached on May 17, 1978, in Radu Voda Church as a part of a new series of sermons announced on May 10. The new series was to be on the theme of "Christ and Culture." It was, however, not held because I was suspended by order of Bishops Roman Ialominteanu, Ilie Georgescu, and Octavian Popescu. Teachers at the seminary were forced to keep watch until 10:00 PM that night to prevent me from preaching. Students in the seminary and institute were confined to their dormitories.[1]—FR. GEORGE

> *He that loveth father or mother more than Me is not worthy of Me: and he that loveth son or daughter more than Me is not worthy of Me.*
>
> Matthew 10:37

I DID NOT INTEND to add this supplementary message to the "Seven Homilies to the Youth," given during Lent, my younger brother theologians, but I am forced to come back to you by internal and external pressures. Thus, I will appeal in a greater measure to our sense of justice, honor, and courage in this homily than in my previous ones.

From the moment I decided to attack openly and publicly the problems of religious freedom, from the moment I decided to protest openly against the demolition of the churches—

---

[1] The sermon was never delivered. See p. 127 above.—ED.

and I mean to use the plural[2]—I knew what would await me: persecution, terror, the tribunal, blackmail. Within a few months I have experienced all these, except for the fact that everything was more inhuman and more degrading than I had imagined. From that moment everything that is bound up with my being, my life, and my public activity indeed became public property. For this reason I will divulge to you a portion of the things that have happened so that you might know what awaits you when your faith, your love of man determines that you act in the way I have acted. I will not tell you everything, for I do not want you to believe that the face of mankind is only hideous, but I will tell you only that which justifies this word.

Two reproaches were brought against me—totally contradictory to each other—regarding the "Seven Homilies." On the one hand, I was reproached—and the term is such a euphemism that it in fact becomes almost insipid—that my sermons were supposed to be addressed to seminarians and therefore my accusations of atheism and materialism would fall exclusively upon the teachers of the seminary. That argument is of such a flagrantly bad intent that it would seem a useless and harmful waste of time to occupy myself in combatting it. On the other hand, some theologians reproached me for giving priority to the lay youth and therefore neglecting the young theologians in my sermons. Here I must defend myself: I have not neglected you, my young friends and brothers. I knew that you were more faithful, more just and more kindhearted than I; that your numerous and assiduous attendance at the sermons which I preached in Radu Voda Church (or on the steps there after the school's directors closed it against me) was a proof that

---

[2] At that time two churches had been demolished: one in Bucharest and one in Focsani. In the years following, the destruction and profanation would continue. We do not have the exact statistics for the whole country. We do know, however, that in the capital [Bucharest] twenty-eight churches and monasteries were destroyed or "translocated."—ROM. ED.

An archival photograph of the Radu Voda Church.

you yourselves were involved in the content of the homilies and that to a great extent your views were being expressed through my mouth. Finally, an inner reason compels me to clarify certain matters concerning us theologians.

It is the time, my brothers, when the words of the Savior that *the time cometh, that whosoever killeth you will think that he doeth God service* (John 16:2) become an actual reality. I do not make such a statement without cause. Rather, I tell you these things because your senior teachers, the very directors of your consciences and the formers of our nation's future priests, have raised themselves up against the things I preached in the name of Jesus, against my protest at the demolition of the Enea Church, and against you theologians who came to listen to truths spoken in courage and forthrightly, in spite of the prohibitions. They rose up, seized by a "noble wrath," strictly watching to keep you from coming on Wednesday evenings to hear the "Seven Homilies." They were not watching to keep you from the temptations of the world: from drunkenness, from dissoluteness, or from any other sin with which the world ensnares you. In that they left you to fend for yourselves. But they jumped up to stop you from listening to the word of God spoken in a new way. They were—to use a phrase from the propaganda brochures on class struggle—"very vigilant." They made you write declarations against one another, becoming informers through official statements and denouncing all those guilty of the grave crime of listening to my sermons, including yourselves. This was the splendid spiritual action by which they transformed the theological institute into an interrogation center. I would like to ask the one who carried out this interrogation, the spiritual father Ilie Moldovan, if he ever took such declarations from his coworkers when he was an engineer? If so, it would mean that here he is continuing his former activity, and that in fact it is not for theology that he is found at the institute. If not, however, I would ask him to explain where and when he learned this system of interrogation.

He who guides his conscience with the statement, "I have children to bring up," or justifies his action by saying, "The dean forced me to make declarations," has a remote-control machine rather than a soul. They should remind themselves of the words of the Savior from Matthew 10:37, which constitute our text today.

I know the fury with which His Holiness [Patriarch Justin] fights against the Army of the Lord[3]—an Orthodox group of

---

[3] Founded in 1923, the Army of the Lord was abolished by the Communist government in 1947 and continued its activities underground. Its emphasis on popular revivalism caused friction between it and the Orthodox hierarchy.—ED.

Enea Church in 1956.

popular Christian piety who dared to put pious verse to popular melodies and non-traditional rhythms. It would be good for them to understand one thing, which is clear to a believing man, namely, that to the extent to which false science secularizes the world, sometimes even helped by priests, to that same extent a simple faith extends into every area of human manifestation.

We know, however, that as risky as it is to combat official and unofficial atheism, it is equally convenient and advantageous to attack the Army of the Lord,[4] even if they should have merely small errors, when they are obliged to hold meetings in semi-obscurity which at times are brutally broken up by the police. In fact there exists only one single solution to the problem of the Army of the Lord: Put all its members into a single congregation under the roof of the Orthodox Church, for they are pious and devout men who want to be

---

[4] The problem of the Army of the Lord has not been properly resolved up to today.—ROM. ED.

received into the fold. Only in this way would you solve a spiritual problem, and not with violence. In spiritual matters violence solves nothing; it only complicates things. I speak of these simple men, honorable in their faith, and who ought to be brought back into the Church, because they are men who burn with faith and who defend their religious belief with zeal, which is something not everyone has or wants to do.

Where was the parish priest of the Enea Church on the previously arranged night that the demolitionists came? Why did he not stay in the altar to defend it, for who would dare to crush a church over its servant?

Where were the priests of Focsani when the party secretary of the region, Mr. Dobrovici, as Romanian by his name as by his actions, destroyed this church? Would this gentleman have dared to blow up the church together with its servants? Surely not! On the contrary, some of the truck drivers and bulldozer workers showed more dignity and courage in refusing to participate in the destruction of the church. I have since learned that for this reason four of them had their work contracts demonstratively broken. What reward was given to those who destroyed these churches, and what sanctions were imposed on the priests who deserted their obligations?

The time will come, and it is not far off, when we shall know the complete list of those who signed in favor of the demolition of the Enea Church. They will be covered in shame. The time will come when we shall know the complete list of those who refused to sign, rightly considering this act of destruction a barbarous, anti-cultural act. They will be honored by all Romanian souls. All I can say now is that those who refused to sign are the most outstanding representatives of our contemporary culture (history, literature, and art), and their names pronounced in public will further strengthen in us the respect which we bear towards them and will prove that only he who is a barbarian in thought could destroy the religious past of our nation to replace it with the crippled puppet of atheism. These men [who refused to sign] have heard the words of the Savior, even if they did not know how to decipher them, with an inner sense of dignity and honor: *What shall a man give in exchange for his soul?* (Mark 8:37).

During the last few months I have received several intimidating telephone calls from people who hide their terrorist inclinations and instincts for moral torture behind the mask of an anonymous telephone call. A whole range of threats have been made against me and my family, ranging from calls for our moral destruction to calls for our civic and physical destruction. To the degree that it becomes necessary I will make these things publicly known, so that you may all see what honor and humanitarianism these individuals possess. Some of these men set themselves up as defenders of the regime, which it seems has been threatened by my sermons. Can there be any falsehood greater than this? What is strange is that these "defenders" strive to convince us that the regime which they defend is one ready to perpetrate any abuse and ready to destroy me, though not guilty, and my family also. These things are happening during a time when I thought our regime acknowledged certain humanitarian principles which do not endorse such abuse....

I have said all this to you, for I want you to make these things public so that the blackmail and moral gangsterism, which is asking for my soul in exchange for my threatened family, may cease for good. I hope that in making them public, these actions will be condemned and our human dignity will be increased according to the words of Jesus: *What I tell you in darkness, that speak ye in the light; and what ye hear in the ear, that preach ye upon the housetops* (Matt. 10:27). For my voice is not sufficient, and it must be amplified by hundreds of your voices, so that the truth of faith and of kindheartedness might reach the ears of all. Let us remain closely united around the hierarchy of the Church and our bishops, for without the hierarchy, the Church would be an organism without a strong skeleton. We shall remain with them and remind them that they are the spiritual leaders of at least fourteen million Romanian believers, among which are to be found the finest men who know how to unite love for one's country with the universality of Christian love, and how to unite faith with true culture.

Should they possess this awareness and should they truly be Christ's apostles on Romanian soil, then we will be their humble disciples. If one single bishop had been on our side, we would not have witnessed the destruction of the Enea Church, or, in the worst case, we would be seeing its reconstruction today. Nor would we have had to painfully look on in the pulling down of the Lord's church at Focsani. We humbly plead with our bishops not to allow a profane tavern to replace the Enea Church, a tavern where drunkenness, violence, and prostitution will take place. They should defend this sacred ground on which our princes walked, and may the church be rebuilt as it was. This is the duty of every Romanian Christian among us.

We will not cease to protest against this sacrilege and this illegality. We will never draw back from opposing any similar anti-cultural acts, such as those committed at Focsani and Bucharest. We will make these transgressions public. It is our right to stop their occurrence.

And who can stop us, if Christ is with us? For what price has our life outside of Christ, since He Himself assures us: *Whosoever will save his life shall lose it; but whosoever shall lose his life for My sake and the Gospel's, the same shall save it* (Mark 8:35); or, *Ye are the salt of the earth ... the light of the world* (Matt. 5:13–14).

Each year thousands of graduates finish the schools of medicine, engineering, law, teaching, etc. They become lost in the anonymity of the masses and of their professions. But if, in a single year, we were to see one thousand priests graduate, full of the spirit of sacrifice, priests as Christ would have them to be, then in less than one year the spiritual face of our country would be changed like that of Jesus on Mount Tabor. For such priests sanctify the world and bring a new spirit of truth and justice, a heavenly love and Christ-centered consolation to a world of suffering.

Our people are like a ripe harvest, waiting to be gathered in for Christ: *Lift up your eyes, and look on the fields; for they are white already to harvest* (John 4:35). But where are the worthy harvesters? Lift up your eyes and, I tell you, you will see how few there really are. And the wheat is wasting in the field outside of the Kingdom of God.

Be most diligent harvesters yourselves. Forget your instincts, which are overpowered by your teachers, whose principles are: "I have a mother, father, sons, and daughters, too large a salary to accept the sacrifice and suffering of Christ and His Church." Lift up the eyes of your spirit to the people who believe in you and for whom there exists no other spiritual salvation than in the Church of Christ.

Be harvesters! Be pastors! And above all, pray to God to give this nation good harvesters who will not love parents and children more than Christ, Who seeing the multitude *was moved with compassion on them, because they fainted, and were scattered abroad, as sheep having no shepherd. Then saith He unto His disciples, The harvest truly is plenteous, but the laborers are few. Pray ye therefore to the Lord of the harvest, that He will send forth laborers into His harvest* (Matt. 9:36–38).

Let us pray to God for the harvest and for the reapers!

A NEW WORD TO THE YOUTH
CHRIST HAS RISEN WITHIN YOUR HEART!

In 1990 Fr. George gave the following homily on a trip to Romania. After the fall of Communism in Romania in 1989, Western culture had rushed to fill the void left by the removal of Ceausescu's authoritarian government. American films and music inundated the country, while non-governmental organizations arrived to "educate" and "enlighten" Romanians with Western values at odds with the Orthodox Faith. Seeing the state of this new generation, numerous young people, especially the students of the Romanian Orthodox College Student Association, asked Fr. George to deliver a new homily. Thus, twelve years after his original "Seven Homilies," Fr. George prepared the following new "word" for the young people of Romania.—ED.

> *Mary stood without at the sepulchre weeping: and as she wept, she stooped down, and looked into the sepulchre, and seeth two angels in white sitting, the one at the head, and the other at the feet, where the body of Jesus had lain. And they say unto her, Woman, why weepest thou?*
>
> John 20:11–13

WHAT NEW WORD can I share with my young friends? Since then[1] many long years have passed. A new generation has arisen, tested by a unique experience and, perhaps, touched by a new skepticism born from contact with the Western world, estranged from the right Faith.

---

[1] The year 1978, when the first seven homilies were delivered.—ED.

Perhaps today, even more so than when I delivered those "Seven Homilies to the Youth," the soul of the young people—whom I consider as much my friends as I did back then (because I still speak in the name of Jesus Christ)—is increasingly assaulted by mental illnesses. This is brought about by the treacherous propaganda from the West, under the mask of liberal democracy, which often takes on the appearance of Christianity, just as Satan dons angelic light to deceive as many as possible.

Back then you were oppressed through force, which created within you a natural resistance against a system of materialistic thinking and formed within you a mystical dimension. You, my young friend, did not believe anything that was told to you then, because, as you know, under the guise of relative truth, which the rulers of the times had proclaimed as absolute truth, a complete and totalitarian lie was hidden.

Back then the voice of the priest reached you through the spoken homily at the price of his liberty and even his life, and the truth of Christ consoled a soul wounded by the violence of political language and physical terror.

Back then you were told of Communist internationalism and of an exclusively materialistic existence, which sought to kill the universal love of the Savior. Then you were told that you were a mere instrument, without freedom, in the social and political mechanism, and that only integration into this necessity would bring you freedom. However, Christ is calling you to a greater freedom of a totally different order when He says, *Sanctify them through Thy Truth; Thy word is Truth* (John 17:17) and, in another place: *Ye shall know the Truth, and the Truth shall make you free* (John 8:32).

Is it not so, my friend, that back then the Christian Truth appeared crystal clear and easily understandable to you?

Today, in the net of lies which surrounds you from all sides, are you still able to distinguish the Truth from the lies as easily?

Under the invasion of American and Protestant-style

"evangelization," in which partial truths of Christianity are preached before a satanic background of rock music and in the form of a "cheap sham spectacle," full of shrieks and false tears, with miracles and healings falling upon your confused heads, how can you find the true Christ in your heart?

Yesterday, under the terror of Communist atheism, you could robe your soul with the body of the Lord, anointed with myrrh, as when Joseph and Nicodemus put Him in the tomb.

Today, seduced by the infernal rhythm of drums and the barbaric rhythm of sectarian preaching, you no longer find God, and you stand, like Mary Magdalene, crying in front of the empty tomb of your soul.

Who stole God from you? Which gardener has hidden Him from you, so that now you are alone and crying?

Return to the simple truth of the Faith and to the account of the Resurrection of Christ! Run like Peter and John towards the Lord's tomb, stoop down, enter, and you shall see and you shall believe, knowing the Scripture, that Jesus must needs rise from the dead!

Perhaps yesterday, when Communism tried to wrench any faith from your heart and to form you into a mere cog in the gears of the social machinery, you, out of a spirit of youthful revolt had more of Christ in your soul than you have today.

Today you are attacked from all sides with the sound of the rhythmic drumming of all the anti-Christian organizations, which wish to create an amorphous mass out of the world's nations, easily led to their intended destination. So it happens in the political world—a few individuals are anointed in secret and installed to govern all people from positions of international power. They determine which nations have the right to bear children and which must abort them; they substitute themselves for God and sketch the destiny of nations according to their pleasures or interests. Whoever does not submit shall perish!

This totalitarianism is expressed, more and more, even

in the life of the Church, through Masonic-style ecumenical international organizations, which actually impose a new religion, a new liturgy divested of sacredness, the Holy Mysteries, and ritual, like a modern theatrical production.

These so-called religious theaters—which you see gathered in all the public marketplaces, led by Western youth—represent the desanctification of Christianity and the Liturgy. Unfortunately, even some Orthodox clergy have taken part in the de-sacramentalization of the Liturgy, as in the case of the brochure *Reconciliation—the Gift of God and the Beginning of New Life*, published in Iasi, Romania, in 1995, where among the editors is found an Orthodox priest (of course, not without the approval of his hierarch). This work, in its liturgical part, is an attack on the sanctity of Orthodox Liturgy and a negation of its Mysteries.

How can you not stand, like Mary, in front of an empty tomb? All these attacks are pointed against you, young man, especially against you, because you are more deprived of protection and you are more sensitive to injustices. Your attackers want to tell you that you are an empty tomb if you don't submit to them.

However, it is written: *Beloved, believe not every spirit, but try the spirits whether they are of God: because many false prophets are gone out into the world* (I John 4:1).

Who can test today if the spirits come from God when the Orthodox and Catholic priests themselves preach an anti-Christian messianic message, similar to the sects established by rebels against the Church? Who protects you from straying, my young brother? Who is to enrobe your heart with the presence of the true Christ and not with the false christs of this age?

As many as received Him, to them gave He power to become the sons of God, even to them that believe on His name: which were born, not of blood, nor of the will of the flesh, nor of the will of man, but of God. And the Word was made flesh, and dwelt among us, (and we beheld His glory, the glory as of the only begotten of the

Father) full of grace and truth.... And of His fullness have all we received, and grace for grace (John 1:12–14, 16).

You were born, young man, not of the desire of the flesh, nor of the will of man, but from God, Who became flesh for you and of Whose fullness you partook, and grace after grace you have received.

This grace is a shield against fornication, to which your modern teachers push you. They tell you that liberty is the eradication of any obstacle facing you; that a good conscience is a talisman; that honor is an old-fashioned, obsolete notion; that sexuality is an unleashing of the beast within you; that your likeness to Christ is a story created by the priests; and that the love of God and neighbor is a new way of inhibiting your personality. Search in your heart, beyond this diabolical thicket of lies, and you will find the Truth, the only one that shall set you free! And the supreme Truth is the Resurrection, the Resurrection of Christ, as the lever for your own resurrection.

Now we approach Passion Week, which we meet filled with pain and repentance for our participation in the slaying of Christ, not only by the mere decadence of the old Adam but through our actions at every moment and our daily falls. Through these we have wounded Him Who is the ideal of human perfection. The priest will proclaim from the altar "the death of God" again and again during the twelve Passion Gospels in a wearying and haunting way. On Great Friday, we will weep like the Holy Virgin for His death: "O my sweet springtime, O my sweetest Child, where has Thy beauty gone?"[2] We will be mournful and full of tears, but never despairing, because we know that the time has come when the Son of man will be betrayed and delivered into the hands of the high priests, who will judge, condemn, and give Him over to death, but on the third day He will rise (cf. Matt. 16:21, 17:22–23,

---

[2] From the third stasis of the Lamentations, Matins of Great Saturday, in Mother Mary and Archimandrite Kallistos Ware, trans., *The Lenten Triodion* (South Canaan, Pa.: St. Tikhon's Seminary Press, 2002), p. 641.—ED.

20:18–19; Mark 10:33–34; Luke 9:22, 18:31–33). This is why we sing during the Lamentations service: "As a lion hast Thou fallen asleep in the flesh, O Savior, and as a young lion hast Thou risen from the dead, putting off the old age of the flesh."[3]

With torn flesh, ravaged by torments, Christ arises as a lion cub, renewed through the total spiritualization of the body. As a lion cub, He comes out of the myrrh-filled linen shroud, leaving it untouched yet retaining its form. As a lion cub He ascends, illumined, through the stone of the tomb without leaving a trace—the stone which the angel would later remove in order to show the women that Jesus was no longer in the grave: *Come, see the place where the Lord lay* (Matt. 28:6).

Christ is Risen!

Paradoxically, the priest who said to you that Christ had died now proclaims, in the brilliant light of the Truth, that He is risen. He knows and he preaches the Truth of the Resurrection with conviction. Friend, you are no longer an empty tomb! The Risen Christ dwells in you and His joy remains wholly in you.

During Pascha of 1981, I was in the prison of Aiud. Early that morning, when the guards were changing shifts, I broke every diabolic rule of the prison by saying to the guard (one of the cruelest): "Christ is Risen!" He hesitated a few moments, in which, like lightning, I saw passing on his face the innocence of childhood, when his mama or grandma led him by the hand to church and when he heard the angelic voice of the priest saying: "Christ is Risen!" After this moment of hesitation, he softly answered me: "In Truth He is Risen!" It was for me the most assuring proof that I was never misled in this regard: the one who was torturing me was confirming the Resurrection of the Lord! I cried in silence, with tears of joy.

---

[3] From the first stasis of the Lamentations, Matins of Great Saturday, in Mother Mary and Archimandrite Kallistos Ware, trans., *The Lenten Triodion*, p. 627.—ED.

Later, Colonel Prisacaru[4] came to prove to me, there, behind the bars, in cold and hunger, through Marxist arguments, that it was stupid to believe and affirm the Resurrection of Christ. He entered the cell and I said, "Christ is Risen!" He gazed fixated a few seconds and asked me in return, "Did you see Him?" "I did not see Him, Mister Colonel, but I believe in the Resurrection through the authority of those who saw Him risen and confessed it: the Apostles and disciples, the myrrh-bearing women, the soldiers who lay as dead men, penetrated by the light of the Resurrection, the millions of martyrs who, in the moment of their martyric deaths, have had the vision of the Risen Christ. You have not seen the North Pole, but you don't doubt its existence, through the authority of those who informed you. You have not seen Marx or Engels or Lenin but you believe in their existence and, I assume, in their theories, through the authority of those that speak to you about them...."

I was wasting myself in a stupid and cadaverous argument, using human proofs, dead before they were uttered, when the supreme Truth consists in its simple proclamation. I was encountering in some way the same circumstances as had the holy Apostle Paul when he made use of philosophy before the Athenian citizens, speaking about the irrational, anti-rational act of the Resurrection (cf. Acts 17:16–34). I was slaying, little by little, the spirit of truth which the previous guard had kindled in my cell through the simple confirmation of the Resurrection: "In Truth He is Risen!"...

Young friend, I can enumerate Biblical proofs of the Resurrection; I can send you to the tomb with Peter and John to see how Jesus came out from the linen cloth, without changing its form, or through the rock, without breaking it; I can tell you of all of His appearances to the Apostles, disciples and saints.

---

[4] Not the same person as the prison guard and torturer mentioned above.—Ed.

They are all, in my mouth, smoke and haze, if the Spirit of God does not speak through me.

Christ has risen in your heart even before I or someone else could tell you. And you knew this fact and confirmed it, the same as my guard, when you cried from the deepest unarguable conviction: "In Truth He is Risen!"

Hristos a Inviat! Adeverat a Inviat!

Do not run after spectacles; do not run after cheap miracles performed on stage; do not run to the senseless babbling of the sectarians: their incomprehensible words are serpents coming out of their mouths! Do not run to the theatrical preaching of any of them: they are all lies; they are all hidden weapons of Satan! Go to the simplest truth, to the most indisputable and even more undisputed:

Christ is Risen! In Truth He is Risen!

Translated from Romanian by Adrian Toma, Elena Chiru, Adrian Ulmer, and Iacob Maziasz.

PART FOUR

Divine Light in the Devil's Lair

Fr. George during his final visit to Romania, in 2006.

LECTURE ONE
FROM HOLY ROMANIA
TO THE DEVIL'S LAIR

The following three lectures were delivered by Fr. George at the St. Paisius Monastery, Forestville, California, in July 1997. The titles and subtitles have been provided by the editors.—ED.

1. ROMANIA

TONIGHT I WANT to share with you my experience, and the experience of my people. Romania was a very strong Orthodox country. Perhaps among all the Orthodox countries, Romania had the largest number of monasteries per capita. In Romania there were monks and hermits living in the depths of the woods, and the land was blessed by their lives and by their deaths. They lived in caves, in log houses, and so on. There was a great number of monks who never slept in beds. They slept on benches, in chairs, and they ate only vegetables. Many of them died without being known by anybody. But you find the memory of the holy monks and nuns kept alive everywhere. Some mountains, for example, are named after a monk who lived and died there.

Because of this, I affirm that Romania was the country with the largest number of monasteries. Nearly everyone was Orthodox. The Protestants and Catholics began to penetrate, but they were small in number. The Greek Catholics [Uniates] appeared at the end of the eighteenth century, and today we have perhaps 200,000 Greek Catholics. The problem today, however, is the invasion of the new Protestant sects in Romania. They have money. They are coming from America, and are supported by American money. They are speculating on the poverty in Romania because, really, never in the history of Romania was the poverty so severe as it is today.

I received a letter just a few days ago from a monastery in Romania, from a nun named Mother Nina, who had been in prison. When I was in prison, she was too. Another nun who is with her now was also in prison. She was tortured very much; now she is paralyzed. Together they started a small nursing home. They have no money, and they write to me: "Father, help us! Because every morning we find on the grass of the monastery one or two old women. The family comes during the night. They are ashamed to leave their mother or grandmother at the monastery, so they leave her during the night, and in the morning the nuns gather the old women—like one gathers fruit."

These women have no money, no social help. And meanwhile the Protestant sects are speculating on the poverty. They are distributing food and clothes but with the condition that everybody becomes a Protestant. They are building big houses of prayer. They have hospitals, they have printing houses, and so on. They have started evangelizing a people that was born Christian. There was no moment in Christian history when the Romanian people were not baptized. The Russians were baptized; they can celebrate one thousand years of Christianity. We were born Christian. The holy Apostle Andrew preached in Romania, in Scythia Minor. Scythia Minor means Bulgaria, Romania, and the southern part of Russia. So everybody was born as a Christian. And now Billy Graham and others come to Romania to evangelize a people that was born Christian.

2. Persecution of the Church

In 1944 Romania was invaded by the Soviet Army. The first

goal of Communism in Romania was to destroy the Church, the intellectuals, and the tradition. In 1948 they started to arrest the intellectuals, monks and priests and nuns, and to put a gap between the old generation and the new. The new generation was supposed to be educated as the builders of Communism. They did not succeed because the Orthodox Christian tradition is too strong in Romania. But the suffering was very great. From the beginning, the attention was directed toward the Church. At this time we had in Romania around eleven thousand Orthodox priests. They arrested more than three thousand. Stalin said if you arrest five percent of the population, the terror has started and nobody moves. In Romania, they arrested fifteen percent of the population. We had eighteen million, and more than two million were put in prison, in labor camps, and so on. And the majority of us died.

The youth, especially, had a very sad experience. I was a student when I was arrested. But I will talk later about this.

The Romanian people, especially the military, started to oppose Communism. They organized a group of resistance in the mountains, and many of the young people went to them. The Securitate, however, started to surround the mountains, to kill them; fights took place between them. Many of the priests were involved in this, though not as fighters. Many of the people in the mountains came down into the villages to have Confession with the priests and to receive some help from the population. When they were arrested and tortured, they made statements about the priests: "This priest confessed me." And when they were shot and killed, the priests were shot with them. So, we had more than one hundred priests shot with the Partisans.

In the meantime, the population tried to gather in the monasteries. In the cities, people who had some position in society—the teachers, professors, or intellectuals—were afraid to go to the churches. Because of this, from time to time they went to the monasteries, where their children were baptized and weddings were performed. When the Securitate discovered this, they put a lot of agents in the monasteries. They even had agents educated to become monks; they entered the monasteries and were spies for the Securitate.

In 1956 the Communist regime made the decision to destroy the monasteries. So they came out with a decree that obliged every monk and every nun under fifty years old to leave the monasteries. Of course, no one wanted to do this; but the Securitate had agents, soldiers and military surround the monasteries, to oblige the nuns and the monks to leave. Many of the nuns and monks went to the forest. They lived in the forest during the day and at night they came into the monastery to take part in the Liturgy or prayers, to make Confession, to receive Communion, and so on. This was also discovered by the Communists, and they made searches in the monasteries during the night. They beat the monks and the nuns very cruelly.

Many of the monks and nuns went into the world. But they were living in groups: they rented houses or apartments together, worked somewhere, and continued their monastic life in the world. After the revolution of 1989, all these monks and nuns gathered together again in the monasteries.

3. Suffering for Christ

Vladimiresti was a monastery founded by a young peasant girl named Veronica. She was fifteen or sixteen years old in 1936 or 1937. The Mother of God appeared to her and said, "You have to found a monastery here. I will help you." And she helped her. So, Veronica started the monastery of Vladimiresti in the south of Moldavia, and in less than three years there were sixty nuns there. All of the sixty nuns were virgins, since the condition placed on the monastery by the Mother of God was that the nuns received there were to be virgins: not to have been married before or to have been concupiscent with somebody. So there were sixty there who were all virgins and, really, the Mother of God worked many miracles there. In 1956 the monastery was invaded by the Securitate. All the nuns were arrested, and the secretary of the monastery was killed by the Securitate during the inquiry after her arrest. Another mother from this monastery had the Holy Gifts with her, and for three months she did not eat anything. She lived only on the Communion. Her name was Mother Michaila. It was amazing for everyone; even the Securitate officers were impressed. God worked a lot of miracles in my country. You know, many of us died, but by these miracles God strengthened our faith and the faith of the people. Everyone was talking about the miracles, and their faith was made stronger and stronger. Where suffering is great, the presence of God is great. He can never abandon us.

Suffering is a very strange thing in the world. It is very difficult to understand why we had to suffer. We were in prison. Every day—perhaps a hundred times a day—we were asking God, "Help us, God, save us." And we got more tortures and more sufferings.

When I was freed, I read a very simple book by a French Catholic writer,[1] who said that Christ did not come into the world to eliminate suffering, Christ did not even come into the world to explain it. Rather, He came to fill human suffering with His presence. That is why where suffering is great, there God is, there Christ is in us. If you want to feel the presence of God, go into the hospitals. There you will see the suffering of innocent children, the suffering of old people. The presence of God, the presence of Jesus Christ, is in all their suffering. When Christ came into the world and suffered, He suffered with me! He suffered with you! Can you imagine how much dignity He gave to human suffering? To suffer with us. To fill our suffering with His presence.

---

[1] Paul Claudel (1868–1955): French poet, dramatist, and diplomat.—ED.

4. Orthodox Movements and Brotherhoods

After the occupation of Romania, many of the priests started the underground Church. The Burning Bush movement started at the monastery of Antim. At this time, I was not a theologian; I was a student of medicine in Bucharest. But because I had a religious education, I was with these people and assisted from time to time. I and other Orthodox practitioners of faith started to spread the word of God in the universities and high schools. We gave shelter to people who were to be arrested by the Securitate—priests, monks, nuns, and so on—and finally we were arrested, too.

There was also a lay organization called *Oastea Domnului*, which means the "Army of the Lord." It was started in 1923 by a priest. They were reading the Bible, singing holy songs, and going every Saturday and Sunday from village to village, from city to city, to preach the word of God. They did this because the workers and the peasants were neglected, and the sects had started to preach to the people and tried to put their hands on them. The Army of the Lord was an organization to fight the Protestants. They used songs, which were very important, especially for the simple people. Song is very important. Members of this organization created hundreds of songs: very beautiful, really, very beautiful.

I was a member of this organization. Even before my second arrest, I worked with them under the Ceausescu regime. I advised my students to be in touch with them. And I have the satisfaction to hear from my students—who are now priests—that they are still working with the Army of the Lord. One of them, in particular, has two hundred members. He is a priest, but he gave up his parish. Every Sunday he goes from village to village with two hundred people, singing songs and preaching the word of God. All the priests accept them because they know that the Army of the Lord is very strong and that the grace of God is present there.

In 1947, during the persecution, all the leaders and members of the Army of the Lord were arrested. They were set free in 1964 or 1965. Sixteen years they spent in prison. (I was in prison the first time for sixteen years, also.) They spent those years in prison just loving God, just working for God, just trying to preserve their Orthodox faith, just trying to build the churches of the heart, not churches of stones—a living church. And this I have seen. They are still working because the protection of God was with them.

5. Two Romanian Patriarchs

In 1945, after the Communists took over, our Patriarch, Nicodemus, was killed. He had studied in Russia and knew very well the Russian tradition. He translated all the important books from Russian. He was a friend of Optina. He was very strong and very committed to the Orthodox Church. So, the Communist regime decided to kill him, and they poisoned him to death. Then the government appointed a new Patriarch, Justinian Marina. At the beginning Justinian Marina was collaborating with the regime. Generally, our tradition is to collaborate with the government, but it is one thing to collaborate with a Christian government and another thing to collaborate with an atheist government.

Justinian Marina had been a simple priest, and had given shelter to Gheorghe Gheorghiu-Dej, who became chief of the Communist Party. He had sheltered him for two or three months in 1944 because Gheorghiu-Dej was being sought by the secret police of King Carol II. So Gheorghiu-Dej wanted to give him an award for this and appointed him Patriarch of Romania. As I said, at the beginning Justinian was totally submitted to the regime. But, with time, he succeeded in understanding his responsibility. God gave him this clear idea—that it is not so simple to be the Patriarch of Romania, to have nearly eight million people as members of your Church and to collaborate against the Church. Little by little, he changed his attitude.

When I was freed in 1965, I started my studies in theology. I studied the French language and, in secret, I studied theology. What does it mean that I studied in secret? I went to the patriarch and said to him that I wanted to become a priest. I told him that I had made a vow during my imprisonment to become a priest, and so I asked him to please let me study theology. But I told him my situation. He said, "It is impossible because the Securitate will not allow you to study theology. But I will give you advice. Do not tell them that you were in prison." At this time, more than one million people were freed from prison. The Securitate was overwhelmed; they could not follow everyone. So, I lied. I said that I was a teacher somewhere in a small village; and the Department of Cults—a special department of the Church—accepted me with a group of intellectuals. I was discovered after four years by the Securitate. They expelled me from theology before I had finished my studies. At the same time I was a teacher of the French language in a secular school. But my patriarch called me and said, "You are to teach in the seminary. You have finished your studies." "Really? I was accepted?" I was made a teacher in the seminary, was ordained a priest, and I started my activity. I was rearrested only after my patriarch died.

So, there was a very big fight between Communism and the people. Every peasant was against Communism. Every intellectual was against Communism. The priests—everyone was against Communism. But, little by little, people gave in. The first ones who fell were the intellectuals. They fell before everyone—before peasants, before workers. They started to collaborate with Communism. These intellectuals had a very high level of education; they had studied in France, England, Germany, and America. And in less than ten years, the majority of them put their skill, intelligence, and ability to express themselves in philosophy, poems, novels, and so on—they put all these gifts from God in the service of the Communist regime. All the poems were dedicated to the Party. All the novels explained to the people how happy the working class was under Communism. They composed hymns dedicated to Gheorghiu-Dej, chief of the Communist Party. Thus, the treason of the intellectual class was complete. Afterwards, the workers were obliged to follow suit, because if they did not accept Communism they had to leave their work and die. The peasants lost everything, just as they did in Russia. They lost their land; they lost their animals—everything. Having been left with nothing, they simply became people who worked for the state. So the resistance diminished with time. Communism took over more and more of the country.

6. The Monasteries

Only the monasteries remained as spiritual lights for Romania. People went to the monasteries to say prayers, to be consoled by God, to get counsel from the monks and from the confessors. God gave us very, very illumined monks. Sihastria Monastery was a center of light. Fr. Ioanichie Balan and Fr. Cleopa Ilie, who is a saint, are still there today.[2] Fr. Paisius Olaru,[3] the greatest confessor in Romania, lived in Sihastria until his repose in 1990. He got his name from St. Paisius Velichkovsky. This was because Sihastria, Neamts and other monasteries received their spirituality from St. Paisius, who brought there the prayer of the heart and the Jesus Prayer.

At Crasna Skete, in the south of the Carpathians, there was another center of light. Disciples of Fr. Cleopa and Fr. Ioanichie

---

[2] Fr. Ioanichie reposed in 2007, and Fr. Cleopa reposed in 1998. See *The Orthodox Word*, no. 261 (2008) for the Life of Fr. Ioanichie and an interview with him. Fr. Cleopa's Life is presented in Archimandrite Ioanichie Balan, *Shepherd of Souls* (Platina, Calif.: St. Herman of Alaska Brotherhood, 2000).—Ed.

[3] See *The Orthodox Word*, no. 272 (2010) for his Life and teachings.—Ed.

Sihastria Monastery.

Balan founded other centers. So, these many monasteries became the true source of spiritual light for Romania. God made it so that the Romanian people would not lose His blessing.

We call Romania the garden of the Mother of God, because all the women's monasteries in Romania are dedicated to her: Holy Dormition, the Birth of the Mother of God, etc. I think only two or three women's monasteries are not dedicated to her. So, really, our country is the garden of the Mother of God. The monasteries that were dedicated to her were always flourishing.

During the persecution, nuns were coming to these monasteries dressed like lay women, in order to pray. They would work somewhere in the world, and from time to time they would all gather together in the monasteries to pray together, to receive Communion, and to refill their souls with the power of God.

In Greek mythology, there is a legend of a giant wrestler named Antaeus. He received his power from the earth. When someone tried to vanquish him, he reconnected with the earth and got the power. And so it was with the nuns and the monks—they came to the monasteries to get the spiritual power to continue life until the next visit. Sure, they were watched by the Securitate, but a spiritual person doesn't care about the Securitate.

7. Childhood

I'm from a peasant family in Dobrogea.[4] I was born in the Danube Delta. I was the eleventh child of the family, the last one, and because I was the last one I was very attached to my mother and my mother was very attached to me. I learned from my mother the true Faith. She was a very simple peasant but she knew a lot of psalms, a lot of prayers. She knew the Lives of the saints. All the time she taught us the prayers and the Faith.

In Dobrogea we lived in a small village, and its church was very small. When we entered the church—my mother and my father and eleven children, my grandmother and my grandfather, fifteen of us in all—it was filled with us! It was very difficult for us children to stand in the church for three or four hours, and we tried to find a motive to leave. But my mother kept me near to her and said, "Stay here." Going home, she told me, "You don't understand that staying there and having pain in your legs—it is your prayer addressed to God." Later, at the table, she said, "I will tell you a story. In a certain village there was a tavern. In my time no woman would enter the tavern, only the men. It was full of men drinking and cursing and fighting and so on. In this tavern there was a single devil. He had nothing to do; he was sleeping, because the men sinned without his help. But in the village there was a very poor house with a widow with six children, and she was praying. Around the house there were legions of devils."

Later, I understood that this was the situation of the Church in Romania. Around the churches and monasteries there were

---

4 Dobrogea is a region shared by Romania and Bulgaria, between the lower Danube and the Black Sea. The village of Mahmudia in Tulcea County, where Fr. George was born, is located in North Dobrogea.—Ed.

Elena Calciu, Fr. George's mother.

legions of devils trying to attack the Church and destroy it. After I was arrested, I remembered this story told by my mother—and I understood that she was a visionary. She could see the situation of the Church perhaps twenty-two years before the events arrived, because God gave her the ability to see into the future.

From my mother I learned the simple Faith. Until I studied theology, my heart was the heart of a peasant, without any theory. I knew only to pray, only to ask God to give me His grace. Becoming a theologian, I lost my ingenuousness. Now my mind sometimes takes over the heart. It's not good.

8. The "Reeducation" Program

In May of 1948 I was arrested with a group of students. At the beginning they arrested priests, monks, and nuns, together with political men: the Liberal Party or the Peasant Party, which were older parties in Romania, not the Communist Party. After that they started to arrest us: the intellectuals, university students, high school students, and so on.

They had a special program for every category. For instance, the political man they put in prison. In a very short time they put into prison and executed people like [Iuliu] Maniu, the founder of the Peasant Party, or Bratianu,[5] who formed Greater Romania after the First World War. They were all old people—seventy, eighty years old. Within five years all these people died. For the intellectuals, they made a prison with a very strong regime in Aiud. For us, the students, they made Pitesti—a place with a special regime. I will tell you about it. For the young boys from high school, they made another prison.

So, they separated us into categories—by age, education or profession—and they conceived a program for everyone. They used the experience of Communist Russia, and they gave it a local color—a Romanian color. You can imagine when the devils from two countries start to work together, what kind of inventions they come up with.

In dealing with my category, they tried to destroy us, not kill us. Because for us, it was a happiness to die. The regime was so strong that each one of us wanted to die. But they did not allow us to die. They wanted our souls, not our bodies. They could kill our bodies at any time, but they wanted to destroy our souls.

There in Pitesti, we were young people between eighteen and nineteen years old, up to twenty-six years old. We were the future intellectuals of Romania, Christians who loved each other. And we started continual prayer. Four people were put into every cell. One of us would say the "Our Father" or other prayers (we learned these other prayers because we had students of theology who taught us). Each one of us would pray for an hour, so that in four hours a cell would accomplish its assignment. Then a person

---

[5] Ion Bratianu (1864–1927) was prime minister of Romania for five terms. In 1919 he aided in the unification of the Old Romanian Kingdom with Transylvania, Bukovina, and Bessarabia, forming Greater Romania.—Ed.

from that cell would knock on the neighboring cell, and the people there would start their prayers. This prayer went around the prison day and night, without any stopping. During one year we prayed and prayed and prayed. Sure, the Securitate knew it. After one year they decided to put a stop to our prayers. It was then that they started "reeducation." "Reeducation" means that they would introduce into our cell a group of inmates who had already been "reeducated," and they would start to torture us. To stay with your torturer for two or three weeks, day and night, and to be tortured all the time: you cannot imagine it! Day and night to be tortured, every minute to be insulted, to be hit, to be beaten, to be obliged to say things against God, against your parents. The aim of the "reeducation" was to change your mind, to change your attitude, to make you a new man. This lasted in Pitesti for three years. Many of us died. Many of us became crazy. The rest made a compromise.

After two years, we were spread into other prisons to spy on the inmates. And there we lost all hope. There we had no vision. Nothing in front of us. Only darkness and remorse. But there we met the priests and the monks, and they knew the history of Pitesti. They received us with love and understanding; and they told us about repentance, about the love of God, about the possibility of becoming, again, a Christian. Then I understood why Jesus Christ said, *Ye are the salt of the earth.... Ye are the light of the world* (Matt. 5:13–14). These priests and monks were truly *the light of the world*.

Then I made my vow. I said to Jesus, "If I go out of prison, if I do not die in prison, I will become a priest." I made this vow, and Jesus noticed it. During those years, until 1965, many of us died; but I went out in good shape. I tried to study theology, but at first I was not allowed to. I studied the French language and became a teacher of French in a secular school. But I was very unhappy because I had made a vow to God and I wanted to become a priest.

Fr. George some time after his release from his first imprisonment, and before he was ordained to the priesthood.

9. Bringing Christ to the Youth

I taught my students, but every summer I took them to visit the monasteries. I did not tell them much about God, but going with them from monastery to monastery for a month each summer—this worked upon their souls.... I put them in the monasteries to instruct them. The monks and nuns always said something edifying to them. My students saw me praying, and they prayed with me. They asked me for the prayers, and they asked the monks to give them prayers. The monks had some small booklets that they gave to them. And many of these students became priests. I met some of them afterwards in the seminary.

I was thirty-eight years old when I was in the university with the young students, and they were nineteen and twenty. They called me "Father," not as to a priest, but because I was like a father to them.

I saw that these young people had no support, no strong foundation under their feet. They were lost. They didn't know God, but they didn't believe in the Communist ideas, either. So, they believed nothing. I think they were a lost generation. Later, after I was received by the patriarch into the seminary, I decided to give something to the Romanian youth—to give them a direction, to give them a light, to clarify their ideas and illumine the darkness in front of them. Being a teacher in the seminary, I talked to my students. They had come from a secular school; some had a religious education from their families, some had no such education. I encouraged them to make friends with students from the secular universities.

The group around me started to have prayers. In the beginning, I had twenty students with me, and every night we went into the chapel of the seminary to pray. We didn't say anything because there were a lot of agents in the seminary. This group increased: in a few months I had more than one hundred students, both theological and secular students. It's surprising—the students in the technical schools came more than the students in the theoretical schools. I had engineers, architects, etc., but very few students of literature. These students from the polytechnic were very dedicated. I think that this was because they had nothing except their technical education, nothing spiritual. They discovered that there was another world—a spiritual world.

10. The Seven Homilies to the Youth

After having this group of other people gather around me, I told them I wanted to take action to evangelize the youth. And they started to talk to one another. When I started my time of preaching, I had more than four hundred young people: seminarians, theologians, students from the lay universities.

I decided to start my preaching time during Great Lent. For this I entitled my sermons, "Seven Homilies to the Youth." Some of you have perhaps already read them in my book. I did not say extraordinary things in them. I just addressed my words to the youth. I told them that they are created in the image of God. God gave them a special dignity because He created them, the youth, in His image, and He gave them freedom. Freedom means dignity. Dignity means responsibility. We have to answer to God if we use our freedom in a bad rather than a good manner. I told them that their dignity was the greatest in the world. No animal has this responsibility, only man. I told them that they had the right to know the Communist philosophy, to know idealist philosophy, and to know theology. Philosophy and technology, I said, are only on the level of high school. Only theology has a doctorate, because theology is working with absolute Truth, Divine Truth. The other ones are on the human level.

I said afterwards that a regime that wanted to destroy churches and to build restaurants and taverns in their place was a regime that was not sure of its situation. (At that time they had started to destroy the churches.) Never can a restaurant replace a church in the soul of a human being. I said, come, let us build a new church. In every place where a church has been destroyed, let us build a church of the heart. They can destroy the churches of stone but never can they destroy the church in our hearts. So, between us and them there is a spiritual fight, and in that fight we are sure to be victorious because we have God with us.

I told them about life and death. I told them that St. Basil the Great said that true philosophy is to think about death. I told them that, with any human philosophy, the first problem is life and death. If you don't understand life, you don't understand death, and in that case you are simply animals. But God promised us eternal life. What does that mean for us? You are now very young men, I said. You have a body. This body is like a box. In a short time, the body dies and will be deposited into the earth and become earth. But we have something more precious than the body. The body is very precious for us because it is the temple of the Holy Spirit (cf. I Cor. 6:19). But don't give your whole attention to the body. Think that you are something more precious, that you have within you a soul.

Amazing! They listened to it. They started to ask me about the soul. I remember one student of the polytechnic said to me, "Father, until now we learned half of the truth. And now we understand that half of a truth means a whole lie." It is true.

During the homilies I said, "Someone is calling you. It is the sweet calling of Jesus Christ. Don't stand on the threshold of the Church. Take courage, and discover Jesus Christ. He has been waiting for you for a long time—before you were born, Jesus has been waiting for you. Because He knew everything before you were even put into the womb of your mother. Jesus knew about you and He prepared something very good for you."

And I said, "I saw you, young man, in the street. You are very savage. You are aggressive. You don't love anything. Why? Who taught you to hate? Who refused to teach you to love? I saw your father and your mother ashamed because of you. You are like an animal in a cage. Who has the right to put you in prison, who has the right to punish you if no one taught you what is the meaning of virtue, what is the meaning of faith, what is the

DIVINE LIGHT IN THE DEVIL'S LAIR

meaning of goodness, what is the devil, and Who is God? A society that is not able to teach you both sides—good and evil, light and darkness—has no rights over your freedom, no rights over your body, because they did not give you the possibility to choose. You are not responsible. Only if you know both sides of things and make your choice in freedom, are you responsible. Now Jesus Christ calls you and tells you what it means to be good, what the soul means, what it means to love. Not sexual love, not orgiastic love, but true love, Christian love."

You've heard it. Every priest says such things in church, right? But these young people had never heard such a word, because the priests were afraid to speak like that in the churches.

I decided to do it. I knew that I would be arrested, that I would finish my life in prison. I never hoped to be free. I was sure that I would die in prison. Nevertheless, I made this decision although the Securitate and even my colleagues tried to stop me and started to threaten me. I have to confess that sometimes I was very, very afraid. I even decided to stop. The director of the seminary said to me, "Father, you will destroy the seminary. The Communists are now ready to destroy it because of your meetings. They don't want to have students influenced like this." They begged me to stop. I was ready to stop. I called my group of students and told them, "I have to stop so as not to endanger the seminary." But they said, "Father, it's too late. We have to go on. You have no right." So I started again. I said, "I will go to prison"; and they said, "We will go with you." And, really, they tried to go with me into prison. "If they arrest you," they said, "we will ask the Securitate to take us with you." I don't think it is possible in free America to hear such words from students.

God placed His blessing on us. He placed His blessing on the souls of the Romanian youth, on the students. He gave me the words.

I delivered my sermons every Wednesday. I started at 9:00 PM and I finished with the discussion after midnight. Then I had to walk six miles from the school to my house. Every time I was attacked by the Securitate, by different agents posing as drunk people who insulted me. The theology students were not allowed to go out after midnight, so the students from the engineering school would accompany me to my house. They kept me from being attacked.

Every Tuesday, I did not know what I was going to say during my sermons on Wednesday. During the whole week, the Securitate, the hierarchs, and the directors of the seminary—they all pressured me. I had no time to think about what I was going to say. I was afraid. My wife was absolutely afraid. I had a son who was thirteen years old; he was watched by the Securitate and was persecuted in school. From all sides they pressured me. So I had no time to think. But Tuesday night, God illumined my mind. In the morning I knew what I had to say. It was not me who said the words, but it was the inspiration of the Holy Spirit. I am so convinced that God spoke through my mouth. Since then I have never been able to say such things. My mind, my soul was exhausted. Can you imagine? I was alone. Absolutely alone, having around me four to five hundred students—young men without any power. I was their support, I was their prophet. They knew nothing without me. And the Securitate was sure that, in arresting me, they would destroy the whole group; but the group was not destroyed.

The Securitate had legions of agents, and even the hierarchs were working with them against me. They closed the door of the church; I preached in front of the church. They closed the gates of the seminary; the students climbed the walls and came to hear the word of God in a new manner. They could have arrested me at any time, from the first week. They did not arrest me because God did not allow them to. So I finished the seven sermons. We had a vacation for Pascha. During the vacation, I was attacked by the Securitate. I was threatened on the telephone by unknown people. They said they would come into my house and destroy me and my wife—put a curse over me and my family. I was insulted with dirty words. I had a most unhappy Pascha. Many times I cried in my soul. But after Pascha I came back to the seminary, I met my students from the university, the students of theology, and they encouraged me again.

I decided to give a new sermon. I didn't care about the Securitate, I didn't care about my hierarchs. I cared about the students. I announced to my students that I had to say something to them. This was because there were two groups condemning me: the theology students reproached me that I addressed more of my sermons to the secular students than to them and that they needed my help more than the other ones. On the other hand, the secular students accused me that my sermons were too theological and that the theological student doesn't need as much help, so I could neglect the theological student to speak in their language. I wanted to explain to them why I had addressed them in such a manner, because, in fact, there was no high theology in my sermons. I addressed them to everyone. It was very easy for everyone to understand them, and they understood, but they needed more. Also, I wanted to tell what kind of blackmail the Securitate tried to submit me to.

11. Arrest

The next Wednesday I was to deliver my eighth sermon. But God said, "No—stop. You asked Me for seven homilies; I gave you seven homilies. I could have let you be arrested after the first homily, but I promised to give you the time to utter seven homilies. Now, an eighth one is not allowed."

I was expelled from the seminary and put under house arrest. So, by being expelled from the Church, I was at the mercy of the Securitate. There was no clerical protection for me. I knew that I would be arrested in a short time.

My bishop, Roman, had been a monk since he was twelve

years old. He was a very spiritual person, and I loved him very much. As a bishop he was still a monk, but he was very afraid.

A group of very good intellectuals, who had been present for my sermons, went to Bishop Roman and asked him to save me. He said, "If I save Fr. Calciu, what will happen to me?" Nothing could have happened to him. The worst thing that would have happened was that he would have been obliged to leave his throne and to go to the monastery. But he was scared.

One day Bishop Roman called me into his office. Bishop Antonie was also there. This bishop was a very well-known agent of the Securitate. So, when I saw Antonie there, I knew that I would be arrested.

The next Sunday I went to the chapel of the seminary because Bishop Roman was serving there. At the end of the Liturgy, when he left the church, he saw me and asked me, "How are you, Father?" I said, "Your Holiness, I came here to kiss your hand because you are committing a very big sin." He was struck in the face by my words, because he understood that I knew he was a participant in my arrest. He was so shocked. He did not allow me to kiss his hand, and left the church. I was on the steps of the church looking at him, and all the time he avoided my eyes; he looked everywhere but not at me. I had made a test. I wanted to penetrate his soul. If he had the courage to look in my eyes, I could be convinced that he was not guilty. But when he avoided my eyes, I understood that I was sentenced to prison. The following Thursday I was arrested.

LECTURE TWO
RETURN TO THE DEVIL'S LAIR

1. Arrest and Imprisonment

Before I start, I would like to read some verses for you: *For the preaching of the Cross is to them that perish foolishness; but unto us which are being saved, it is the power of God. For it is written, I will destroy the wisdom of the wise, and will bring to nothing the understanding of the prudent. Where is the wise? Where is the scribe? Where is the disputer of this world? Hath not God made foolish the wisdom of this world? For after that in the wisdom of God the world by wisdom knew not God, it pleased God by the foolishness of preaching to save them that believe* (I Cor. 1:18–21).

Please don't pay any attention to my foolish words. Don't look for the sensational in my speech. Look for the humility and the power of God which preserves us. This same power has preserved me just to come here and tell you about the suffering of the Church in a Communist country and how God is working wonders for His servants.

I told you that when I had delivered the "Seven Homilies to the Youth," after Pascha I wanted to deliver an eighth homily, explaining to the students what had happened to me during the vacation of Pascha and how the Securitate had tried to blackmail me, to discourage me, knowing well that I had the intention to continue with my preaching. I had just announced before I had finished my seven homilies that my intention was to start a new cycle of preaching—something about Christianity and culture. Because our culture was Christian. I wanted the young men to see that, in Europe, nothing was created outside of Christianity, and that a creation outside of Christ has no value.

The Securitate tried to discourage me from this, to threaten me and force me to give up. Because I continued to follow my intention, they obliged my superiors, my bishops, to expel me from the school and the Church. The bishops left me without any protection against the Securitate. I was just a simple man. They could arrest me without any opposition from my hierarchs. I told you that I said to my bishop, Roman, trying to kiss his hand, that he was about to perform a very big sin, which was my arrest. Since he avoided my eyes—he had no courage to look at me—I understood that my freedom had come to an end. I was arrested. Around twenty agents came to my house. I was with my wife and my son (my son was thirteen years old). They searched the whole house looking for some documents by which to accuse me. Of course, they found nothing. Then they arrested me and brought me with them, and for a half a year I was under interrogation. My wife knew nothing about me. They told my wife that I was sick. Later they told her that I had died, that my bones would rest somewhere in the earth in the prison and nobody would find my body to pray for me at my grave.

Of course, my wife didn't believe this. It was incredible for such a thing to happen at that time, 1978. Between 1948 and 1965 it was possible for the Securitate to kill a public figure without having the body discovered, but in 1978 it was difficult. Christian and human rights organizations had all adopted me. As I said earlier, my sermons were smuggled outside of the country and transmitted on Radio Free Europe in Romanian; they were published in German, French, and English, too. Mother Alexandra translated them. I was so known throughout the world that Ceausescu had no courage to kill me.

At one point they decided to sentence me to death; they held me under an article [of the penal code] and assured me that I would be executed. They assigned a lawyer to me, but the lawyer was my accuser. I remember how, during my trial, the lawyer declared in front of the jury: "It is true, Your Honor, that my client was an agent of the CIA. But, please, don't kill him. Let him live and let me really tell him to be a useful man for the Communist party." Can you imagine? It was a plea for my forgiveness.

They had nothing against me. I did nothing underground. Everything I did was public. I told my students, citing Jesus Christ, "What I say to you in secret, now you have to preach on the housetops" (cf. Matt. 10:27, Luke 12:3). That was my position. I exhorted my bishop to preach with me, to go out with me, because it was time for the word of God to be made public without any fear of human power. It was time to conquer the world with the word of God. No one followed me. I thought, my voice is very weak, but the voice of a bishop is a strong voice. It can be heard all over the world. They had no courage. They needed only a very small piece of courage, but they didn't have it.

2. Interrogation and Psychological Torture

So, they had nothing against me, but they tried to press me, to stretch my mind and my soul. I was beaten, but not too badly. The psychological pressure, however, was unbearable. The interrogation was very simple: night and day I was asked: "What is your name? What is the name of your father, your mother? What is today's date? How old are you?" This was repeated thousands of times. I felt that I became crazy. Of course, I was not able to answer anymore. I forgot my age. I forgot the name of my mother. I forgot what day it was. How was I to know what day it was? When I mixed things up and gave the wrong answer, they accused me of trying to deceive them. "What are you hiding?" they said. "What kind of bad things against the Communist regime have you done?"

After three days and nights of this, I refused to answer. They continued interrogating me, and I answered nothing. I just tried to pray to God. It was impossible. I wanted to pray the "Our Father." After three or four verses I forgot the rest: I was not able to pray. Then I remembered that there is a prayer to Jesus Christ: "Lord Jesus Christ, Son of God, have mercy on me." It is a very short prayer. I put my fingers like this over my heart and was praying all the time. I was able to say the whole sentence: "Lord Jesus Christ, Son of God, have mercy on me." They were asking me ... and I heard nothing; I heard none of their questions. I was no longer scared. And, little by little, I regained the peace of my soul and heart. I had felt sick, not only psychologically but physically as well, and my heart had been pounding. But through this prayer of Jesus Christ I received peace of soul. Everything in my body became quiet, normal, and I was able to resist.

I told them, "I have no answer for you. You know very well what I did. I did nothing underground." Like Jesus Christ, I was preaching in the temple. If I preached outside of the temple, it was only because they closed the doors, not because I wanted to go into the streets. I understood that my mission was to preach in the church. If not in the church, then in the yard of the church. So I said, "I have nothing to tell you. You know everything. Perhaps you know more than I know" (And they probably did, since they had hundreds of agents around me.) "If you want to kill me then you can kill me; if you want to let me free, then let me free. I will go and continue preaching because I cannot give up. It is my duty to preach the word of God everywhere, even in prison." They began to be very furious with me and started to hit me; I did not answer. One of the agents said to me, "I know that you are praying for us now." And, really, I was praying for them. "I know that you are praying for us, but in the end you won't be praying for anyone, because we will convince you to give up Jesus Christ." I did not answer, but in my soul I was determined not to give up.

At this time there was big pressure on the Ceausescu regime not to kill me. Perhaps even among the Securitate agents there were [foreign] spies. At the beginning of my arrest, I was known in the West. So Ceausescu, under this pressure, decided not to sentence me to death. They held me under a new article to be sentenced to ten years in prison. But Ceausescu asked the Securitate to kill me in the first two years. They told me this. They said, "Comrade Ceausescu is very angry with you. He's decided not to sentence you to death, but to have you killed within the first two years. And be certain that the word of Comrade Ceausescu will be accomplished." I am sure they were convinced that this would happen. I, however, was thinking in my soul, in my mind: God is stronger than Ceausescu, and Ceausescu can do nothing against His will.

I was not scared by death. During my imprisonment, I wished very much to be tortured and killed, to become a martyr. This thought persecuted me for a long time. I really wanted very much to become a martyr. I was thinking of the martyrs during our persecution, and I started to be proud, thinking that I could be a martyr with them. Little by little I realized that this was not right, it was not from God, not from Jesus Christ. It was a demon in me, trying to persuade me that it would be very good for many people and for my memory if I were to die like a martyr. And I gave up this prayer.

They judged me. My wife knew nothing about my trial; nobody knew about me. They sentenced me to ten years and sent me to a prison called Jilava. Jilava is a prison eight yards underneath the earth. It was a hospital for crazy inmates. In this hospital for mental illness, they put me with two crazy inmates. They were not that dangerous, but the Securitate tried to influence me by their madness so that, little by little, I would change my normal attitude and borrow their deportment.

But this also became known in the West. After three months I was moved to Aiud Prison. Aiud is in the north of Transylvania. It is a very, very old prison with very bad conditions. I was isolated in a cell, absolutely alone for seven months. In fact, I saw no man except the guards. I heard no words except the insults of the guards. They were instructed to insult me all the time. Sometimes they hit me, but not too bad. I was accustomed to this. What was worse was that these guards were instructed to strike me in the most sensitive points of my soul: to insult me as a priest, to curse Jesus Christ, to mock me during my prayers—because I was all the time in prayer. They disturbed me every time I prayed, so as not to let me concentrate or meditate or do my prayers in peace. I was watched all the time through a "Judas" in the door. This was very difficult because I had everything in my cell. I had water in my cell. I had a vessel for physical necessities. And all the time I was watched by them. It was impossible for me to make so much as a gesture, or to go to the vessel for my physical necessities without being watched. That shamed me very much and they knew that. They wanted to torture me psychologically, not by beating.

3. Regaining Mental Order

I had a wooden board that served as my bed during the night. During the day it was put against the wall. On the side facing outward, toward me, it was black. With some chalk from the walls I could write on this board. At the beginning I composed prayers, because my mind was very sick after the interrogation, and I was not able to remember the prayers. I tried to write "Our Father." I remembered "Holy God" completely; I remembered "Our Father," but I forgot prayers to the Mother of God, evening prayers, and morning prayers. So I tried to make my own prayers. They entered my cell, they insulted me and beat me and did not allow me to write.

Then I started to do something else. Pascal was a French philosopher and a mathematician. In his childhood he loved mathematics very much, but his father wanted to make him a lawyer and confiscated all his books of mathematics. At twelve years of age he remade in his mind the geometry of Euclid. So I said, I am fifty years old; I can remake the geometry that I learned in high school. I started with a point: what can I do from this point? Two points, a line; three points, a triangle. Thus I started to remember geometry. This put an order in my mind! I was obliged to think logically, to imagine, and this ordered my mind completely. It was not geometry of space, only of surfaces—there was no flesh in this geometry, only lines and surfaces. There was great purity in this; it was like a prayer. This order—not with three but with two dimensions—made in my mind a spirituality. Since there was no flesh in this, no third dimension, there was nothing outside of the spirit in the mind. So I succeeded in remembering geometry in two dimensions. The profit of this was very great for me, not because I remembered geometry—I have forgotten it now—but because it put my mind in order. I was able to think logically, and was able to go out of the passions—the psychological passions.

4. The Divine Liturgy

As a result, I started to remember all the prayers. Before I was arrested I learned the Liturgy by heart. Not the whole Liturgy because the Liturgy is like an ocean of prayers. The priest prays all the time in the altar. Only from time to time, islands come out of the water to be heard by the faithful in the church—I mean, *ektenias*[6] and certain other prayers—but the rest of the time the priest is submerged in this ocean of prayers. I was not able to learn all these prayers, but the islands—the *ektenias*, the *epiklesis*[7]—I learned by heart. So I was able to recite the Liturgy in the cell. At the beginning I recited the Liturgy in my mind, answering the *ektenias* with "Lord, have mercy," and so on.

With time I remembered that in the catacombs the Christians

---

[6] *Ektenia:* a litany recited by a deacon or priest.—Ed.

[7] *Epiklesis:* the part of the Eucharistic prayer in which the descent of the Holy Spirit is invoked.—Ed.

performed the Liturgy on the tombs of the martyrs. I said to myself, "This prison is full of martyrs because thousands of Christians have been killed here. So everywhere I have some relics of the martyrs; I can perform the true Liturgy."[8] I had no wine, but I remembered that Jesus had transformed the water into wine, and I was sure that God would make the same miracle in prison. So I had a small piece of bread, I had wine, I had my cup, and I decided to start to celebrate the Liturgy. And I did it. I did it in the presence of the angels. To this day I am sure that during the Liturgy my cell was full of angels. They protected me. At the beginning, the guards came to my door and insulted me and made noise and hit me. They tried to disturb me so that I would not be able to pray, but in the end they said, "He is a crazy man; let him do anything he wants." It was to my advantage. I was very quiet. I could celebrate the Liturgy. I partook of Communion: truly it was the Body and the Blood of Jesus Christ. I had no doubt. After I was freed and people heard about this, there was a dispute among the priests as to whether the Liturgy I performed in prison was valid or not. I had a part of the priests maintaining that the Liturgy was real; and I had some priests, even priests who had been in prison the first time between 1948 and 1965, who did not admit that my Liturgy was real. I had no doubt. I am sure. God considered the Liturgy a true Liturgy; and the bread and water that I was drinking was the Flesh and Blood of Jesus Christ.

5. Friends in Prison

Before I established my mind and did the exercise with geometry, I was as if crazy. I was so alone. I was surrounded only by hatred. There was nobody around me to love me. And I tried to find a friend. The first friend I got in my cell was a fly. I don't

---

[8] According to Orthodox tradition, Divine Liturgy should be performed on the relic of a martyr, which is sewn into the antimension on the altar table.—ED.

know from where the fly entered my cell. I tried to domesticate it. I received food only every second day—three times a week, Monday, Wednesday and Friday. Sometimes on Saturday and Sunday I received no food because it was Jesus' day, His Resurrection, and they wanted to punish me. With the bread I received every second day, I got a small piece of marmalade, and I kept it for the fly. I tried to domesticate and talk to her, but she moved all the time in the cell and this commotion exhausted me.

One day a cockroach entered my cell and I considered it like a messenger of God. He was not as lively as the fly. He was quiet, very cautious—extremely cautious. He would look at me. I was quite silent in my corner, looking at him and trying to domesticate him. In high school I had read *The Little Prince*, and there is a chapter in it on how the little prince domesticated the fox. The fox told him, "You have to approach me little by little, a step every day, and I will become accustomed to you. Be quiet; approach me every day with caution because I like to be domesticated, and we will become friends." The fox spoke to the little prince about ritual. "What does ritual mean?" asked the prince. "In the village," said the fox, "every Sunday the young people are dancing. They gather on Sunday and go to church and then have dancing. During their dancing I can enter into their kitchen. So, that is a ritual. Something is being repeated at the same time, periodically, and it allows you to enter a special rhythm of life." In this way, through ritual, the prince domesticated the fox. In the end the fox said, "When you go back to your country, I will remember your blond hair whenever I see the wheat in the wind."

I tried to apply this method of the little prince. I put the piece of bread on the ground and stayed far away from it. The cockroach came and looked at the bread; he looked at me, and after some days he started to eat. Every day I moved closer to the bread. Finally, I was lying on my back and looking at the bread, and I saw that the cockroach was approaching. You know, he is awful. He was like a monster—from very near he looked like a monster in a science fiction movie. After perhaps one week I succeeded in talking to him and he would listen to me. He was not afraid of me. So I had ... not a dialogue, but a monologue. Nevertheless, I felt that the cockroach answered me. When we had become friends, I was moved from the cell. So I lost my friend, and in the new cell there was no cockroach.

6. A Miracle of the Heart

I forgot to tell you that the cells had no windows, no light. During the night the light would come in from the corridor, but only very small beams of light. I lived in a kind of semi-darkness.

A new guard was sent to me. He was president of the Communist organization of the prison. He was a very bad man. I never saw such a bad man as him. Really, I think he was possessed by the devil because he knew exactly where to hit me—I mean by words, by insulting me. I was never so humiliated by anybody in the world as by this man. He was a simple man without any education; but the devil taught him how to hit me in my soul, in my faith, in my sensibility. The time that he was with me was like a day in hell. With a devilish perseverance, he disturbed me every time I was in prayer, every time I was celebrating the Liturgy, and during the time of my meditation. He knew exactly the times, even if I was walking in the cell. He knew when I was meditating. The devil knew that I was in touch with God. He always disturbed me.

I told you that I got a piece of bread like we are eating here [i.e., a regular slice of bread]. It was for the whole day—for two days, in fact. So if I got a piece of bread on Friday, I would preserve a small piece for the Liturgy on Sunday.

It happened from time to time that the guards would enter the cell in order to search it. It was a tradition. They would find nothing: I had nothing in my cell except the water, the vessel for physical necessities, the wooden board against the wall, and a pillow and a kind of blanket. (They gave me the pillow and blanket at night, and in the morning I had to give them back to them.) Everything was visible, so this searching of the cell was done only with the aim of terrorizing and humiliating us. There were ten or twelve guards; the corridor was full of them, and we were obliged to divest and to stand naked in front of them. I was very skinny because of the situation and they would make all sorts of jokes to insult me. "Look at him," they would say, "he is a man of God. Look at him, he wanted to throw Ceausescu out of the country," and so on. To stay for ten or fifteen minutes in front of them completely naked—this was a most humiliating situation, and they knew it.

So, once a month, they came into the cell to humiliate me. Taking this opportunity, they confiscated everything in my cell. A little piece of chalk or the piece of bread—anything I had—I was not allowed to have in the cell. One Saturday they confiscated the bread I had saved for the Liturgy, so the next day I had no possibility to serve the Liturgy. At that time the especially bad guard was on his shift. I needed the Liturgy, because it was the supreme consolation of my soul. To celebrate it on Sunday provided me with spiritual power for the rest of the week. Not having Liturgy this Sunday would mean to have nothing for the whole week, to have no means of support. I thought that it would be good to ask the guard for a piece of bread, but I knew he was possessed by the devil and I was sure that I would get nothing from him. During the next two or three hours, I weighed the consequences of asking for the bread against the consequences of not asking for it and not being able to celebrate the Liturgy.

Finally I knocked on the door. Normally, if you knocked on the door, the guards never answered. They would make you wait for one hour. Because of this, we avoided knocking on the door. During that hour of waiting, your mind would begin to imagine what would happen, since the guard could call other guards to come into the cell to beat you because you knocked at the door. Or two or three of them could come and insult you and search the cell, and so on. Our mind was so excited and our imagination was so overwrought by this waiting that it seemed better to be tortured.

So my soul was troubled by my imagination, and I regretted very much that I had knocked at the door. After one hour, the guard opened the *vizeta* [a small window in the door], and asked me what I wanted. I said, "Sir, give me a piece of bread because I want to celebrate the Liturgy." He looked at me like I was a crazy man! You know, he had been a guard in prison for perhaps twenty years, and thousands of prisoners ask for bread because they are hungry. But to ask *him*—a man possessed by the devil—for bread to celebrate the Liturgy: this was absolutely crazy. So, he looked at me and closed the door and went out. I was very sad and my imagination again began to work; really, it seemed like the end of my life. Then after another hour he came and gave me the bread. He gave me a whole piece—not a small piece but my portion for a day. I couldn't believe it. I held the bread in my hand and was not sure—maybe it was my imagination. I was very happy. I celebrated the Liturgy and the guard never interrupted me. The whole corridor—the whole section—was absolutely quiet. I never had such a Liturgy! Really, I felt the presence of God and I felt the presence of Jesus. The small napkin was my antimension. I have kept it. I was so happy. I prayed for him. Very late in the afternoon, before the next shift was to come, he came again. He said, "Father"—it was the first time that he called me "Father," not "Popa" (a derogatory word for Father)—"don't tell anyone that I gave you the bread. If my superior learns of it, I will be destroyed." I said, "How can you imagine this? You are an angel of God who brought into my cell the Body of Christ. You celebrated the Liturgy with me! You are like a priest." Since then, he never insulted me, and during his

DIVINE LIGHT IN THE DEVIL'S LAIR

time of service I had the most quiet time to pray, to meditate, and even to celebrate the Liturgy.

So you can see the miracle. I did not ask God to make the miracle for me. The most important miracle that God performed during my imprisonment was a miracle of the heart: not breaking the doors, not setting me free, not sending His angels flying into my cell, but *changing the heart of my torturer*. There is no miracle greater than this miracle.

7. "Christ Is Risen!"

There are certain other events which I will tell you tomorrow, because they are connected with Uncreated Light. But I want to tell something now. After this, I was moved into another section. One of the guards there was a young man—truly a beautiful man. He was like an angel: blue eyes, blond hair, thin, always very well-dressed. But he was so cruel. This man could not accomplish his shift of eight hours without beating people. The biggest pleasure for him was to hear the people crying, asking for pardon, calling, "Mother, come and save me!" In prison it is easier to be beaten than to hear others being beaten, because your imagination begins to work. You ask yourself, "What happened there in the cell? Who is being tortured? What happened?"—and you are very afraid. Truly, I was more afraid of hearing other people being beaten than of being beaten myself.

It was incredible—how could such a beautiful man be so cruel? Generally, the guards were peasants from the neighboring villages. He was perhaps twenty-six or twenty-eight years old. I would ask myself, "Where did he learn to be so cruel?"—because he was educated in a peasant family with a tradition, with faith, with love. Certainly he had a mother. How could he look into the eyes of his mother after torturing the people here?

We were approaching Pascha. I tried to fast as long as possible. During the last week, the week of the Passion of Jesus Christ, I ate almost nothing. I drank water only on Tuesday, and on Thursday night I ate a piece of bread. They were very astonished at how I could fast so hard.

Aiud is full of churches. Catholic churches, Greek Orthodox and Romanian Orthodox churches, and Uniate churches. There were perhaps ten or eleven churches with big bells. At midnight on the day of the Resurrection of Jesus Christ, all of the bells started to ring. The sound of the bells arrived very lightly in my cell. It was so beautiful—it was like in Paradise. Being alone in the cell, I realized for the first time how beautiful the sound of the bells is. That night I did not sleep. I was lying on my bed and remembering in my mind all the traditions from when I was a child until I was a professor in the seminary. All the time I was singing, "Christ is Risen from the dead, trampling down death by death, and upon those in the tombs bestowing life." I was so happy!

At 7:00 AM the shift changed. Coming into the corridor, the new shift opened the doors. We were obliged to turn our backs to them, to be against the wall and to not look at them until we heard the door close. It was a tradition. But on this day of the joy of the Resurrection of Jesus Christ I did not turn to face the wall. The above-mentioned young man came in—he had just come on his shift—and I looked at him, directly into his eyes, and said, "Christ is Risen!" He looked at me, not with anger, and then he looked at the others guards, because it was forbidden not to face the wall. He looked at them and then he turned to me and said, "In Truth He is Risen!" I was very shocked. I was not able to move. How could he say to me, "Christ is Risen"? I understood that it was not him—it was his angel. It was perhaps the angel who said to the myrrh-bearers, "You are looking for Jesus Christ Who was crucified. Come and see. He is not here; He is Risen. Go tell this to the Apostles" (cf. Matt. 28:5–7). I am sure it was this angel who came and spoke through his mouth.

Then occurred something special. I will tell you about this special event in tomorrow night's talk.

Later, around eleven o'clock, the officer in service was a colonel. He wasn't a bad man. He was very bad when he was sober, but generally he was drunk, and being drunk he was not bad. I heard his steps in the corridor, and I knew that the guard was about to tell him what had happened in the cell. He was approaching the cell—I was sure it was the colonel—and I prepared my answer. Now, it was like in a theater, in a play or a movie: I knew he would come, I knew his question, and he knew my answers. He opened the door and, as I had done with the guard, I looked at him and said, "Christ is Risen!" He looked at me and said, "Did you see him?" "No, I did not see him, but I believe that Christ is risen because of those who testified: the apostles, the martyrs, the bishops, the patriarchs and all the Christians who for two thousand years affirmed that Christ is risen and answered, 'In Truth He is Risen!' You believe in things you have never seen. Did you see the North Pole? It exists, and you believe in it on the authority of the men of science. Did you see Marx and Engels? You didn't see them, but you believe in them because people of authority told you that they existed. You didn't even see Stalin, our contemporary. But you know that he existed because someone told you. Because of this authority concerning the Resurrection of Jesus Christ, I believe in His Resurrection."

He did not have an answer for me. But I felt something false in myself. No argument is able to convince somebody about Jesus Christ—it is enough to say, "Christ is Risen!" Can you bring forward some proofs that Christ is risen? No. Only faith.

I remember reading something in a Russian newspaper or book, how at the beginning of the revolution in Russia, the Communists sent people of science—people with higher education—from village to village to speak to the peasants and show them with scientific arguments that Jesus could not have risen from the dead. Trotsky, with a group of such devoted Communist scientists, came into a certain village on Pascha. The police obliged the people and the priest, on the day of Pascha, to come to a big hall to hear the scientific arguments that Jesus Christ could not have risen. They said a lot of things—very intelligent—and at the end they asked if there were any questions. Then the priest, who in fact was a peasant, said, "I have a question." They said, "Come here," and he came up to the front and said, "You are very intelligent people: the intelligentsia of Russia. I think what you said is true, but I want to say something. People, CHRIST IS RISEN!" And he heard the answer: "IN TRUTH HE IS RISEN!"

This is the single argument we have for the Resurrection of Jesus Christ. We can invoke information from the Bible: to the unbelievers it means nothing. We can speak from the Holy Fathers: again, it is nothing to them. Therefore, it was enough for me to say, in front of the colonel, "Christ is Risen!" We need no other proof. Because of just trying to prove to the colonel that Jesus really rose from the dead, I felt something wrong in my orientation. Since then I gave up trying to give proofs to the guards or to the inmates, the criminals. I had learned from experience that people are changed only by the fire of your faith, by the dedication in your attitude to them and to God, because this is the most powerful proof.

8. The Story of the Two Criminals

I passed already two years in prison, and they did not kill me: they didn't have the courage to kill me with their own hands. I don't know how, but anytime they moved me from one prison to another, the West knew about it. If the West, through Radio Free Europe, spoke about me being in Aiud, then they moved me to Galati. When Radio Free Europe spoke about me being in Galati, they moved me to Gherla. So they moved me three times, but I spent the longest time in Aiud.

They decided to put an end to my life, so they put me in a cell with two sadistic criminals. One of them killed his own mother. They tried to convince me to work in the cell, to make some baskets. I said, "I don't want to work for the prison. It is the creation of the devil. I do not work for the Communist regime, because this regime serves the devil. I am here in prison to testify that God exists, that Jesus resurrected, and that the true Faith is Holy Orthodoxy. I am not here to work." I had denied the right of the regime of Ceausescu to put me in prison. He had no grounds on which to imprison me—I did nothing against the regime. What I did was for Jesus Christ, not against Ceausescu.

So I refused to work, and they decided to bring into my cell those two criminals to make a team. We had to work eight hours a day and to accomplish the normal work quota. If not, the whole team would be punished. What did it mean to be punished? It meant that the criminals lost their usual right to receive letters and packages from their families, and to be visited by their parents and children and so on. Unlike the criminals, I was not given these privileges in the first place, so working or not working was the same for me. But it was not for this reason that I opposed working. I opposed it because I contested the right of the regime to put me in prison and to force me to fulfill their orders. But now that I was with these two criminals, they had to be punished with me. Thus the administration of the prison told them that, if I refused to work, they were to beat me and even kill me. Such things happen—you read in the newspaper about inmates killing inmates. So, if the criminals killed me in prison, the regime would say, "It was merely a conflict between Fr. Calciu and the inmates—and they killed him. We could punish them, but we can't give life back to Fr. Calciu."

The inmates told me, "You have to work. You must; if not, we will beat you, we will kill you, for we have permission to do this from the administration." I said, "I cannot work. Excuse me." I tried to explain. Perhaps they understood, but they did not accept my explanation. So, they started to work—I did not work. They did not accomplish the normal quota, but they did not get punished. I said, "See, God protects you. Nothing happened to you."

Once or twice a week, they were called by the administration. They came back very excited. I think the administration threatened them and asked them why they did not kill me. They were very angry with me. They insulted me, they hit me. It was nothing ... a small thing, but I was very stubborn in my position. For two months we lived together. They worked, I did not work. They got food and visits and everything, and I was punished. They reduced my portion of food to half. I said, "See, I am punished—you were not punished." After two months, they came to me and told me—they talked to me in a very low voice—"We decided not to force you to work with us and not to forbid you to pray." They said that because for two months I had had no right to speak with them or to pray without their permission; I could not eat or go to take care of my physical necessities without their permission. Now they said, "From today, you are free do to anything you want."

Can you imagine? Considering this, I thought that I still wouldn't be given the right to celebrate the Liturgy. They were working every day, even Sunday. The next Sunday, I asked them for permission to celebrate the Liturgy. "You are free to celebrate," they said. They were very curious to see what was meant by the Liturgy. For them, the priest was a kind of man who exploited and got money from the people. Or perhaps they saw the priest as a magician. They knew nothing about the Faith. Maybe they knew a few things about religion and church, but I am sure that they knew nothing about the Liturgy.

So, on Sunday I began to prepare my bread, my water, my napkin. They were looking at me. This Sunday, they stopped working, so we had a Church holy day. They were looking very fiercely at me, thinking perhaps that they were the instruments of my magic work. I started my prayers in a very low voice because the guards did not permit me to celebrate with a loud voice. My cellmates approached me just to hear what I was saying. With time, with the advance of the Liturgy, the fire of my faith and the transporting of my soul touched them—I am sure. There was no movement. They didn't move. They didn't talk. They were with me to the end. I didn't even turn to them, but after the transformation of the Holy Gifts, after taking Communion, I turned to them to tell them to approach, and I was astonished. They were kneeling! They were kneeling and were praying with me.

At this time the same thing happened in the cell as happened when the guard said to me, "In Truth He is Risen!" I will tell you about it tomorrow. It was something special.

The rest of the day passed in friendship and love, talking about Christ. For the first time I was allowed to tell them about Christ, about faith, about love. They asked me, "Can Christ love me? I killed my mother. How can Christ love me?" The other one had killed two young men. "Can Jesus Christ love me after I killed two young men? Perhaps I will go out and kill other ones. Can Jesus Christ pardon me for the crime I did?" I said, "He can. Perhaps human justice cannot pardon you, but Jesus will pardon you, if you repent. He will give you His Body and His Blood, if you repent and if you decide not to do other crimes." They believed and didn't believe. It was very difficult for them to understand, because all their lives they were in continuous conflict with the society. They tried to kill, to steal, to deceive the society and the society tried to catch them. It was a continual fight, and in this fight there was no space for love. The first one did not love his mother—he killed his mother. The other one did not love his friends—he killed them. They didn't have a moment of love. Perhaps as children they were loved by their mother and father, but as they grew up, their life left no space for love. But I realized, *they were fascinated by love.* They did not understand exactly what the meaning of love was—Jesus' love—but love was a fascinating word for them. On that day I insisted on love and told them, "Jesus said, 'Love one another ... by this shall all men know that you are my disciples, if you have love one to another.... Love your enemies. Bless those who curse you. Do good to those who persecute you.'" They said, "This is impossible; it is not human!" "You are right," I said, "it is not human. But such love exists in this world—I am a living example for you." The next day we were separated. The administration realized that it could do nothing with me and that these men refused to kill me, so they left me alone in my cell.

9. No Compromise

From time to time some senators or some representatives from America, from the State Department, came to Romania to ask about me. Even Bush,[9] who was the vice president, came to Romania with a list of arrested people, and I was the first on the list. Anytime that senators or anyone came from America to Romania, I was brought to Bucharest by the Securitate and well fed. My wife was invited to come to me, and my son was allowed to visit. They said, "You see, Father, that you are well treated here. Now your wife can come every week to visit you." This lasted two days; and after two to four days, when the Americans left Romania, I was sent back to the prison. I already knew their system; it was nothing new for me.

But one of the American senators wrote me a letter. The Securitate gave the letter to my wife, and my wife brought it to me. This senator told me that if I signed a letter requesting Ceausescu to give me pardon, I would be set free. He talked to people who were close to Ceausescu and they assured him that if I would sign, I would be free in three days. My wife brought me the letter. She said nothing. My son, however, was very impressed by the Securitate. They told him, "Your father is very proud. He is not a true priest. Because of his pride, he refused to sign this request to be with you. He abandoned you just now when you

---

[9] Later, when George H. W. Bush was president, he said of Fr. George, "His story proves you can't kill an idea, you can't destroy the human will." ("Remarks at the Annual Convention of the National Religious Broadcasters," Jan. 29, 1990, The American Presidency Project. http://www.presidency.ucsb.edu/ws/print.php?pid=18087.)—ED.

DIVINE LIGHT IN THE DEVIL'S LAIR

The reception of Fr. George at the White House by President and Mrs. Bush, 1989.

need a father to guide you, to protect you, to tell you what is good and what is bad." My wife said nothing because she was against the Securitate, but my son was influenced by them. He said, "Father, you are so proud. You don't love me. You left me alone. You abandoned me and prefer to stay in prison to die here, to make yourself a hero of the Church in Romania instead of being with me." This hurt me very, very deeply. I was so distressed! I had no words except to say, "Andrei, if I signed this letter and came back, in two years you would completely lose respect for me and would deny me as a father. Let me stay here." He accepted this.

So I went back into prison. I was moved to Galati—perhaps the worst prison was Galati. I did very badly there. Galati was the very worst: the last was the worst. They assigned to me two other criminals, but they were not dangerous. These criminals knew something about the Faith, and they asked me to talk to them about Jesus Christ. We passed three months together, praying together. I don't know if they were convinced; I don't know if after I left them they did bad things again. But during these three months we prayed together, we meditated together. I told them about Jesus Christ and about the Bible and so on. I told them about my mission and why I was in prison. In the beginning they did not believe that I was in prison just because I preached the word of God, but I explained to them what had happened and they believed me. We realized a kind of friendship in faith through living together.

After three months, I was sent back to Aiud. I was very sick; they sent me back to Jilava, to the hospital. A guard was sent to me who was very cruel, and he really beat me very badly. Perhaps they tried by this to pressure me to sign that letter. Then somebody came: he was a minister of state (they never told you their names). "Father," he said, "I warn you: if you don't sign this request, you will die in prison. We have decided not to set you free, because we want to compromise you. We cannot let you go out from the prison without a compromise. You know very well that your students still adore you. They are ready to follow you. But we cannot allow to happen what happened five years ago. Without a compromise, we will never let you out of prison. And I assure you again that you will die and your wife will never know where your body is. You know very well that there are hundreds of thousands of dead people in prison—political prisoners—buried in different places. Until the end of the earth, no one will know or discover your body."

Today we see that the bodies of those killed in Russia and Romania are being discovered. But at that time the minister was very convincing and, really, he gave me a contention to think about. Since I was very sick he said, "You are very sick—we have documents that you were very sick and died because of this sickness. So no one can accuse us that we killed you."

I was impressed by this. It was the first time that somebody was sincere with me. Many times they were trying to drive into me the principles of Communism, and so on. No one was ever very sincere with me. And I was scared.

Fr. George with his wife, Adriana, on her eightieth birthday.

But I said, "Sir, I know that I am really very sick and I know that I will die here, but I can die outside as well. Why should I make a compromise—just in order to die outside in my bed? I prefer to die here without any compromise." So he left me, and no one visited me. Then one day the chief of the Securitate called me to the Bucharest Securitate and called my wife and son there. He said to my wife and son, "Look, they gave him the possibility to go out. He refused to sign. This is the last time you will see him. From this moment you will never see him again unless he signs the request." My wife, my son, and I were all crying, because it was the last time we were to see one another. The next day I was set free. At the last moment, they were trying to convince me to sign.

I have to say that my wife was so courageous, more than I was. She succeeded in raising my son, educating him, making him a faithful young man, giving his soul an education, so that when he came here to America after so many privations, so many persecutions, so many pressures put on him, he was very strong.

He never did bad things here: no alcohol, no drugs, nothing. He studied without having money. He succeeded in getting grants and now he is preparing his doctorate in law, and I hope he will be a lawyer for the Christian society, not for the money.

So, I think that in refusing to leave, in refusing to follow what my son asked me to do, I contributed to my son's education. If I had left as a compromised priest, he would have been ashamed of me in a short time. So God gave me the strength to resist any temptation.

Now it is very simple to tell you that my son said such-and-such and that the senator wrote me that letter, but you have to put yourself in my situation. It was a matter of life and death. It was not so easy to make a decision, to choose death—because I really considered that I was condemned to death. The Communists never allowed someone like me to leave without compromise. I was sure that the consequences of my refusal would be death. It was not at all easy for me. But God gave me strength! As a human being, with my sins, with my weakness, with my indecision, with my impossibility to reach God, I could do nothing. It was Jesus. It was His angels. God told me through His angels that indeed Christ is risen, that Jesus would give me the power, that He would place on my lips the words to answer. In my soul I doubted: perhaps I should sign? Yet something stronger than me wouldn't let me. Something that came from somewhere outside of me forced me to say no. I prefer to die. I am scared to die, but I prefer to die than to make a compromise, than to betray Jesus Christ, to be a Judas.

You should know that at that moment, when I decided to stay in prison, my family meant nothing to me: all that mattered was my position before God. I knew I was a sinner, and I knew that I was without any value, but I also knew also that Jesus Christ loved me. Only by His love I was able to do what I did. Without His love, without His support, I was nothing—and everyone else is nothing. Put not your trust in the sons of men (cf. Psalm 145:2). I didn't trust the sons of men. I didn't trust myself. I didn't trust the senators. I didn't trust the ministers of state, because every one was a son of men. I trusted Jesus Christ, and I was right to trust Him. Otherwise, I would not be here in front of you. I could not speak to you. I could not say that Jesus made miracles with me. Jesus saved me. If I had signed the letter, it would have been the devil who saved me. Now I am saved by Jesus Christ. Glory be to Jesus Christ!

QUESTION: Do you know where your prison guards are now?

ANSWER: I don't know, because when I came out of prison, I was put under house arrest for one year with my wife and my son. I had the right only to go to church, but not to go into the same church two times. So I went from church to church and I was not allowed to receive Holy Communion. When I was going to church, I had behind me six or seven agents of the Securitate, and everybody knew it. So the priests were very scared. I did not even want to go into the same church twice, so as not to put the priest in a bad situation. Therefore I preferred to go from church to church.

A single priest in Bucharest invited me into the altar. He said, "Father, I know that for years you have not received Communion. (It was not true: I had received Communion when I served Liturgy in prison, but he didn't know that.) I said to him, "Behind are the Securitate; don't put yourself in a bad situation." He said, "I am not scared, Father." He was a young man; he was not my student, but he invited me into the altar. I received Communion. I was so happy—for the Communion, sure, but I was happy also for his courage. I don't know if anything happened to him.

I visited perhaps thirty priests and only one invited me into the altar. I don't blame them. I only tell you this so that you will realize how scared the population was in Romania—what terror there was. I do not accuse anybody.

Fr. George with Fr. Paisius DeLucia during the Great Entrance at the chapel of St. Innocent's Academy in Kodiak, Alaska, 2004.

LECTURE THREE
UNCREATED LIGHT

I. What Is Uncreated Light?

GENERALLY EVERYONE SPEAKS about light and dark, light and shadow, because light is given us by God and we work with light and shadow. As I look around this room, due to the light and the shadow I can recognize everyone. I can see your presence by your face; I can see your eyes. Without light and shadow nothing is discernible. But I want to speak to you about another light, the Uncreated Light. This is real light but is not created.

God is one in Essence, but in Him there are three Persons. God is not a closed entity—He is in touch with us, with the universe. How is He in connection with the universe? By His Uncreated Energy. From God there is continuous Uncreated Energy going out, reaching all of creation, and coming back towards Him.

Dionysius the Areopagite, a very mystical writer of the sixth century, wrote of the Divine realms and of the Heavenly Hierarchies. He said that up and down exist only for man, while for God there is no space, no time—nothing. In the center is the Holy Trinity. The Holy Trinity spreads the Light—the Uncreated Energy—around.

In the spiritual creation there are three triads of orders of heavenly beings. The most near to the Holy Trinity are the Seraphim, Cherubim, and Thrones; next are Authorities, Dominions, and Powers; and finally there are the Angels,

Archangels, and Principalities. Between God and the spiritual creation there is the Mother of God. She takes of the Energy and distributes the Energy to the chief commander of the Seraphim. This is passed to the first member of the Cherubim, and so on. The Light goes from step to step through the Heavenly Hierarchies and reaches afterwards the visible universe. Everyone can be perfected by it. No one reaches the absolute perfection of God, because God is infinite, but each being can be continuously perfected by the Light by means of aspiration towards the Trinity. This Light, which has its source in the Holy Trinity, can be seen by some people who have undergone special exercises and have been especially perfected. If God wants to, however, He can reveal this Light to anyone, without any merit on their part. I can prove this by my own experience.

2. Uncreated Light in the Old Testament

In the Old Testament you find many times when this Light appeared to people. I can tell you about the burning bush. The burning bush was seen by Moses, and he understood that God was there. He tried to approach, and the voice of God said, *Put off thy shoes from off thy feet, for the place whereon thou standest is holy ground* (Ex. 3:5). The bush was enveloped in Light, but the Light did not consume it. It was the same Light that God gives to man, which in touching us does not consume us. Only sin is consumed in us, as this Light gives us perfection or makes us better.

You know that this burning bush represents the Mother of God, who received in herself the absolute Light of Jesus Christ, the fire. We say in our prayers before receiving the Body and Blood of Jesus Christ: "Rejoicing and trembling at once, I who am straw partake of fire, and, strange wonder! I am ineffably bedewed, like the bush of old, which burnt without being consumed."[1] It is true:

---

[1] Prayer of St. Symeon the New Theologian.—Ed.

we take in our mouth the fire—God, Jesus Christ—but we are not burnt because the fire consumes nothing except for sin.

In Exodus we read: *The glory of the Lord abode upon Mount Sinai, and the cloud covered it six days: and the seventh day He called unto Moses out of the midst of the cloud. And the sight of the glory of the Lord was like devouring fire on the top of the mount in the eyes of the children of Israel* (Ex. 24:16–17). This means that the mountain was covered by that very Uncreated Light which cannot be comprehended by us.

God said to Moses: *Thou canst not see My face: for there shall no man see Me, and live.... Thou shalt see My back parts, but My face shall not be seen* (Ex. 33:20, 23). No one can see God and be alive because we can never see or understand the Essence of God. He is above everything: above every mind, above every possibility of being understood. Even the angels cannot see the face of God, that is, His Essence. They see only his "back parts," that is, His Uncreated Energies.

What did Moses see? He saw precisely the Uncreated Light or Energies. After that, he lived: this means he did not see the face of God, but saw only His Uncreated Energies. The Holy Fathers say that we, like the angels, can only see the "back parts" of God. We can see only from the back, and never see His face.

Afterwards, when Moses was invited by God to the top of Mount Sinai and wrote down the Ten Commandments, the glory of God again filled the mountain. Moses didn't see the face of God, he saw only the Uncreated Light.

Sometimes this Light makes the body and soul come near to perfection, and thus the body begins to shine. The Light is incorporated by the body and becomes visible to the physical eyes. That is why Moses, when he came down from the mountain, covered his face with a veil: the shining of his face was unbearable for the Jews to look at (cf. Exodus 34:33–35). The Uncreated Energy was present in his body, not only in his spirit.

3. The Transfiguration

I won't talk more about the Old Testament, but will go on to talk about New Testament times and about what happened in my life. One of the most important terrestrial events in the life of Jesus Christ was His Transfiguration. Jesus Christ, who was God, was at all times surrounded by Uncreated Energy, and by this Energy He made His miracles. No one can see the true face of God, but people could see the body and human face of Jesus Christ. His Uncreated Energy could not be seen by anyone, but on the mountain of Tabor, Jesus Christ opened the spiritual eyes of the Apostles and let them see this Uncreated Light. Don't imagine that Jesus Christ took from His Father the Uncreated Light just for that moment. He was surrounded by this Light all the time, and He only opened the eyes of the Apostles to see His Light on the Mountain of Tabor in order to make them understand that He was truly God. The Apostles were not prepared to see the Light of Jesus Christ, and because of this they fell to earth. We don't know how long they lay on the ground before they recovered.

And He was transfigured before them: and His face did shine as the sun, and His raiment was white as the light (Matt. 17:2). How can my ryassa [cassock] become light? Only by being covered by Uncreated Light. If God has enveloped me in His Light, you can see me in Light if you open your eyes. You can see my ryassa not black but white. Again, it was not the Essence of Jesus Christ, of God, that the Apostles saw; they saw His Uncreated Light when Jesus opened their spiritual eyes. This mystical Light has no shadow.

I read something written by a man who had clinically died and come back to life. He said he saw a light that he could not bear. He asked himself what kind of light this was. "I tried to cover my eyes with my hand," he said, "but the light was just as strong, without any diminution." Because this Light has no shadow, nothing can stop it.

4. Hesychasm

The Christian monks in the East—they knew this Light. They were prepared to receive this Light because they had started a special movement called hesychasm. Hesychasm means peace, silence. The hesychastic monks prayed in their cells, alone in absolute quietness; and the prayer they uttered was, "Lord Jesus Christ, Son of God, have mercy on me," or, "Jesus, have mercy; Jesus, have mercy." They uttered the prayer while looking in their heart—not just in their heart but above the heart—trying to put their mind in connection with their heart and to submit the mind to the heart, to the *kardia*. The *kardia* is very important in Orthodox theology. In Catholicism the reason is exalted, but in Orthodox theology the *kardia* is regarded as the most important faculty, by which alone we arrive at true knowledge.

The monks submitted prayer of the mind to prayer of the heart, and with time they realized the rhythm of the prayer. Although it is not absolutely necessary, they sometimes timed the prayer with their breathing, saying, "Lord Jesus Christ, Son of God," as they breathed in, and, "have mercy on me," as they breathed out. By this they inhaled the name of God into their bodies, and the name of God inspired them, entering through the lungs and spreading all over the organism. The last cell was touched by the name of God, by the name of Jesus. Thus, little by little even the body was sanctified by the name of Jesus Christ, and the body became a true temple of God.

This practice was very common in Orthodox monasteries, especially on Mount Athos. With time the mind submitted to the *kardia*. The saints were all the time saying, "Jesus Christ, Son of God, have mercy on me." A monk could be accomplishing his obediences; he could be preaching or teaching his disciples, but all this time his heart (and part of his mind which was connected with his heart) would be repeating, "Jesus Christ, Son of God, have mercy on me." I tell you this not from my experience, but because I have met many monks who confirmed what I read in books. It is absolutely real; it is not an invention. This practice is so common in Orthodoxy that the monks consider it as nothing special.

In the fourteenth century there lived a monk named Barlaam. We don't know if Barlaam was an Orthodox monk who converted to Catholicism or whether he was a Catholic in the first place. In any case, he was a monk who was to be instructed about the prayer of the heart, and for this he asked permission to enter Mount Athos, and to talk with the monks who were practicing the prayer. We don't know to whom he spoke or from where he got his information. We suppose that he talked to some very simple monks. They were not scholars; they could not explain anything. They were simple practitioners, but the Holy Spirit was in them and the Light of God appeared to them. They could not explain to Barlaam what this Light meant. For this Barlaam started to criticize the monks on the Holy Mountain, saying that they practiced idolatry, that they were worshipping the One God Who is the same for all Christians and also a second god who is created light—an idol. In the Catholic conception, everything that touches the world is created; even grace is created. In their jealousy to keep the Essence of God as far as possible from us and to lock God in His Majesty, they declare that everything from God that touches us is created. They do not understand the Orthodox conception that God Himself is experienced as Uncreated Light, Uncreated Energies.

Several monks from the Holy Mountain asked St. Gregory Palamas to answer Barlaam, and St. Gregory wrote three treatises about this Uncreated Light and Energy. He said, "Don't ask the practitioners of the Jesus Prayer to explain to you what happens, because there are no words to explain this miracle of God. And if they are very simple people, it is because Jesus Christ said, *Blessed are the poor in spirit* (Matt. 5:3)." And they were really poor in spirit.

St. Gregory said that the prayer of the heart to Jesus Christ is the prayer that the human mind performs inside the heart. St. Paisius Velichkovsky was a practitioner of this prayer who came from Russia and renewed and spread the practice of the Prayer of Jesus Christ in Moldavia, Romania in the eighteenth century. He said that the mind is the minister and the heart is the altar where the mystery of the Prayer of Jesus Christ is accomplished.

You've read, I believe, *The Way of the Pilgrim*, about the man who was looking for perpetual prayer. When this book entered Romania in the nineteenth century, it created a true spiritual revolution in the life of the monks. The monks and other people who practiced this prayer were after long exercises able to see Uncreated Light. This Light is not visible to the physical eyes—only the spiritual eyes can see it. As I said, however, in receiving this Uncreated Light the body can start to shine.

5. Fr. Benedict Ghius

I will tell you of my experience. Before I was arrested, I always liked the monasteries. So every time I had the possibility to go to a monastery, I was there. Very near to Bucharest is a very important monastery called Cernica. The prayer of the heart to Jesus Christ was taken by George, a disciple of Paisius Velichkovsky, and brought to Cernica. From then until now—nearly two centuries—in Cernica every monk performs this prayer. Even during the persecution by Ceausescu, nothing could stop them from praying, nothing could make them unworthy to see the true Light, the Uncreated Light.

One Sunday I was there in the church of Cernica, officiating at the Holy Liturgy with some monks. At the beginning of the Liturgy Fr. Benedict Ghius [1904–90] was there, a very spiritual monk. He had been the spiritual leader (not the organizer) in the Antim Monastery of the Burning Bush, which was a group dedicated to prayer, formed by monks for the sake of the most important intellectuals in Bucharest during the Communist regime. People from the Burning Bush were arrested until the group was exterminated, and many of them died in prison. Fr. Ghius was arrested, too, but he was set free at the same time I was—1965. And he gave up everything and entered the Cernica Monastery, where he practiced the Prayer of Jesus. He was perhaps the most loved by God. I never saw him sad or angry.

Because he was very old, he didn't serve.[2] As we started our Liturgy, he was sitting in a chair in the altar, without moving. At a certain moment I felt something strange in the altar. I looked at my left and saw that in the corner where Fr. Ghius was—a Light started to shine. The Light covered Fr. Ghius completely, but it did not spread through the altar. It was just around his body. I am sure Fr. Ghius was not aware what happened to him. The other monks saw what I was seeing, but they paid no attention because they were accustomed to this. They had seen it many times; it was something very normal to them. I was very shocked. And this Light persisted until the Liturgy was finished. When Fr. Ghius came to take Communion, his hands were hands of Light. I bowed in front of him, and he felt very, very ashamed—I think because he felt he was unworthy of such respect. He left the altar without looking at anybody. As he went out, I saw how the Light disappeared and he became a normal person, a normal man.

He was sitting on a chair in the altar, without moving. But if you looked at him, knowing nothing about the Light of Jesus Christ, about Uncreated Light, you could see his face full of Light.

6. A Childhood Experience

I kept in my mind what I had seen; and passing through

---

[2] I.e., he did not celebrate the Liturgy.—Ed.

DIVINE LIGHT IN THE DEVIL'S LAIR

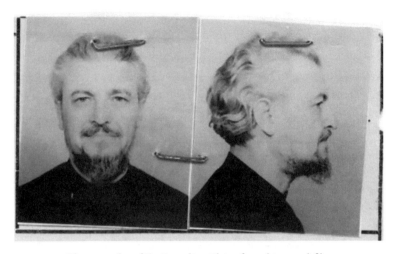

Photographs of Fr. Benedict Ghius from his penal file.

my mind different events from my life, I remembered another situation like this. I myself have had this experience with the Light of God. I told you that I was the son of a peasant family, a very simple family, and that I was guided in my spiritual life by my mom, who was a true lay ascetic herself. She taught me how to listen to the Liturgy and the prayers; she taught me how to pray. She had no words to explain this. She only told me, "To direct your heart to God, you have to stay in the church without making noise or moving or anything like that, and listen to the priest. He is the servant of God; he is the visible image of Jesus Christ." She also told me about Communion. It was difficult for me to understand how the bread and the wine I was taking was really the Body and Blood of Jesus Christ, but I believed because my mom had great authority in my eyes. Because my mom said, "It is the Blood and the Body of Christ," I was convinced without any explanations. No theology can understand it, nobody knows how it is, but we believe it and it is true.

When I was eight years old, I was standing in front of my parents' land. I remember this exactly—I have been followed by this image all the time; it was especially strong during my imprisonment. I was looking over the fence; the field of wheat was very great, and I was really moved in my soul thinking about God Who created the world. I was remembering what the priest had said the previous Sunday, I was remembering what my mom had said to me—and then in a moment, I realized that the field was full of Light. I could not understand what it was: this Light had no shadow and no perspective. Perhaps because I was accustomed to the image of natural light on the land, I could see all the details, but only in light, not in shadow. I was as if petrified. I don't know how long I was like that; and when I recovered, the field was normal. I said nothing about it to my sister or my brother. But, later, when I was a student in high school, I told my mother about it. She was not astonished. I suppose she knew something about it, but she only made the sign of the Cross on me. Then to my surprise she kissed my hand. I did not understand this at that time; later I understood that she was kissing not my hand but the body of this child who had seen the Light of God.

7. The First Experience in Prison

When I was in prison I had two other experiences of this Light. Yesterday I told you of some events and I said that there were other aspects of those events that I could not say to you yesterday. But I will tell you of them today.

I'll repeat what happened on Pascha in 1980 (I was arrested in 1978). In 1980 I was in Aiud Prison. That night I heard the bells. I remembered Paschas in the past. They were very strong in my imagination: a Pascha when I was a child, a Pascha when I was a student, a previous Pascha in prison.

In the morning the new shift of the guards came. When the guard came into my cell I didn't turn my face to the wall as I was supposed to, but said to him, "Christ is Risen!" He looked at me and at the other guards. As you will recall, that guard was the most sadistic man I had ever met in my life. He could not accomplish his eight-hour shift without beating and torturing the inmates. His face was like that of an angel, very beautiful, very elegant, but I never saw such cruelty in a man. Nevertheless he answered me, "In Truth He is Risen!" This shocked me very much. He shut the door and I was petrified because of what he had said. And little by little, I saw myself full of Light. The board against the wall was shining like the sun; everything in my cell was full of light. I cannot explain in words the happiness that invaded me then. I can explain nothing. It simply happened. I have no merit. I was perhaps the biggest sinner in that section, but nevertheless God gave me this Light. Perhaps when I was a child He gave it to me because I was innocent then, but why did God choose me for this and not another one? In my village there were perhaps a hundred children more innocent than I was. So don't ask me why God chose me and not another one.

In a short time this Light disappeared, but the happiness lasted many hours. Later I had that incident with the colonel when I started to give arguments to him, to explain to him why I believed in the Resurrection of Jesus Christ. But can you imagine?—I felt then that I was like a fallen angel. I tried to explain to someone what the Resurrection of Jesus Christ meant and why I believed in it; but as I told you yesterday, there is no explanation, there is no justification in human words. I think God gave me a lesson when I said to the guard, "Christ is Risen!" My affirmation was so strong, my faith in it was so overwhelming, that he answered me, "In Truth He is Risen!" And now I was trying by syllogisms to explain to the colonel, a grown man, an atheist, why I believed in the Resurrection of Jesus Christ. And really, I did feel like a fallen angel. I had fallen from that vision of the Uncreated Light of God entering human life.

8. The Second Experience in Prison

The next experience I had with Uncreated Light was a year and a half later, when I was in prison in the same cell with those two criminals. I told you that something else happened when I was celebrating the Liturgy with them.

This is what happened: When I turned to them after receiving Communion, I saw them on their knees and surrounded by the Light. They were in this Light, visible Light, Uncreated Light but visible.... God just opened my eyes to see this Light, and they were surrounded by it. I noticed that the whole cell was full of Light. I didn't know then and I don't know now when this Light appeared. Perhaps when I started the Liturgy the Light was around us, but I was concentrating only on the holy service. Perhaps the Light appeared at the moment when I uttered the *epiklesis*—and from the Body and Blood of Jesus Christ the Light spread into the cell. Or perhaps the Light appeared just at the moment when I turned to them, or perhaps they had been surrounded by this Light all the time.

This Light transformed their souls! Not my prayers or my serving at the Holy Liturgy. God transformed their souls by pouring this Uncreated Light upon them. By this Light we were able to love one another, to pray and to feel that we had something in common. It was the presence of God, of Jesus Christ.

I do not know if they realized the presence of the Light that I saw in the cell, but this Light operated in their souls and transformed them into my brothers. The Energy of Jesus Christ changed them from criminals into, perhaps, saints. I cannot believe that after that they became criminals again. I am convinced that they were saved, and I pray for them all the time; even today I am praying for them. Never in my prayers do I see them as criminals. I am sure they were saved.

The Light brought about a very sweet consequence in my

soul. I didn't fall to the earth. I don't know why I didn't, for I was not prepared for it.

9. The Jesus Prayer

I tried more than once in my life to practice the Prayer of Jesus Christ. I did not succeed. I think God exercised a kind of "censorship" with me. During the months in prison, I advanced in doing the Prayer of Jesus Christ until I arrived in a space of darkness, complete darkness. I must tell you that in practicing the Prayer and trying to be in touch with Jesus Christ, you arrive in a given moment at complete darkness. You know very well that Jesus Christ is there—Jesus Who is God—but it appears to you like an abyss. Every time this happened, I wanted to throw myself into the darkness, because I was convinced that God would send His angels and bear me up in their hands, lest I dash my foot against a stone [cf. Psalm 90:12]. I was convinced that He could do this for me, but I had not the courage to jump. When I had the courage to jump, I found myself at the beginning of the Prayer. Because of this, I understood that Jesus Christ "censored" me.

During the night of my second arrest, when they tried to make me mad with their stupid interrogation, I used the Prayer of Jesus Christ like a shield, not like a prayer for myself. During the interrogation I repeated the Prayer as quickly as possible, "Jesus Christ, have mercy on me." Because there were spaces when the interrogation entered my ears, I started to repeat, "Have mercy on me, have mercy on me, have mercy on me," with the greatest speed possible. And so I created a shield. I didn't ask for the Light of Jesus Christ; He didn't give me His Light, but He did give me this shield of prayer that stopped the interrogation from reaching my ears and putting my mind in disorder.

What I wanted to say to you is that God gives His Light not only as He does to certain monks after they have made long exercises, sitting in the loneliness of their cells in concentration, uniting the mind with the heart, submitting the mind to the heart; He also gives His Light as a present to someone without merit, without asking anything from that person. He gave me this Light without any merit from me, without asking me to do something for Him. So, if sometime you see a Light around you—it can happen—don't be afraid, and remember what I said to you today. Don't ask why God has chosen you, or you, or you. He is God. He does His acts, He has no necessity. If He wants to give you Light, He gives it to you. If He does not want to give you His Light, He does not give it to you. Your response is to praise God; it is to say, "God, thank You very much. God, I love You, I praise You. You are great, You are glorious, You are good. You loved me, a sinner, and You gave me Your Light." May God give you His Light.

I assure you that in every good thought and every good intention there is the love of God for you. I assure you that monks and nuns are loved more than others by Jesus Christ. And I assure you that, even if you cannot see it, you are surrounded by the Light of God. The blessing of God is on this place, and the Light of God is above this place, and He will jealously preserve this place against any devilish matter. I am so sure of this. I don't prophesy but it is my ultimate conviction that this place is blessed and you are under the blessing of Jesus Christ. It's obvious.

You accomplish the will of God only by prayer, only by being the Light-bearer. May God bless everybody. May God give you peace in your soul. May God give you His Light in your mind and heart. May God, Jesus Christ, give you the love He had for His torturers. There is no love bigger than this, than to love your enemy; and He taught us by His example to love our enemies.

I hope I succeeded in telling you what I intended to tell; I hope you understood that the experiences I had don't mean that I was chosen by God for something big or exceptional. No, not at all. God wanted to teach me that without His goodwill I am nothing, without His love for me I am nothing. And for this I am very grateful to God.

10. Questions and Answers

QUESTION: The Light of Christ is overwhelming and it is hard to say what it is. But can you tell us, is it a certain color or is it all white?

FR. GEORGE: All white; no color, no outline. But nevertheless I knew that the table was there, the chair, the inmates.... I cannot explain. I didn't see them in white and black, or in other colors. I saw them only white, but I recognized everything. Even now when I close my eyes, I can see the cell or the field, I can recognize everything, but in my mind I don't see shadows, only light. This image was so strongly imprinted in my mind that I cannot see that moment without this Light. It was caught in my memory like that. There is no shadow, no outline, but I see Light and I recognize everything, every detail.

QUESTION: You suffered and you had God's grace from childhood, but many of us converts are very crude in spirituality. When some converts pray, they hope to see Uncreated Light. They want to see miracles, they want to measure the size of their halo, how many inches it is. That's a dangerous thing, because the devil can appear as an angel of light, too.

FR. GEORGE: Absolutely! You know, I told you that the gifts of God are not a reward for us. We can do nothing to have merit before God. We receive gifts from God just out His love for us. I was the biggest sinner in that corridor; nevertheless, God chose me. Why? There's no explanation. Those two guys were criminals, and yet God loved them in the Light. Why? Because He wanted to transform their souls—and I am sure He did transform them. So don't ask God to give you the Light.

Fr. George on a boat while traveling to Spruce Island, Alaska, in 2004.

PART FIVE

Other Homilies, Talks, and Interviews

Fr. George at the gates of a monastery in Romania.

THE INNER CHURCH

*This talk was given in 2001 at the Holy Transfiguration Orthodox Church, Syracuse, New York.—*ED.

1. WHAT IS THE CHURCH?

I HOPE GOD WILL put in my mouth the words to make you understand the subject of my talk. At the same time I invite the Holy Spirit to place in our hearts faith and Christian ideas.

I passed my youth under the Communist regime in Romania. I was in prison for twenty-one years, and I don't think that it is easier to be a Christian in America than in Romania under the Communist regime. In America we don't have to suffer imprisonment, torture, and so on, but spiritually, it is very difficult to keep the true Faith here. There are so many temptations on every side that it's a true fight to maintain your faith in Christ.

I decided to talk to you about the Church—not about the visible church but the inner Church. There are two Churches: a visible church (I mean a church built of stone) and the inner Church, a spiritual Church. There are many definitions of the Church. The majority of them are legalistic, but I think the best definition of the Church is the definition given by St. Paul, who says the Church is the Mystical Body of Christ and every one of us is a member of this Church (cf. I Cor. 12:12–27). We are connected like parts of the human body; each member is a part of the body. If a member suffers, the whole body suffers; if a member rejoices, the whole body rejoices. This is an organic, biological vision of the Church, applied to the spiritual realm.

I agree with St. Paul because, while in prison, I felt what it means to be in the Church of Christ, what it means to be a member of the Church of Christ. During my imprisonment I felt that people were praying for me. I had moments of joy in prison when nothing justified my being happy, yet I was happy in prison. It was the spirit of the Body of Christ that circulated between the other Christians and me—imprisoned and behind bars.

I want to start the conference by reading my definition of the Church from my book, *Christ Is Calling You!*

> Where then is the Church of Christ to which you are called?
>
> She is everywhere. She holds within her all human life, and, more, she contains all heavenly beings, too. For the Church knows no history; her history is the spiritual present. Family and society bear within them the tragic fate of their own limitations within the boundary of history. History is, by definition, the chronology of unhappiness, yet the road to salvation. But you, my young friend, are called to the Church of Christ which was conceived in God's eternity and which bears within her perfection, just as the world bears within it its own limited nature. Society considers you simply a component part, one brick lined up alongside other bricks. Your freedom in it is to function as a brick, fixed for all time. This freedom is the freedom of constraint and in this lies your tragedy. For your true freedom lies within you, but you know neither how to discover it in its true meaning, nor how to use it when at last you have found it. You have been told that you are not free, that freedom is the understanding of necessity, and that necessity is imposed upon you from the outside by factors entirely exterior to yourself, as in a lifeless construction.

THE INNER CHURCH

The Church of Christ is alive and free. In her we move and live through Christ, Who is her Head, and have full freedom, because we learn the Truth and the Truth makes us free (cf. John 8:32).

You are in Christ's Church whenever you uplift someone bent down in sorrow, when you help someone elderly walk more easily, or when you give alms to the poor and visit the sick. You are in Christ's Church when you cry out, "Lord, help me." You are in Christ's Church when you are patient and good, when you refuse to get angry with your brother, even if he has wounded your feelings. You are in Christ's Church when you pray, "Lord, forgive him." When you work honestly at your job, returning home weary in the evenings but with a smile upon your lips, bringing with you a warm and kind light; when you repay evil with love—you are in Christ's Church.

Do you not see, therefore, my young friend, how close the Church of Christ is? You are Peter and God is building His Church upon you. You are the rock of His Church against which no one and nothing can prevail, because you are a liberated rock—a soul that is fulfilled within His Church and not one condemned to stagnation.[1]

This is a fragment of one of my sermons delivered in Romania under the Communist regime. I had a group of young people, young seminarians, supporting me, and we decided to start during Great Lent a series of sermons fighting against the Communist, materialistic philosophy, the belief that freedom means the understanding of necessity. Plekhanov, a Communist writer,[2] said that freedom is the understanding of necessity, and I said that this is not true. You are not a brick; you are a living being. You are created in the image of God, and we know that freedom

---

[1] See pp. 161–63 above.—ED.

[2] Georgy Plekhanov (1857–1918): a Marxist theorist and founder of the Social-Democratic movement in Russia.—ED.

means to know the Truth. To know the Truth means to know Jesus Christ because He said, *I am the Way, the Truth, and the Life* (John 14:6). This is my definition of the Church. You are in the Church, in the holy institution that was mystically founded by Jesus Christ on the Cross on Golgotha.

Mystically, the Church is built by Jesus Christ, established by Christ on the Cross, by His blood, on His blood. But historically, the Church was founded in Jerusalem on Pentecost with the descent of the Holy Spirit when, through the preaching of St. Peter, three thousand people were baptized. The Church has survived every tribulation, persecution, and martyrdom because it was founded on the rock of faith and the devil cannot destroy her, according to Jesus' reply to Peter's confession of faith: *Thou art Peter, and upon this rock I will build My Church; and the gates of hell shall not prevail against it* (Matt. 16:18). Hundreds of years of persecution confirm what Jesus said. The devil has never succeeded in prevailing against the Church of Jesus Christ.

Nevertheless, we can be within the Church or not be in the Church. I insist more on the mystical significance of the Church, not on the physical, because we can be churchgoers for years and years, yet nevertheless not be in the Church. We are outside the Church; we are only on the threshold of the Church. To be inside a church of stone or brick or wood does not mean you are really within the Church; spiritually you can be outside the Church. If we don't have enough faith or we don't accept the commandments of God and of the Church, we can stay the whole of our life on the threshold of the Church, being merely churchgoers! To be in the Church is a spiritual state—it is to be contained, body and soul, in the Church. And even more than that, it means to contain within you the whole Church, which is a supernatural phenomenon.

If you enter a visible church, you can see that you are really inside a church. On the mystical plane it is not like this. To be in the Church means to accept Christ in your heart, to be united to

Jesus, and more than that. It is very difficult to understand that you must have the Church in your heart. It is a mystical state. We confess that the Holy Trinity is of One Essence but that the *Prosopa*, the Persons, are Three. God the Father contains the Holy Spirit and Jesus Christ; at the same time God the Son contains God the Father and the Holy Spirit; and the Holy Spirit contains God the Father and the Son. In Greek this is called *perichoresis*. It is difficult for our mind to understand this; nevertheless, mystically, it is possible. So the Church contains all of us, yet we contain the Church within us. We bear the Church with us everywhere in this world. Whether we are outside, at our job, or somewhere in the city, we are bearing the Church within us. We are in the Church at all times, and we contain the Church in our soul. Otherwise you are outside the Church or only at the threshold. For this reason I stated in my sermon that you are in the Church whenever you uplift someone bent down in soul, when you help someone elderly walk more easily, give alms to the poor, visit the sick, and so on.

2. The Church Militant and the Church Triumphant

There is also another conception of the Church. We have the Church militant in this world. It contains righteous ones and sinners alike. Not everyone in the Church is a holy man or a holy woman, because the Church's mission is to heal our wounds, to transform us from sinners into righteous men. This is the Church militant. And there is another Church, the Church triumphant; it is in heaven. This Church is in heaven, but there is a communication between these two Churches, a circulation among spirits.

More than other religions or Christian denominations, we the Orthodox care for the dead. We have memorial services, and not simply memorial services, but a whole celebration of the dead. We remember them at every Liturgy. At every Liturgy an Orthodox priest remembers the dead: my father, your father or sister, and so on, all those who have passed away. So, it is a continuous prayer from us for them, and at the same time they are praying for us.

While I was in prison, I was completely isolated in solitary confinement for two years. During those two years, I saw no other person except the guards. I heard no kind words; I received only insults and torture from the guards. Sometimes I felt abandoned by everyone, abandoned by Christ, abandoned by God, abandoned by my mother. My mother was dead, and there was a very strong connection between my mother and me, even after her death. At one point, however, some days or weeks passed when I was absolutely alone in spirit and body, and I started to call on my mother. It was after two years of isolation and torture, and I was upset. I called on my mother, her spirit I mean, and I said, "Mom, you abandoned me. Until now you were with me, supporting me. For the last two or three months you have abandoned me completely. Where are you? Why don't you answer my questions, my cries?" That night I had a dream. I saw my mother. She was in front of me for the first time. My mother's face was sad. She was upset, and she said, "How can you imagine that I abandoned you?" After a few minutes she disappeared. The next day someone—I think it was [Vice President] George Bush—came to Romania and asked for my liberation. The following day my wife and son visited me.

The connection between us and a dear person—a member of our family or a friend who is dead—is real. It's not just our imagination. It's not a joke or some magical system. Really, if you love somebody, if you call somebody, he or she will answer you. So I say to you that between the Church militant and the Church triumphant there is a continuous circulation among spirits. We can call upon our dear departed ones and they will answer us. When I face difficulties, I ask my mom to pray for me: "I am in difficulties." And she prays for me. I felt that she prays, and I felt the result of her prayers, because I am sure my mom is in heaven and she has a very important place among the spirits.

What does it mean to be in the Church? What does it mean to have the Church in your soul, in your heart? In Pitesti Prison there were seventeen hundred young people, students. We came from different universities, both schools of the sciences and schools of the humanities. We were educated in the family and in the Church. We were under pressure from the guards: we were assaulted, tortured, in confinement. We kept the Church in us. It was a mystical Church. Our parents, teachers, and we ourselves had built in us an inner Church. This Church was with us even in prison. Deprived of any spiritual assistance, subjected to starvation, psychologically and physically abused, we preserved with jealousy this unseen Church in our hearts, and it saved us. In complete secrecy, we decided to establish a continuous chain of prayer in the prison in which each person had to be a link. In practice, our cell started to pray at six o'clock in the morning for an hour. After that hour, we knocked on the wall of the next cell, and they started to pray, and so on throughout the whole prison. This circulation of prayer, day and night without any interruption, continued for two years. A continuous prayer, uttered by seventeen hundred students, was circulating through the prison. The Spirit of God and the angels were with us. We were in the Church; we transformed the prison into a church, and every one of us was a living stone in this building of the church. It was a church built by ourselves in our soul, in this huge and deep soul of the prison community, built by seventeen hundred students arrested by the Communists for faith in Jesus Christ....

3. Temptations and the Church

The Church is under the continuous attack of the devil. The

evil one knows the Church is the Kingdom of God on earth, and he wants to destroy her. He was so furious that he tried to tempt Jesus Himself after His Baptism by John the Forerunner in the Jordan River. After the Baptism, the Spirit of God led Jesus Christ up to the mountain of Qarantal, a mountain in Israel, and the devil came and tempted Jesus Christ three times (cf. Matt., chap. 4; Luke, chap. 4).

The first was the temptation to turn the stones into bread; the second, to submit Himself to the devil, so that the devil would make Him the king of the world; and the third, to perform a miracle (to cast Himself down from the temple). From this we see that the devil tempted Jesus Christ in His human body with three temptations.

The first of these was bodily temptation: to feed oneself well, to gain riches, and so on. The second temptation was the offer to make Jesus Christ the king of the world. The devil placed Him on the top of a mountain. Satan let Him see the whole world, and told him that everything would be His if He worshipped him. To the devil's other temptations, Jesus Christ merely answered with a quotation from the Old Testament, but this time he rebuked the devil. He said, *Get thee behind Me, Satan* (Luke 4:8). This signifies that we shouldn't argue with the devil, because he is cleverer than we are. He is entirely spirit. In an argument with the devil, using rational arguments, we would be vanquished every time by the devil. Our attitude toward the devil, when he tries to tempt us through our egotistical mind— our desire to be great in this world—is to say, "Go back, Satan, leave me alone."

The third temptation, the thirst for miracles, is something that we all have. We are looking for miracles, we ask God to perform miracles, we ask the Mother of God to perform miracles. And miracles are everywhere in the world. But Jesus Christ refused to perform the miracle. He refused to perform it because He knew that faith cannot be established entirely on miracles. Faith is

THE INNER CHURCH

Fr. George with his mother in 1972.

established by the spiritual connection between us and God. St. Paul said that *faith is the substance of things hoped for, the evidence of things not seen* (Heb. 11:1).

Yet the devil still attacks us all the time. He attacks the Church especially. When I was a child, my mom used to take us to church. (We were eleven brothers and sisters, so the church was filled with our family!) She taught us to see that the devil attacks the Church all the time, and that his goal is to destroy the Church of Christ. She told us a little story. She said that in a village there was a restaurant, and it was filled with men drinking, cursing, and fighting. In this restaurant was a single devil, sitting on the counter, napping. He had nothing to do. Everybody was doing bad things without being tempted by the devil. But in the village, there was a widow, a very poor one. Sometimes her children went to bed without eating anything, but every evening, they knelt and prayed to God. Around the house of the widow there were legions of devils. At the restaurant there was just one devil, napping on the counter, but around this poor widow praying with her children, legions of devils were tempting them in their attack against them. Can you imagine how many legions are around the Church? Can you understand now why there are conflicts in the Church? It is because there are devils. You probably have experienced the devil's temptations during prayer. When you start to pray, hundreds of thoughts start to go around in your mind—all kinds of things, all kinds of remembrances, all kinds of imaginings—because the devil is attacking you. He doesn't like anyone praying.

My mother was a very simple woman. She was a peasant, but she was very faithful. I learned more from my mother than I learned from my teachers in theology because my mother put in me the foundation of the Faith by her simple words, by her example. I remember when I was a child, and I saw my mother praying. My mother was a devout person of faith who had the Church in her soul. My mother was talking to God as if she were talking to my father. I was a child. I was sleeping in my mom's bed, and she prayed for a long time before going to bed. She talked to God: "God, my child is sick," or, "My child doesn't listen to me! He doesn't obey me! Do something!" "Our cow is sick. Take care of it!" And so on, about the hen, about the cows, about the sheep, she was praying for everything and I am sure that God answered her. It was a dialogue, not a monologue! I am sure that my mother was speaking to God, and God answered her. I never heard God speaking, but the next day everything was arranged. The cow was in good shape, I was better, and so on. My mom was in the Church. She was never on the threshold of the Church. She was always in the Church, and the Church was always in her soul.

4. Building the Inner Church

I would like to move your hearts. I would like to succeed in making you understand what it means to be in the Church. And I would like to force you, because God forces, He makes violence on our souls. The Holy Fathers called it "the sweet violence of God." This means that in a certain manner, spiritually, He forces our mind and our soul to think of Him, to worship Him, to love Him. He wants our soul. The violence He inflicts on us is the violence of love. He loves us, and by His love, He calls us to Himself and obliges us to love Him.[3]

I want you to have this love, to answer the love of Jesus Christ, the love of God, to be in the Church, to be connected with the visible and invisible Church, to be in touch with the souls of your reposed dear ones, to call on them as I called on my mother in prison, and to build a church, a spiritual church as we in prison built this church by praying day and night for two years without stopping the prayer for even one minute. It was a true church because in prison you had no right to pray. Just to make the sign of the Cross in prison was a crime. You had to suffer greatly. Sometimes priests in prison would perform the whole Liturgy.... They performed it in a low voice, and we heard it and participated in the Liturgy. It was always under the threat of death. While in the midst of performing the Liturgy or services or while confessing us, many priests were surprised by the Securitate, by the guards. They were killed or put into isolation without food. They would become ill and in a short time die. They sacrificed their life for the Church.

A few people had the happiness of receiving Holy Communion, and I was close to some of those people. There was an Orthodox nun in prison. She [Michaila] lived for three months only on the Holy Communion that she had sown into her shirt. Three months! The Securitate were amazed. They could not understand it. At the beginning they supposed some

---

[3] Here Fr. George is not denying that man has the freedom to reject God and His commandments. He affirms this freedom later on; see p. 292 below.—Ed.

guards were giving her food, and they changed the guards many times, but for three months she lived only on Holy Communion and water, nothing else. One year later, she was killed by the Securitate, because they realized that they could not sentence her. She was innocent. They had no justification for sentencing her, but they were scared that if she went outside, she would be a great preacher, an attraction for Christians. And so they preferred to kill her. I pray to her always because I know she is a saint.

5. Questions and Answers

QUESTION: In Christ's parable of the Prodigal Son, the father (who represents God) just let his son go off. He didn't stop him. Could you talk about this?

FR. GEORGE: You know what often happens: God lets us act according to our will. He doesn't oblige us to be saved. He gave us freedom. We are free. We can follow the commands of God, or we can choose not to follow them....

You go to a doctor, and he says that you will die in two weeks. He knows that you will die, but he doesn't force you to die. Likewise, God knows everything from the beginning, but He doesn't force us to be saved or lost. We have the freedom to be saved or lost.

QUESTION: So where do we get the courage to let our children just go?

FR. GEORGE: Before you let the children go, you tell them everything you can to change their minds. [Before the coming of Christ] God did everything to change the minds of the Gentiles. He took care of them. Now, we know He took care of the chosen people, the Jews, in many ways, but He also cared for the Gentiles. Nevertheless, they started to forget and forget and forget. We have a theologian, Nichifor Crainic, who writes in a book called *The Gnosiology of Paradise* that we can forget everything, we can

THE INNER CHURCH

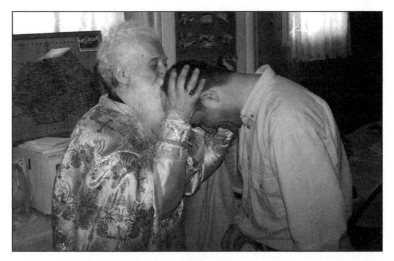

Fr. George with his spiritual son Marian Popa in Alexandria, Virginia.

be completely lost, but the memory of Paradise remains in us. We try to remember, but we do not succeed. We have the memory of a happy time in the past. Every philosophy, every mythology affirms that in the beginning was a golden age.... Mythology knew something that we are ignoring, that in the beginning God created man with a very strong connection to Himself, and this connection was lost more and more, until man denied God. Man turned to idolatry, and then God chose the moment to send His Son into the world.

So, if your son leaves you to go somewhere and stay, you are not completely guilty. If you examine everything you have done, you'll see that you made some mistakes in his education. You are partially guilty, but you did not force him to leave you. You can't stop him. God does not force the prodigal son to stay in his house. The son needed experience, and God let him leave his parents and eventually turn back. Immediately he said to his father, I am guilty before you, before God. I am not worthy to be called your son. Accept me as one of your servants. This humility brings down the grace of God.

Did your son come back in humility? I'm sure if he came without humility, you would accept him, because you are his father. But can you imagine your joy when your son comes in humility and asks pardon, saying, "Father, I am not worthy to be your son. Accept me like a stranger." This is highly satisfying. It is the same with God. He is very happy when someone comes back. But this parable can be applied to everyone, each person. I like my interpretation, because it explains exactly what I said. You can live all your life in the church and not be in the Church, only on the threshold of the Church. You can be a churchgoer all of your life and never have the happiness of being a son of God. What is even more tragic is that a churchgoer who is, in fact, only on the threshold of the Church, doesn't realize his situation. He never comes and says, "God, I am guilty in front of You. Pardon me." But the sinner, he comes. He comes and says this.

QUESTION: After your experience in prison and having come to this country, how do you maintain, or how do you recommend us to maintain that spiritual closeness to Christ and being in the Church, and not standing on the threshold of the Church? We have so many things that are trying to capture our attention.

FR. GEORGE: Unhappily, Romania is no longer a Communist country. If Romania were still a Communist country, I would give you this advice: Go to Romania and enter prison to resist temptation [laughs].

I know the temptation, the American temptation. I know what the "American dream" means. I know what it means to fight against the devil in America. But if we were able to resist physical torture in prison, you can resist the temptations of the devil in America. Pray, worship God, be good to other people, love everyone, and you'll be a follower of Jesus Christ. The devil is very strong, but not that strong. No one can vanquish the devil except through the grace of God. Through prayer, we become stronger than the devil.

Fr. George at a Romanian Monastery.

QUESTION: Could you say something about our attitude toward enemies? It seems to me that your attitude toward your enemies changed a lot while you were in prison.

FR. GEORGE: Yes, under torture, under the conditions of prison, it is very difficult to love your enemy. It is very difficult, but I told you that I was not a theologian in the beginning. I was a student in medical school. I was very faithful. I had this from my mother. But I was a young man, and many times I raged against my torturers, my enemies.

In prison, I met some priests, some monks, and from them (and especially from living with Constantine Oprisan in my cell) I learned what it means to love your enemies. When they let us out of prison, everybody, every prisoner, tried to put on paper his memories from prison. The Securitate knew our psychology very well because they were very good psychologists. They had the experience of fifty years in Russia and twenty in Romania. They knew each mechanism of our soul. I mean each psychological mechanism, not spiritual. And they knew that after liberation everyone would try to put his memories on paper. They started to search our houses. They confiscated everything, but they didn't search me. I started to put down my memories on paper, and all the rage began to well up in me. The torture, my imprisonment, and the wounds, the spiritual wounds, became very present in my soul, and I started to hate. I started to hate my enemies. I wrote eighty pages, and because I felt that the hate started to grow in me, I destroyed the pages. In the moment that I destroyed the pages my soul became quiet, free of all hatred against my enemies. After I came to America, I was invited to speak in many cities and states in America, churches in America, in Europe, everywhere. I never pronounced the name of any of my torturers. I considered that pronouncing their names was to deliver them to the hatred of the people. God knows the name of everyone. God knows what to do with them. It was not my right to judge them, or to deliver them to the rage of the people, since I was already a free man. Often, I was a free man in prison, more free than now, because I knew the Truth, and the Truth gave me freedom. So it is very simple to understand why I did not hate my torturers, my enemies, and why I don't hate my enemies now. I try to be good. Sometimes I succeed, sometimes I—anyway, I strive to be good.

QUESTION: Father, a follow-up question. In America, when we are hearing Confessions as a confessor, we hear this many times: "I will forgive, but I will not forget." I am hearing from you that by burning that account of what happened, you are trying to forget. You also have to forgive, I imagine, but you still have the memory of what happened to you.

FR. GEORGE: It doesn't bother me. I consider that my suffering in prison was to my advantage.... I had a lot of sins, but the suffering purified my soul. But regarding this "forgive but not forget": There was a monk called Nicolae Steinhardt. He was a Jew. He was arrested, and in prison he converted to Orthodoxy. He was baptized by a monk in prison, and his godfather was another prisoner. He wrote a book called *Journal of Blessedness*, which told about his suffering in prison. What a paradox to give such a title to a book telling of the sufferings he had passed through in prison. Nevertheless, he considered all his sufferings as happiness for him. He said, "I met many people in prison who said 'I forgive, but I cannot forget.' Imagine you are with the priest in the chair of Confession. You are in front of him and you say, 'Father, I cannot forget but I forgive.' The priest gives you absolution, but at this moment Jesus Christ comes in front of you and says to the priest, 'Father, you can forgive him, but I cannot forget his sins. I forgive him, but I cannot forget his sins.'" What kind of feeling would you have if God said to you, "I forgive, but I do not forget"? It is the same with you! So this is a problem. You cannot forgive without forgetting, because the memory is always in your mind and at difficult moments, you remember that hatred. And I experienced it.

QUESTION: Do you see a persecution of the Church in this country at all?

FR. GEORGE: That is a difficult question. I know that America is a free country, at least in word, and I don't think that there will be a political philosophy in America [that says] to kill and to torture people. This is specific to pagans and to Communism. But looking at the mass murders in America, looking at the cruelty in this country—that young boys, fourteen years old, kill people *en masse,* and premeditate doing this—I think we have to ask God to protect America and not allow such people to gain important positions in this country. Because with the technical means that America now possesses, they are able to check or control any thought that you have. Technology is so advanced in America that they can follow you everywhere. Think about the credit cards. If the American authorities wanted to check on you, they could take your credit card and see everything you bought. They could ask you, "Where did you get so much money? Your salary is not this big." They have the

Fr. George with Monk Andrew at St. Herman's Spring, Monk's Lagoon, Spruce Island, Alaska, in 2004.

means to control your every movement. May God protect us and not allow bad people to arrive in positions of leadership in this country. But I think God is good.

Just today I was telling the fathers and some others that I visited France. I was completely disappointed, because I love the French people. I love French culture. I used to be a professor of the French language in Romania. The connection between my country, my people, and the French people is very strong. We borrowed elements of the French culture, so the second language of my country was French. When I went to France, I saw that it is a lost country. The French people are a lost people. You cannot find a religious book in a public library. You cannot find a religious book in a secular bookstore, only in the bookstores that specialize in religious literature. If the president of France dares to say, "God bless France," the next day he has to resign. It is not allowed for officials to publicly pronounce the name of God in France. Since the French Revolution, the devil has been victorious in France.

When I returned to America from France, I took a cab from the airport to my house, and the driver started to talk to me about God, about the Bible. In shops people often start talking to me about God, about the Bible. As long as simple people speak about God, as long as simple people read the Bible, America is saved. For despite all the mistakes America has made, despite the war against Yugoslavia, despite all the killings of people, despite everything, America is blessed by God—not because Clinton or another president says, "God bless America," but because of these simple people who speak of God, worship God, read the Bible, and preserve America against every evil and every attack of the devil.

Fr. George serving in Bucharest, Romania.

A WORD ON PIOUS PRAYER

I DO NOT WISH to discuss the piety that we must have at the time of prayer, but rather the method of prayer in order for it to become truly pious prayer. From my personal experience, from discussions I have had with different people, monks, priests, and also laymen, I have employed a certain technique of prayer—not in the mechanical sense, but in the sense of a certain course of action one takes which opens the spiritual heart in order to understand what holy prayer means.

I must affirm that most of the discussions which I have had about prayer and which laid the foundation of my spiritual life took place in prison: there I had discussions with different men. They were men whose relationship with the Savior Jesus Christ had been opened to a more personal and deeper degree after long years of detention. These were men who were not clergy or monks, but who, as a result of years of suffering and introspection, had acquired self-knowledge and attained to a life of deep spirituality. They lived in close proximity to the great spiritual fathers: Valeriu Gafencu, Constantine Oprisan, Virgil Maxim, and many others, who were models of holiness and character for those of us who passed through the prisons and knew them, or at least had heard about them.

Prayer is an act of concentration and detachment from material reality—one's anchoring into a realm that is new for any man, even if he is a believing man, because genuine prayer does not mean the mechanical reciting of some texts and the directing of attention, every now and then, to the meaning of the words. In prayer one is to be seized and carried off. It is a going out of yourself and making straight for God in a mysterious way which is not even understood by him who practices it. Prayer is the gift of the Holy Spirit.

In the first place, one who prays knows that he is engaging himself in an activity full of demonic snares. Anyone—no matter how rarely he has prayed—who has desired to feel the sweetness of prayer knows by what difficulties and temptations he will be hit. On the other hand, stay in front of the television for hours on end and watch a movie full of trivialities and the commonplace, and not one other thought will distract you from the dissipation that occurs on the screen.

Set yourself to prayer—I am not speaking of those who pray mechanically, but of those who come with the good intention to pray—and a thousand other thoughts will assail you, contrary to your good intentions. Memories and stupid and unimportant preoccupations will invade your mind, as well as anger, bad words, jokes, and whatever else can distract you from prayer which would unite you with God.

This experience, which is painful for those of us who pray and live with it for years, gradually improves through very simple exercises, such as I will set forth further on.

He who wants to have his prayer improve must, before anything else, realize that he is a sinner. He must watch over his attitudes, actions, and thoughts and realize how sinful he is every day and every hour, just as the prayer from the Rule for Holy Communion says. Then, step-by-step, he must make a shield against the temptations of the world, as much as possible, and not be frightened if, at the beginning, this shield is easily penetrated by the temptations of Satan. In time, the shield strengthens him and it is more difficult for the devil to penetrate beyond it. No one, however, is spared temptations as long as he lives in the flesh. The roads of temptations are many: some come to us through our feelings, others through the imagination,

A WORD ON PIOUS PRAYER

Fr. George censing the chapel at St. Innocent's Academy, Kodiak, Alaska.

others through impious memories, others through the heart, and others through the rational mind. The most advanced fathers themselves confess the temptations which they suffered in their earthly life. St. Symeon Metaphrastes, in a prayer from the Rule for Holy Communion, says, "What sin is there that I have not committed? What evil is there that I have not meditated in my soul? I am guilty of fornication and adultery, of pride, arrogance, condemnation of others, censure, idle conversation, unworthy laughter, drunkenness, gluttony, hatred, envy, cupidity, avarice, usury, self-love, etc." And St. Symeon the New Theologian, in the seventh prayer from the prayers before Holy Communion, after he has laid out all his sins, adds: "Thou knowest also my wounds, and Thou seest my bruises. But also Thou knowest my faith. And Thou beholdest my willingness, and Thou hearest my sighs. Nothing escapes Thee, my God, my Maker, my Redeemer. Not even a teardrop, nor part of a drop...."

It is good that we know that just as God knows all our deeds and thoughts and intentions—"All things are naked and manifest before Thine eyes"[1]—so also He knows our repentance and tears and regrets. If someone lives all these things, he begins to be integrally formed in the Spirit. That is, he gains a sort of immunity from the evils of the world; he is no longer so strongly disturbed by the malice of Satan, offences from his neighbors, and all that usually creates sufferings for us. According to the expression of St. John of the Ladder, "I have partly closed the windows of the soul to the world." In this case, prayer begins to become all the more devout, all the more genuine.

The Holy Fathers say that the devil tries to agitate us at the time he sees us praying. This explains why we are so tempted at the time of prayer. Temptations which we have never had in our lives rush at us during prayer with a fury which we would not be able to withstand if we did not cry out to the Savior to help us. Prayer is a conversation with God in which he who prays takes his position on the lowest step of humility. The devil fell because of his arrogance, and therefore humility enrages him, because he cannot do anything against it. He can perhaps turn a good deed against you through self-praise or by having someone else praise you. Anything performed with good intentions can be subverted unto your destruction if you let yourself be tempted. But humility and repentance are untouchable by him.

As I have already said, at the time of prayer satanic assaults are innumerable—thoughts besiege you, memories abduct your mind from prayer, past anger [i.e., remembrance of wrongs] becomes very present. All of a sudden, some unimportant matters—for example, "What time is it?" or, "Is it raining outside or is the sun shining?"—become very important, and the evil spirit drives you to interrupt your prayer "just for a moment" in order to look at the clock or the weather or some other unimportant thing.

---

[1] From the Prayer of Blessing of Water at the Baptism of Catechumens.—Ed.

A WORD ON PIOUS PRAYER

The experience of the saints or of men of prayer gives us some solutions in the fight against the spiritual temptations to which we are subjected by the devil at the time of prayer.

As soon as you prepare your heart for prayer and have purified your mind of the cares of the day which, no matter what, you will not be able to vanquish completely, set yourself to prayer. In that moment, the angel of prayer who watches over you comes to your right side, and the devil cunningly and covertly sets himself on your left. You must take a pious position, appropriate for the attitude of prayer: be it on your knees, or standing—your position must express a relationship to prayer.

Fr. Roman Braga from the Dormition of the Mother of God Monastery in Michigan says that, at the time when you set yourself to prayer, "you must empty your mind of any imaginations and not imagine anything during prayer, because God will put His Holy Spirit into your mind when it is empty of all images, and will fill you with His Presence."

This is, however, for a more advanced state of prayer, and, especially for those who practice the prayer of the heart. For us common folk who pray, it is better that we have before us icons of the Savior and of the Mother of God and of the saints to whom we wish to pray. The icon, however, is only your step toward the spiritual—toward the heart of Jesus, toward the compassion of the Holy Virgin, and toward the goodness of the saints. In fact, do not see the icon except as a gate of entrance into the world of divinity.

If you pray aloud, do not be carried away by the sound of your own voice; do not embellish the words with a kind of soft wave which accentuates the sounds and blurs the meaning, leaving you with only the monotonous sound of your voice. In that moment, prayer abandons you, leaving you with only the barren prayer of the lips, which, in any case, is better than no prayer at all, because at least the flesh prays. Be careful in your pronunciation of the words and put the accent, through the modulation of your voice, on their spiritual meaning, and keep yourself alert and your heart directed toward God.

If you pray mentally, know that thought is more rapid than the uttering of words, even if it is just in your mind. The word is slower than thought. Linguists have ascertained that at the moment we think, we are thinking in words. Especially when we are praying or speaking with someone mentally, our phonetic organ imitates the uttering of the words, even though the vocal cords make less movement than when we speak out loud. Nevertheless, these imperceptible movements have a certain inertia, so that the thought proceeds much further before the sub-vocal pronouncing. Additionally, the thought skips over many words which remain only intended, so that the accumulation of many unsaid words diverts us from the meaning of prayer, and we lose its sweetness. That is why we must carefully pronounce every word mentally, with the same care that we pray aloud.

Often our mind abandons prayer and goes to and fro, far from God. However, what remains is a light of vigilance which is kept alive by the angel of prayer. When your mind runs off, stop the prayer for a moment and call your mind back. The presence of the angel who helps you to pray will immediately be felt in the sense that the angel will remind you of the exact moment in which your mind wandered off—even the words which you had said the moment it fled. Resume the prayer from the phrase where that word was, and continue to pray. Repeat this calling back of the mind, no matter how many times it wanders and, with patience, you will manage to discipline it.

In order to preserve the vitality of prayer, it is important to change the position of your body when you feel that you are tired and that the mind is ready to run off. Some changes can be more significant, as, for example, the falling onto your knees if you had been standing. Others are less extensive, but have the same exact effect. A simple change of the positioning of the hands, such as, lifting them up or rotating the palms so that they are turned up in supine position, or joining together the palms and bringing them up toward your lips with your index fingers on the edge of your lips, or raising them above your head—all of these movements express actions of bodily piety which call your spirit back to prayer from its wandering.

All prayer requires certain obligatory prayers, called the Beginning Prayers, which are composed of: O Heavenly King, Holy God (three times), O Most Holy Trinity, Our Father, Psalm 50, the Creed, and at least one prayer to the Mother of God. O Heavenly King is addressed to the Holy Spirit; Holy God and O Most Holy Trinity are addressed to the Father, the Son and the Holy Spirit. Our Father (The Lord's Prayer) is addressed to God the Father; Psalm 50 is a prayer of repentance. These prayers are obligatory even for those who practice the prayer of the heart.

It is very important to read the Akathists to the Savior, the Mother of God, and (if it is available) the saint of the day; the Supplicatory Canon to the Mother of God, and the Canon of Repentance. Finally, add prayers for special purposes: parents, relatives, friends, enemies, for the dead, etc.

All of these endeavors and personal prayers are only a drop of water. The great prayer—saving and unifying—is the Holy and Divine Liturgy, from which the Christian cannot be absent on the days that are fixed by the Church. Confession and Communion are obligatory. They are the crown of our endeavors and put upon our prayers the seal of the Holy Spirit and deify us through the Body and Blood of Our Lord Jesus Christ, true God and true Man.

Translated by the St. Herman of Alaska Brotherhood from the Newsletter of the Holy Cross Church in Alexandria, Virginia (in Romanian).

A WORD ON ANGER

Be angry and sin not: let not the sun go down upon your wrath. Neither give place to the devil.

Ephesians 4:26–27

FROM MY PERSONAL experience, from my experience as a spiritual father, and from my observations in society, I have found that one of the endemic sins of contemporary mankind is anger. This sin can be of a personal nature and also of a group nature. The first is individual anger and the other is the anger of a people which can lead to destructive war, for a short or a long time, but executed with a cruelty which the technology of past centuries could not carry out....

Personal anger transforms the heart of a man from a dwelling place of the Holy Spirit into a demonized house, because it changes the spiritual structure of the soul, orienting it toward the dark regions of the human being. History knows disastrous events brought about by anger and tragic incidents caused by impetuous anger, which created regrets and hopelessness in he who allowed himself to be seized by it.

The Holy Scripture is intensely preoccupied with the problem of anger. In comparison to ancient times, our times give greater occasion for anger to manifest. This is due to the great increase in the density of the population, which has reduced the personal security of the individual to a minimum. The appearance of anger presents a major temptation which the devil uses to lure us, knowing that anger darkens the mind and equips the tongue and hands with a violence which gravely wounds....

In chapter thirty-four of Genesis, there is a reason for the anger of Jacob's sons. The son of the prince of the country of Shalem dishonored Dinah, the daughter of Jacob and Leah. This deed provoked anger in Jacob's sons who decided to avenge their sister, even though that youth asked Dinah to marry him.

The place where Jacob had settled, not far from Shalem, was very convenient for this family to live for many reasons. But his sons were roused to anger and the desire for revenge. When the youth from Shalem asked for the hand of Dinah, his brothers answered deceitfully—that it would be shameful for their sister to marry one who is uncircumcised. And they asked that all the males of the town be circumcised, and they accepted. After two days, when all the men were still in pain, Jacob's sons entered the city at night with their servants and slew the fiancé, his father, and all the men with the sword. Then they robbed the city of all its wealth and took the women and children captive. Thus, under the impulse of anger, they used the token of Abraham's sacred covenant with God (circumcision) as a means of deception through which they carried out their revenge, disregarding the holy for their personal gratification. When Jacob found out, he said to his sons, *Ye have troubled me to make me to stink among the inhabitants of the land, among the Canaanites and the Perizzites* (Genesis 34:30).

And Jacob had to depart from that place with all who were with him and all his wealth, where he had desired to stay, because of the uncontrolled anger of his sons. Behind him he left a spoiled city and murdered men, and he was followed by the hate and anger of the inhabitants of that region.

This intervention of the devil in arousing the anger of the sons of Jacob and, as a result, the inhabitants of the region, was unto the fulfillment of the journey toward the Promised Land. The meaning of this story is like all that happens as part of God's will, through which He communicates something to us or drives us toward something which we must fulfill, but this does not mean that the sin of anger remains unpunished.

The Christian, however, must not get angry. He knows that God watches over him and that not a hair of his head falls without the Lord's knowledge. In relation to his neighbors, he must moderate his anger, because the Savior was not angered against those who mocked and crucified Him. Will we get angry with our neighbor, knowing that he is created in the image of God? Indeed, how can we utter words of anger against him if he did something to us, knowing well that we have done the same thing to him or to another, and even worse?

Man today lives under such overwhelming pressure that his nerves are strained to the limit and even the slightest provocation arouses in him the sin of anger. Causes for anger could be the child who does not listen to us, or the husband or wife who contradicts us, or the driver who cuts us off with his car, or only seems to us to cut us off, giving a motive for us to be roused to anger. Even if, through self-restraint, our anger is not outwardly expressed or is not heard by the one who provoked it, it is still a sin, because it harms our soul and our heart. It is an action against ourself, under the temptation of the devil to anger.

The Savior warns us in severe terms concerning anger that gives birth to verbal conflicts and the use of abusive words.

I say unto you, that whosoever is angry with his brother shall be in danger of the judgment:[1] *and whosoever shall say to his brother, Raca, shall be in danger of the council: but whosoever shall say, Thou fool, shall be in danger of hell fire* (Matthew 5:22).

See, therefore, that Jesus sanctions neither anger expressed

---

[1] St. John Cassian writes: "This is the text of the best manuscripts; for it is clear from the purpose of Scripture in this context that the words 'without a cause' were added later. The Lord's intention is that we should remove the root of anger, its spark, so to speak, in whatever way we can, and not keep even a single pretext for anger in our hearts. Otherwise we will be stirred to anger initially for what appears to be a good reason and then find that our incensive power is totally out of control. (St. John Cassian, *On the Eight Vices*, in *The Philokalia*, vol. 4 [London: Faber and Faber, 1979], p. 86.)—ED.

outwardly nor anger in one's thoughts. No one thinks evil without corrupting the heart in which God should dwell. Whoever is angered in thought against his brother tears apart a sacred tie between him and the other. And this tie is difficult to reestablish, because the demon of anger, once it has penetrated the heart, fabricates numerous arguments in your defense that stop you from reconciling. In the Epistle to the Ephesians, the holy Apostle Paul gives a series of counsels to the inhabitants of the city of Ephesus and emphasizes the sin of anger in a special way. The quotation from the beginning of this article is from his Epistle. Knowing that man gets angry for many reasons and that this anger has the tendency to remain in the heart of man and to transform it into hatred (or at least to dig a gulf between us), the Apostle counsels us not to allow the sun to go down upon our anger. Through this counsel, the power of anger—which often hurts and eventually becomes a deep-rooted sin—is swept away and its power dissolved.

I am concerned about the sin of anger as an everyday sin committed against those who are close to us: against our family, friends, colleagues, and anonymous strangers who happen to cross our path. In an instant, anger expressed through fiery words against our wife or husband wounds the sensitive bond between the married couple. In the mystery of marriage, the Bridegroom is the symbol of Jesus, and the Bride is the Church. The holy Apostle Paul, in the Epistle to the Ephesians—the Epistle that is read at the crowning service [the marriage ceremony]—in this sense speaks about the family as a family church in which the bridegroom loves the bride with the love with which Jesus loves the Church, and the bride loves the bridegroom with the love which the Church loves Christ.

If the husband and wife would ponder on their marriage as the relationship between Christ and Church, the sun would never set upon their wrath, and they would never separate. Neither would the children be delivered over to state or private institutions, like some worn-out objects no longer needed by these two, separated through the sin of anger, which was not extinguished at the setting of the sun. The love of their family becomes a hollow word, which no longer matters before the demon who took complete mastery. A word said in anger wounds just as seriously as a physical blow. If he who wounds does not rectify the spiritual damage, little by little, a gulf is dug between the two, a deadly coldness kills the sentiment of love and respect appropriate between husband and wife; time deepens and enlarges the gulf. Later, it is very difficult for them to be able to throw a bridge across it—only with great effort and suffering.

I have seen spouses—who had maintained a good marriage for many years—divorce after many years, causing pain for their children, who were, perhaps, already married. I have also seen happy spouses divorce after a short time, all caused by anger over time, leaving small children to grow up in frustration and confusion, not understanding who is father or mother. Later, following the example of their parents, they no longer consider marriage to be a sacred bond, like that between Christ and the Church.

I have seen brothers who loved each other in Romania, but after arriving in America became estranged due to the pressures of being in a foreign land and the difficulties of adapting. They remained enemies until death, because their anger burst out fiercely into strong words and because they allowed the sun to go down upon their anger.

An Arabic proverb says that when you become upset, count to ten, and if you are roused to anger, to count to one hundred. I do not know how effective this solution is, because it does not contain a mystical element; it merely appeals to the reason to moderate the outward expression of anger. I counsel my penitents that before they express their anger, be it in speech or gestures, be it only mentally, to utter three or five times, "Lord Jesus Christ, Son of God, have mercy on me, a sinner." And if they say the prayer quickly and inattentively under the oppression of anger, then they should concentrate with humility upon the word "sinner," and their anger will abate. Many of them have succeeded in making their life, their family relationships, their relations with other people, and even their interior life change for the better.

All the conflicts in the world have their origin in unabated anger. One is angry and wounds the other, who then responds with greater violence and strength. Once this chain is begun, it cannot be stopped except through the appeal of prayer—genuine prayer.

Change the conditions of this equation and substitute groups of people for individuals and you will realize the immense dimensions of the disaster spawned by anger.

Try to put an unshakable obstacle before the demon of anger. Put a guard on your mouth (cf. Ps. 140:3) and change the evil thoughts originating from the impulse of anger, and your interior life will be transformed. The blessing of the Lord will work in your heart, your tongue will no longer be so sharp, and the Jesus Prayer, uttered at the necessary times, will convince you of your sinful state, thus stopping you from either exteriorizing anger or keeping it in your mind and heart.

The name of Jesus is sweet to utter. It casts out the demons and brings the angels back into the heart, into the mind, and you will bear yourself in meekness before others.

Translated by the St. Herman of Alaska Brotherhood from the newsletter of Holy Cross Church in Alexandria, Virginia (in Romanian).

A WORD ON THE "SPIRIT OF THE TIMES"

THERE IS A "spirit" unveiling itself in Europe and the world in general, a New Age kind of spirit that frequently changes its appearance and speech, striking the Christian world from all sides. Its image is generally gentle, its discourse attractive, but its intent perfidious. This spirit can speak in beautiful words about family, but its intent is to annihilate it. It can also sermonize on the Church, full of "love" for all, a sort of religious syncretism, but its urge is primarily to dispel Orthodoxy. It can speak about nations and their homelands as something that it tries to support, but its intent is to destroy both the Church and the nations. This spirit is called ecumenism.

And this whole "beautiful" discourse, which takes on many faces, has only one purpose: the destruction of nations, the abolition of the Orthodox Church in particular, and the establishment of a group of leaders, anointed by I do not know whom ... to win over all nations to their spirit, to initiate them into certain social, political, and religious orders, so that those leaders may always direct [world events]. Let us not be deceived! I live among these "spreaders" of prolific and protean discourses that cover the world. And I know their hearts. They have no good intention for our Church! Under the guise of Christian love, of Christian peace, they hide their perfidious intent. And I came here to say: Do not be allured by it!...

In this New Age spirit I'm referring to, nothing exists with an absolute value.

For their intent is to destroy all the elements of the Faith,

A WORD ON THE "SPIRIT OF THE TIMES"

Fr. George speaking at a church in Romania in 2005.

the moral elements, the elements of kinship, on which we have relied, since (so they say) there is no absolute truth. The truth, according to them, is that which I possess [i.e., subjective truth]. And therefore, when my neighbor is wrong I cannot tell him, "You are deceived!" Nor can he tell me that I have erred, because we are absolute entities [unto ourselves]. We have our opinions which are absolute, but before others, they hold no value! This game of hiding the truth is an insidious invention of Satan.

Translated by Elena Chiru from Diaconesti Monastery, ed., Fr. George Calciu: Living Words *(in Romanian) (Bacau: Bonifaciu Press, 2009), pp. 86–87.*

WALKING ON THE SEA OF LIFE

WHY GET INTO the boat? Because it represents the Church. The Church is built very much like a boat or in the shape of the Cross. A boat keeps you away from the waves of the sea, but the Church, from the waves of this life. And the Cross saves you from all hardships, for Jesus Christ was crucified on it; and in that mystical sense, it is through the Cross and our Savior's Blood shed there, that the Church was founded. As for those who abandon the Church, they are neither in her nor can they be in Christ.

Peter wanted to leave the boat (the Church) so that he could be greater than the other disciples, standing on the waves next to the Savior (cf. Matt. 14:24–33). It was a temptation for him to desire Jesus to give him the power to walk on the sea. So Jesus bid him to walk, and he did as long as he didn't doubt and his faith was strong.

The Church is the only salvation for our souls. He who places himself outside it is a lost man. We are saved only in it. We are washed from our sins inside this ship and never outside it. He who ventures to leave it—as did Peter, desiring to wander further above the seas, towards the heights of God—had better maintain great faith that the waves do not rise or disturb him no matter how the winds blow, his heart and mind directed towards Jesus. But how many can really be saved outside this ship, in order to speak directly with God?

The Protestants say, "I have my own relationship with God and have no need of a priest or the Church, I need no sacraments, and I speak directly with God Himself!"

I do not know how much they're speaking directly with

God …, but from what I have seen, they are conversing more with their earthly interests than with God.

Our Savior will save you from certain trials, if you cry out to Him. He will reach out His hand and catch you, and say, "O man of little faith, why did you doubt?" (cf. Matthew 14:31).

We often travel the waters of this life, and the temptations are many. In this world, so troubled by snares, by wars and horrors, and by all the ways that will lead to its end, who can really come to Christ by walking alone on the sea? Who can venture forth so earnestly to cry out at his last moment for Jesus to stretch out His hand and save him? For our own good and our salvation, it is best to remain in the Church. Amen!

Translated by Elena Chiru from Living Words, *pp. 206–7.*

HOW TO BATTLE AGAINST THE DEMONS

They cried out, saying, What have we to do with Thee, Jesus, Thou Son of God? Art Thou come hither to torment us before the time?
Matt: 8:29

BECAUSE THE DEMON is a fallen angel, it is very difficult to defeat it with our intellect or even with our (weak) faith and repentance. A demon possesses greater "intelligence" than us and greater power (to deceive), since it understands and sees things more clearly than we do.

Prayer is one of the most powerful tools we have received from our Savior Jesus Christ, a weapon from which the devil flees. The prayer of St. Basil (the Great) was so powerful that when the saint began to pray, all the demons fled. God granted St. Basil this extraordinary power, which He can also bestow on us ordinary believers. Strive towards deeper prayer, perhaps not one that would move "mountains," but at least one that would cleanse us from sins and keep demons away. The way of fasting is also the way of purifying the flesh, making it more transparent, for a corpulent body is impenetrable to the Holy Spirit. The Spirit of God does not abide in flesh that is satisfied. For the fast that thins the flesh will make it hungry for the word of God, and we'll better understand His commandments and receive power to overcome the devil. However, the devil is not always defeated by everyone.

I have my own experience with this. Some years ago I encountered a young man possessed by an evil spirit. He was not acting evil, that is, throwing himself down or other frightful acts, but he had a total distrust of people. He feared God and the Church, but he was in great distress. While I was reading the prayers (exorcisms) of St. Basil over him, he was seized by a great tremor. At that moment, perhaps because his thoughts were in so much distress, he responded by making the most inhuman and strange sounds. The demon inside him never attacked me: the man didn't try to hit me or to escape from under the epitrachelion [priest's stole]. But he passed through these "states" which were from the demon that dwelt in him, and he was not freed until he opened his soul to Confession. When he falls again into temptation, he returns to me, and I pray these prayers (of St. Basil) over him. If the devil takes possession of his heart, he manifests it in the way I mentioned above, but if not, then he's only overcome by evil thoughts.

With time, the prayers began to work, but many temptations also arose: he fought against all sorts of images, he had suspicious thoughts that God had no power over him and that the prayers I read do not have the same power as those of St. Basil—all sorts of doubts to further distance him from the influence of prayer. But if you have a powerful prayer and have also fasted, know that the devil flees.

Our Lord Jesus Christ works in those who believe and have received God's grace through the Sacrament of the priesthood, regardless of their virtues or sinfulness. Some are attracted to the intellect of the priest, others by the power of his prayers, while others by his counsel. There is always something that draws you to the priest, and through this, God grants him power. This is the grace that was given to him by the "laying on of hands" (cf. Acts 8:18, I Tim. 4:14), by which he can "bind all that can be bound on earth and absolve all that can be absolved" (cf. Matt. 16:19, 18:18) according to the Gospel. Amen.

Translated by Elena Chiru from Living Words, *pp. 44–46.*

ON THE IMPORTANCE OF HOLY TRADITION

FAITH HAS ITS place in a balanced Orthodox environment and a natural relationship with the world. What I mean is that we live in the world and must do what it takes to survive in it, but not at the cost of compromises, betrayals, or renouncing Christ. Orthodoxy gives us balance.

We [the cradle Orthodox] possess a very ancient tradition. I look at the American Orthodox. They are very passionate for Orthodoxy, but they're lacking Holy Tradition. So, in a sense, they are streams branching off the Russian, Bulgarian, Serbian, or Romanian tradition, since they do not have that traditional instruction from their ancestors, as we do. We stand on a firm rock: the teachings of the Holy Fathers, the ascetic experience of the desert monks, the entire Orthodox Tradition handed to us in patristic books or by oral tradition, and these, regardless of our sins, constitute a stone foundation, that unshaken ground where our feet may walk and not sink—like a boat in which Jesus is present. We do not sink because we hold fast to tradition. Yes, we are sinners, but God preserves us when we follow Him and the teachings of the Holy Fathers, even though sometimes we fail.... But is there anyone without sin? Is there anyone who has not been tempted? Who does not dirty his soul with evil thoughts, deeds, or lusts? But aside from all these failings, we have unshaken ground.

This ground is the Orthodox Church, the tradition of the Holy Fathers, the Seven Ecumenical Councils, the struggle of the saints in the wilderness of the Thebaid, Sinai ..., in our

ON THE IMPORTANCE OF HOLY TRADITION

Fr. George on his final visit to Romania, in 2006.

country [Romania], and in the monasteries found everywhere. Having these riches, we will not sink.

Translated by Elena Chiru from Living Words, *pp. 76–77.*

THE CENTURION'S FAITH AND THE HEALING OF THE HEART

THE CHRISTIAN FAITH is not a conditioned, devised attitude. The Centurion described to Christ his relationship with his servants: "Lord, if I say to one of them, 'Go!' then, he goes; if I say to another, 'Do this!' then, he does it" (cf. Matt. 8:9). Even more did he believe that if the Lord commanded an evil spirit, "Free the man!" the spirit would free him, or if Christ said, "Do not enter this man again!" the spirit would not enter him again.

The Centurion had great faith before any miracle had been accomplished.

Quite often we are guided by good deeds. We hear that an image of the Mother of God has appeared somewhere in the sky. We go there to see it, and maybe we'll believe. And we do not know what our faith is about....

I was in Chicago to see a weeping icon of the Holy Mother of God. It was in 1987. We were three priests, and we served the Divine Liturgy for the Romanian nation. During the Liturgy, the Holy Mother of God shed tears from her icon three times. Her garment was soaked in tears. I saw people who came there to see that. And we also saw. Then we forgot. For the faith that rests only on miracles is weak.

If God strikes you this moment, you'll definitely cry out, "Lord!"

If an earthquake or a war were to occur now, you would cry, "God, save me!" But after the earthquake passes, you'll forget God again.

Distinct from this is the faith based on a close spiritual

THE CENTURION'S FAITH

relationship with Christ, when you know that you're nothing without Him and that everything is in His hands: that He can lay you down or lift you up. He can heal you or let you perish. He can free you from tragedy or let you be pounded by it.

The teaching is this: do not establish or base your faith on wonders! Many times our Savior employed His word, and the sick were healed. The Centurion did not need our Lord to first perform a miracle for him to believe. Indeed, he only needed Christ to confirm that his servant would be healed. He came to Christ as to One Who he knew would cure his servant, to someone in Whom he truly believed, although he was not a Jew, but a new Samaritan, a Roman.

When you're longing for a miracle to happen, you might say, "Lord, if You exist, perform this miracle!" And God does not hear you. Or perhaps He will, if your soul really needs it. More importantly, believe in God before any miracle occurs! Do not expect miracles; the deepest relationship with Christ is spiritual. Pray to the Lord and be in His presence, have Him abide in you! And God will answer you with His unseen wonders, through the strength of your spirit, rousing you to greater understanding of His judgments. Not as we tend to understand historically and rationally, but in a deeper spiritual sense, when you see the hand of God in everything.

There were many great Fathers who lived a lofty spiritual life, and God rewarded them with great gifts. They performed many wonders, but when someone would come to thank them for a miracle, they would answer, "It is not I, but Christ Who made it happen. Give thanks to the Lord."

And Christ elevated them in His Light: either with a halo around their heads, as Fr. Benedict Ghius[1] from Cernica had, or with the ability to move with great speed from one place to another—they were in one place, and within minutes they

---
[1] See pp. 269–70 above.—ED.

were many kilometers away. All these were miracles that Christ performed through them and for them, because they had a deeply spiritual, personal relationship with Christ.

Here is that personal relationship: when you offer your soul to Christ and He sends you the Holy Spirit, Who works within you. This is beyond any earthly reward. What does it mean when your car breaks down and God sends someone to help you? These are small things ... but what of your spiritual relationship with Christ, Who dwells deeply in the Christian soul, and the presence of the Holy Spirit in your heart? They make you gentle, forgiving; you neither become angry with your neighbor nor hold it within you; you are a beacon of light for all, even if you're small—all these are true miracles which Christ calls us to perform.

Preserve your relationship with Christ as did the Centurion and you'll receive godly rewards. Think rightly, and do not allow the evil spirit to conquer you. Do not tempt God, or say, "O Lord, come and abide in my heart," while you are conversing with the devil, even though you may feel you're fighting against him. But like the Centurion cry out, "Lord, speak Your word only, and my heart will be healed" (cf. Matt. 8:8). Amen!

Translated by Elena Chiru from Living Words, *pp. 211–12.*

THOMAS SUNDAY

The Apostle Thomas represents those who are dominated by rationality and who need evidence. They are not unbelievers, but they need evidence to strengthen their faith. The moment they are given proof, their faith deepens, up to the ultimate sacrifice, as it was with the holy Apostle Thomas.

Why was Thomas not with the disciples? All the disciples were gathered together in a house for fear of the Jews, as the Evangelist John relates in today's Gospel. But Thomas was not with them. It is possible that Thomas was the most courageous of them and went outside to gain information and hear what else was said about Jesus, or perhaps he went out to bring food because the other Apostles didn't have the courage to do so.

Thus, when Jesus came, he was not with them.

When they told him, *We have seen the Lord*, Thomas answered, *Except I shall see in His hands the print of the nails, and put my finger into the print of the nails, and thrust my hand into His side, I will not believe* (John 20:25).

The day when Jesus appeared to His disciples and Thomas was not with them, the disciples doubted Him. Even when our Savior said to them, *Peace be unto you* (John 20:19), they did not believe it was He until *Jesus showed unto them His hands and His side* (John 20:20), saying, *Behold My hands and My feet, that it is I myself: handle Me, and see; for a spirit hath not flesh and bones, as ye see Me have* (Luke 24:39). So who is unfaithful: Thomas, who had not seen the Lord and doubted, or the disciples who saw Him and doubted?

Our Savior knew of Thomas' doubt and came especially for

him. Jesus came into this world not only for believers and sinners, but also for those who live in doubt.

To doubt is a demonic act. The demons constantly seek to afflict our souls with doubt by suggesting to us: "Well, I believe in God, and I believe that Jesus Christ came into the world, died, and was crucified for our salvation, but was He the Son of God?" Or perhaps: "I believe in a certain miracle, but ... is it really authentic?"

In the book of Revelation, the angel of the Lord, addressing the Churches of Asia Minor, said to the one in Laodicea, "I will spit you out of my mouth because you are neither hot nor cold, but lukewarm" (cf. Rev. 3:15–16).

God does not love the lukewarm. Perhaps, God knows that he who advocates strongly "against" Him can be converted. St. Paul was a great persecutor of Christians, but when our Savior met him on the way [to Damascus], he turned to the Faith and became one of the greatest Apostles. It is easier to convert such a man than one who is lukewarm. The lukewarm man lives in warm water: he neither "boils" nor "freezes," nor is he good for anything.

Thomas was a not a lukewarm man, he had faith, but he needed some evidence. Our Savior appeared to him and said, *Reach hither thy finger, and behold My hands; and reach hither thy hand, and thrust it into My side: and be not faithless, but believing.* (John 20:27).

The Evangelist John does not mention whether Thomas put his hand in our Savior's side, but we know what Thomas said, *My Lord and my God!* (John 20:28).

He saw Jesus and understood that the proof was right before him. There was no other evidence for him to seek when Jesus was right there in front of him, shining in the light of the Resurrection, entering through the locked doors and through the walls, a bright Savior shining forth everywhere.

Our Savior said something not for Thomas but for us: *Because thou hast seen Me, thou hast believed* (John 20:29).

Jesus did not say, "Because thou hast touched Me, thou hast believed!" ... instead He said, *Because thou hast seen Me, and blessed are they that have not seen, and yet have believed* (John 20:29).

This blessing is for all of us pious Christians. This blessing is for us who come to church to confess that Christ is the Son of God, Who suffered, was crucified, died, was buried, rose again on the third day according to the Scriptures, and ascended into heaven. This is the foundation of our faith!

The lesson that we draw from today's Gospel is that Jesus Christ came for everyone. He didn't come only for those who believe or for Jews, or only for sinners. He came for the lukewarm as well, if they "warm up."

So, He came for the doubtful. And all of us have doubts ... We doubt because we once asked for something, and God did not grant our request! But merely one cry in a "time of need" does not show faith. It rather shows human weakness. We must have a strong, steadfast faith, one that is indisputable. And today's Gospel is for all of us who doubt.

When Jesus appeared to Thomas, who doubted Him, Thomas, seeing our Lord, fell at His feet and said, *My Lord and my God!* Let us also fall at the feet of Jesus and cry out, *My Lord and my God!*

Translated by Elena Chiru from Living Words, *pp. 235–37.*

Fr. George with Fr. Ioanichie (Balan) (†2007), in 1998.

THE HEALING OF THE PARALYTIC AND THE LONELINESS OF CONTEMPORARY MAN

WHAT IS MOST striking in today's Gospel (John 5:1–15) is the loneliness of the sick man.

Have you heard? *Sir, I have no man, when the water is troubled, to put me into the pool: but while I am coming, another steppeth down before me* (John. 5:7).

The most tragic state of man is loneliness, his total isolation. According to St. Cyprian of Carthage, "Everyone falls alone, but we are being saved in the community," in the community of the Church. To be alone means to fall, to get lost. Being alone implies thinking only of oneself ..., because you're overwhelmed by the suffering in which you lie. You are overpowered by the futility of life. If your life is lonely and bereft of God, it becomes useless and lost—a life whose meaning has vanished from the moment you became isolated.

This paralytic did not even have a relative or a friend to put him into the pool when the water was troubled, so that he could be healed.

How many times do we find ourselves in this situation? How many times do we feel alone or sick or disabled or bereft of anyone to help us to be healed or relieved from our suffering? Or perhaps, in our loneliness and pain we cannot find anyone to share [our suffering], because, as a German proverb says: A pain shared is halved, but an unrequited pain is doubled. So it happened with this man.

But our merciful Lord asked him, *Wilt thou be made whole?*

(John. 5:6). Such a question addressed to the sick may seem unnecessary. Of course he wants to be healed.

However, our Savior was alluding to something else. This man was sick because of his sins, and when he was asked, *Wilt thou be made whole?* our Savior was in fact asking him, "Do you want to repent of your sins?" The proof of this is revealed to us later, when Jesus met him in the temple and said, *Behold, thou art made whole: sin no more, lest a worse thing come unto thee* (John 5:14).

What is even more striking to us and to others, is that the moment Jesus healed the paralytic man, instead of rejoicing at seeing him healed, the scribes and the Pharisees became angry and said, *It is the Sabbath day: it is not lawful for thee to carry thy bed* (John 5:10). They did not say, "We are grateful that you are healed! Go and give thanks to God." Rather, they were only interested in the formality of the law, which stated that on Saturdays one should not work. They sacrificed man in order to obey this law.

And they asked him, "Who is the Man that healed you?" But he didn't know who it was (cf. John 5:12–13). But when Jesus met him in the temple, he went away and told the Jews that *it was Jesus, Who had made him whole* (John 5:15).

His intent was not to denounce Jesus to the Jews; rather, he had a sincere will to tell everyone, "This Man helped me! He healed me! He stood by me in misery!"

We all feel the need to proclaim it when someone has helped us. We feel the need to reveal a miracle. Not for praise, but to escape the loneliness, the sickness, and the pain! I feel the need to proclaim who brought me to the Faith, who absolved me from my sins and the wickedness of my heart: a priest, a believer, a friend.... I feel the need to say, "He helped me!" So it was with this paralytic.

My beloved faithful, our contemporary society and most authorities—not only the Communists—are increasingly isolating us, in order that we may become lonelier, less bound to each other, and less communicative, in order that they may lead us to their intended destination. They are trying to isolate us, because communities are much harder to lead than isolated individuals.

The Communists have done this through violence. The West doesn't use violence but another method: proclaiming that you are "unique," that you have "many rights," that you are an "independent man," that you need to be alone, not confined by your parents, not obedient to them or to anyone as a child, because you are a "free man."

This misunderstood freedom is a revolt against God, it is nihilism.

Thus, we have reached the state that we see today, with all the crimes that haunt the world ... where fourteen-year-old children shoot their teachers, their friends, and their parents.

We have broken the human ties with those we live near. That spiritual relationship between my brother and me, between my parents and me, between parents and children, between friends has vanished. And in this disintegration of the personality, which leads towards a demonized world, we are growing increasingly isolated.

Let us remain united in faith and love with one another, through Jesus Christ our Lord. Let us stay united in the community of the Church, because the Church of Christ is the only beneficial social group. Other groups lead to self-destruction. They attempt to destroy humankind, to make man an instrument of business, a mere cog in this complicated mechanism of human society.

Translated by Elena Chiru from Living Words, *pp. 213–15.*

ON THE MEANING OF SUFFERING

*Fr. George was often asked about his suffering in prison. Presented below is his answer to one such question.—*ED.

WHAT CAN I tell you? In my arms people have died who were a thousand times more valuable than I. In prison many who were more valuable than those who survived have died in the arms of other men, and yet I, a sinner, am here. And to speak of myself again—whether to say what good I did or what wrong I did—it would still come out as bragging. So, I find it very difficult to talk about these things.

Generally many words of praise have been said (in relation to this); all this is dust and ashes, all vanity, but we continue to hold onto what we have received from God and what we have managed to keep through suffering, or through success, praise, or blame.... Thus, we remain faithful to the Church and our nation.

My life in Romania was full of events for better and for worse. I do not accuse or blame anyone, all these were sent by God to exercise my soul.

Someone asked me if my sufferings in prison helped me in any way. I answered, "No, they have not helped me, but I'm the result of this suffering. If I do something, if I am anything, if you see something in me, know that it is because of suffering. Without this suffering, I have nothing!"

Perhaps of all the difficult questions for the human person, suffering is the most inexplicable. Why is suffering necessary? I have lived an experience of suffering that enriched my soul, and I believe that suffering was necessary for me. But it is very difficult for someone to accept this principle.

ON THE MEANING OF SUFFERING

When we were in prison, we asked each other, "Why suffering, why us? Of all the millions of Romanians, why have we been chosen to suffer? What is the purpose?" And God wouldn't reveal anything to us. Every day we cried out to God to give us less pain, and He seemed to grant us even more suffering.

Even after I was liberated from prison, I held within me this imprint of the pain, which seemed to mark my whole life thereafter. After the second imprisonment, I immigrated to the West and traveled through every country in Europe and America, speaking about the results of Communism. My intention was this: I could not keep silent as long as suffering, injustice, Communism, the destruction of churches, and the destruction of the human personality took place in my country. In my wanderings I came upon a monastery and slept in its library. It was a Catholic monastery. In its library I found, among many books, a small booklet with Christian sayings. I opened it randomly to a page where I saw a reflection of Paul Claudel, a famous French writer. He said this: "Christ did not come into the world to eliminate suffering, Christ has not even come into the world to explain it. Rather, He came to fill human suffering with His presence."

Have you heard? To fill human suffering with his presence! Then I understood that when we weep, or when we revolt or cry out, "God, what are You doing to us?!" He is present within us more than ever, despite all our sins, all our infirmities. He filled our suffering with His presence. Thus, I understood exactly the deep meaning of this pain: God is present in us!

Translated by Elena Chiru from Living Words, *pp. 138–39.*

THE GREAT SUPPER

Let us clothe our souls with the sincere garment of repentance! Let us clothe our souls with the shining garment of good deeds and prayer! Let us renew ourselves inwardly through Confession and Communion! I have always counseled you: Confess! Commune! There is nothing greater in this world—no greater Supper—than to bear Christ in your soul and body.

Fr. Dumitru Staniloae used to say, "If I walk on the street after the Holy Liturgy and I see a priest and an angel coming out of the church, I bow before the priest, not before the angel, because the priest bears Christ in him." He can be a sinner, he can do many wrongs, but at that moment he bears the Body of Christ. So great is this Supper!

When you commune and leave church, the angel bows before you! You stand before the angels, because you are bearers of Christ! If you do not understand this, I am not saying that you come to church in vain, but that you are not truly penetrated by the significance of coming to church, of the fact that you have to be saved, of the fact that you did not come into the world to perish, like any other animal. You did not come to live a life which terminates in death, but you came into the world with a mission. This mission possesses a social aspect, but at the same time it is a sacred mission: to spread the word of God, to be an example to all, to exhort others through that which you do, to do good, because this saves you, too.

Translated by Adrian and Mihaela Ulmer from Living Words, p. 58.

ON THE COMMUNION OF THE SOUL WITH GOD

Your relationship with God—when you feel that God has answered you—is a special relationship which cannot be explained. As much as I would try to define faith, prayer, and the mercy of God, I can only use human and rational words, which have nothing to do with the super-rationality of God.

God is outside the world; God is only in love. I won't try to explain all these things to you because they cannot be explained. They belong to a mystical relationship of man with God, which someone feels or does not, puts into practice or does not. There is no middle way. There is no way to talk with God today, curse Him tomorrow, praise Him the day after tomorrow, and so on. You need to be in a constant relationship with God: constant in your faith, in your knowledge of your nothingness before Him, in your understanding that you are nothing before the face of God, because you are filled with sins—but not because God created you impure. God created you pure, but you have bemired yourself in every sin; you have trod through all the mire; you damaged your soul, heart, and mind. Your mind works against the good. Your heart has cooled toward God; it does not love anyone. You are hardened. All of these are things which change your relationship with God, weaken it, or even sever it.

We have to restore this relationship through love, perseverance, and prayer—to have love for God and love for our neighbor, because no one could say that he loves God Whom he cannot see, but doesn't love his neighbor whom he can see. It is not possible for someone to love God and to not love his neighbor (cf. I John

Fr. George in Romania in 2004.

4:20). This is our relationship with God: it has one end in our heart and the other end in His hand. Through this relationship of faith, of love, of our good deeds, we enter into God's will, and God dwells in us. It is, as I said, hard to explain. Only those who have faith, who endeavor on the path of this life, who act for the good, who strengthen their faith, will establish this relationship. I don't say that it [this relationship] is permanent. We perhaps sever it through our sins, but there is, nevertheless, a spiritual channel through which we speak to God.

I remember when I was small: we were eleven children and there were difficult times.... And my mother was praying to God just as I am talking to you. She was crying to Him that her son was sick, that the cow stopped giving milk, or that it had no calf and that the chicken didn't lay eggs... She was telling God everything, as if she were in a direct relationship with Him. And God answered, just so you know. There wasn't any kind of impiety. My mother knew that God is with us, and she talked to God the same way we speak to one another as friends. You tell your brother or friend all your pain, to the smallest details. God knows them, but it is also our duty to tell Him and to bring Him praise. I want you to understand that you can have a relationship of kinship with God, as between a son and a parent, or a relationship with a friend.... It is this kind of relationship that God asks from us.

In silence, simplicity, humility, we can establish this relationship with God so that we can have a place to go when we are in trouble and nobody provides refuge. When everybody abandons us, when our life seems to be lost, nevertheless God opens His arms and receives us. This is an extraordinary mystery.... This is why I tell you: try to pray! Try to talk to God constantly! Prayer is the path which connects you with God. It is not a conversation with God, but a spiritual state, which I cannot explain in words, but which we can all feel. The mercy of God, and the echo in our heart of a spiritual joy otherwise unknown to us, and the suffering of our heart for a dear one who is in pain: all these things form the ladder of ascent to God.

An enormous ladder ... Ascending on it step by step, we come nearer to God. God comes to us at the midpoint of the ladder, and extends His hand and tells us, "Maybe you have doubted; don't doubt yourself anymore! Here is My hand!"

Translated by Adrian and Mihaela Ulmer from Living Words, *pp. 22–23.*

PRAYER IS A STRUGGLE

I DO NOT LIKE definitions. But regarding prayer I must say, without a doubt, that it is a work proceeding from God, which returns to God. The spirit of prayer is a gift which the Holy Spirit puts in each of us, some more, some less. We cause it to be more or less active. And at the same time, prayer destroys the barrier which comes between us and God.

The greatest miracle is to know God. If we call on Him with all our strength, God reveals and makes Himself known to us. Search in the depths of your heart and you will find God there. Cry wholeheartedly and God will respond to you, and miracles will occur in your soul, and your spirit will become pure, the eye will open, and you will see the Divine Truth, which is the only Savior.

Prayer has such strength that it can change the unchangeable will of God. Prayer can bring bodily and spiritual health to the one praying; it softens the hearts of families that are embittered, and it turns from sin the one committing sin.

I have stayed in prison with many people: with hierarchs, with good priests, with monks, and I understood that prayer is a struggle, a very great struggle.

In the moment when you begin to pray, the devil attacks you; and after the first words, after the first short prayers you make, he puts all kinds of unimportant, worldly thoughts in your mind. Even curiosity about the time of day or whether it is sunny or cloudy works in your mind. All of these appear as innocent behavior, but they disrupt the voice of prayer in our heart. Fr. Paisios[1] says that these thoughts which appear in our mind at

---

[1] Elder Paisius of Mount Athos (1924–94).

the time of prayer are like airplanes. First, you hear them from afar, very faintly as a noise without much intensity, then the noise grows and grows and grows, and when they arrive over your head, they overwhelm you with their noise and then go away. But if you enter into conversation with these thoughts, they will make your heart into an airport.

Some Christians ask me what to do when fighting against the thoughts which come to their mind when they pray. The first thing is to pay no attention to them. Namely, to let them pass over your head. The second thing is to call for the help of God and of your guardian angel. And the third thing is not to open your heart to a conversation with the bad thoughts, because the demon is stronger than we are. The devil goes mad when someone prays. This can explain why we are especially attacked when we pray. An army of demons brings all these vile thoughts.

If your heart is truly penetrated by the Holy Spirit, if your prayer melts your whole heart and soul, then you do not need to say many prayers, but only, "God, do not forsake me!" or, "Lord Jesus Christ, Son of God, have mercy on me, a sinner!" which is the strongest prayer. The name of Jesus is sweet when pronounced, it banishes the demons and brings the angels back, and it brings to the heart and mind a good-hearted concern for others. But if you do not attain to this, follow the rule of prayer from the prayer book, because by calling on the name of God through all the prayers, you call on Christ, the Mother of God, the Holy Spirit, the Holy Trinity, God the Father, the saints, all the martyrs, and your heart will enter into an interior resonance with all of them.

Sometimes I come here to the church and no one is inside. It is quiet. I enter, and the moment I come through the door, I have the feeling that all the saints have their faces turned towards me, that they have turned their gaze upon me. I feel that I am not alone. I feel surrounded by spiritual powers. And often I hear feet walking through the church.... I do not see anything, but I hear soft steps. A movement is heard. Surely you will say, "Fine, but the church is old and it creaks." Perhaps the church creaks, but perhaps God lets me know that the saints are with me, that I pray with them, or they pray together with me. God lets me know.

And truly I know, in that moment, that I am not alone here. Even if it is night, as late as it may be, I am not afraid. I do not feel boredom, but only a sort of joy which does not belong to me, which is foreign to me. It does not come from my heart, but it comes from somewhere else.

Translated by Adrian and Mihaela Ulmer from Living Words, pp. 24–25.

THE CHURCH AND THE SPIRIT OF THE WORLD

THE CHURCH IS persecuted in a spiritual way. The most horrible movies and books appear about Jesus, about the Apostles; the most detestable worldly passions become a spectacle for the whole world. What else do we see on television except this spectacle of fornication and sins?! From time to time something else is presented. Have you seen the Romanian press? Nothing good is ever mentioned. Only wickedness and misfortunes ... We live in a sinful world, which tries to prevent us from going to the church of God, so that we might not be part of the mystical Body of Christ, because the Church is the mystical Body of Christ our Savior, in which every one of us is a member.

The holy Apostle Paul says that if one of the members suffers, the whole body suffers, and that it is impossible for a member to live alone, without others. The eye cannot say, "Body, I don't like you and I won't serve you anymore!" nor can the heart say, "I don't like you, I won't serve you anymore," because all of us form an organic body, and this spiritual unity is manifested in the Church. Each is a member, each helps the other, and all of us form the mystical Body of Christ. (cf. I Cor. 12:12–30)

In the Church, nobody remains indifferent when someone is sick. In the Church, nobody stays away from someone asking for help. In the Church, nobody passes by someone who has fallen into misfortune, even if he does not know him. Christianity is like this, God is like this, the Church and sanctity are like this. All the members of this Church, both the living and the departed, together make a community, a being united in spirit. This is why we perform memorial services. The Church triumphant from the other world and the Church militant here are one single Body. And this Body is the greatest enemy of politics, of atheism, of human wickedness, and of the regimes of this century.

The Church, while being a communal Body, cannot be maneuvered or controlled by an international atheistic government or by its own [national] government, because there is a mystical, spiritual resistance by the Body of Christ to this world. Because of this, all the adverse powers direct themselves against us. As our Savior says, *Thou art Peter, and upon this rock I will build My Church; and the gates of hell shall not prevail against it* (Matt 16:18). The Church will always remain in this world as a nucleus of faith, as a nucleus of spiritual truth.

Translated by Adrian and Mihaela Ulmer from Living Words, *p. 75.*

A WORD FOR THE FEAST OF THE HOLY GREAT-MARTYR GEORGE

THE CHURCH NUMBERS among the saints and the martyrs an entire line of military saints who were enlisted in the Roman army. Christianity had spread greatly [by the third and fourth centuries]. During the time of the persecutions against the Christians, these soldiers preferred, instead of worldly military glory, the eternal praise and unfading crown of martyrdom, confessing before everyone their faith in Christ, never renouncing it: the price being their lives.

St. George was martyred at the beginning of the fourth century. He is also venerated by the Catholics. However, in our Orthodox Church, the veneration of the saints is much more developed than that of the Catholics. We have special feast days for these saints, Canons, and special hymns for them, which the Catholics do not have. Their communion with the other life lacks the power of our communion. Likewise, their communion with the departed is much weaker than ours. You know how many memorial services we perform for the departed: on the third day, on the ninth day, on the fortieth day, at six months, and so on. Thus, we always maintain an indelible, enduring communion with the departed through prayer, because they are a part of the invisible Church, and we are a part of the visible or militant Church.

The holy Great-martyr George lived during the time of Emperor Diocletian, who reigned between the years 284 and 305. The emperor was very faithful to the pagan gods. Because of this he had a disposition to persecute Christians. His cruelest and longest persecution lasted until 305. In that year he became mentally sick, imagining that he was being chased and persecuted by his own victims. He was always terrified that he would be killed. He retired from the throne to one of his palaces on the Dalmatian coast and lived there in seclusion, not receiving anyone except his guard; but he was afraid even of him, living a very anguished life. It is assumed that he died in the year 311, about the same time the persecution of the Christians stopped. He died in loneliness, terrified by all the threats surrounding him. We received all of this information from Lactantius, who was a teacher in Diocletian's court, a very learned man. Early in his reign Diocletian did not persecute the Christians very much, that is, not in a vicious way. In the meantime Lactantius became a Christian and lost his position, but continued to write his chronicles during Diocletian's reign. In his book *On the Deaths of the Persecutors (De Mortibus Persecutorum)*, he shows how the persecutors who attacked the Church of Christ ended miserably, and the greatest example is Diocletian, whom he knew during the height of his reign and during the period of his madness. Diocletian had a dark madness and was persecuted by his own interior fears. He always had the impression that the Christians were coming, that Jesus would come and punish him for the crimes he had committed, and because of this he persecuted the Christians more and more.

In the beginning, as I said, the persecution was not so cruel. The first form of persecution was the decree that everyone in the army must worship the gods if they wanted to remain in the military. If they did not [worship the gods], they would be discharged. This was his initial persecution. But later, around the year 302, he searched out the pagan oracles, who always gave obscure answers. And those oracles told him that he must persecute the Christians. So, in the year 303, he delivered a very harsh edict of persecution, in which it was said that all the Scriptures owned by the Christians must be rendered to the authorities, to be burned in the public markets. In this atmosphere, his son-in-law Galerius started two fires near the imperial palace at Nicomedia, where Diocletian was residing, blaming the Christians. Diocletian then ordered the arrest of all the bishops, priests, and deacons and tried to force them to worship the gods. This is why they were tortured; they were given over to wild beasts, and many Christians were killed. And so, Christianity produced an extraordinary number of martyrs. This persecution extended to the whole empire. This happened even as far away as here [Romania], where martyrs like Zoticus, Atallus, Philip, Camasius and others with them were killed at Niculitel.[1] It was a general persecution. Then he ordered all the soldiers who were Christians, not just the officers, to confess in order to be punished.

In these circumstances, St. George decided to confess his faith in Christ. He was a member of a prominent family, he had a good education, and his family was Christian. He was handsome and the bravest of soldiers. Being so gifted and remarkable in battle, Diocletian very quickly promoted him, naming him commander of the imperial guard. In this position, he was caught by the decree of Diocletian, which by this time had extended to all Roman citizens, who were obliged to worship the pagan gods once a month in the public markets. Many Christians, probably tens of thousands, hundred of thousands, suffered. In these circumstances, St. George decided to confess his faith in God and Christ before the emperor and the senate. While the emperor was in the senate attending to business, St. George entered and spoke about his faith and about Christ as an Emperor. He said that instead of serving an emperor and a pagan empire, he preferred to serve Christ, and that his duty to Christ would not entail the sword or fighting competitions but would consist in his sacrifice for Christ. He confessed before all that he was ready to receive martyrdom. This confession of St. George, who was greatly loved

---

[1] They were martyred in 320 at Noviodunum (present day Niculitel, Romania). Their commemoration day is June 4.

by the emperor and admired by the senate, sparked confusion and sadness, but also anger. The emperor ordered that St. George be arrested. He was put in prison and was asked to renounce his Faith. Because he refused, he was submitted to every possible torture, being probably one of the most tortured martyrs. He was forced to wear red hot metal sandals studded with nails, he was tortured on the wheel, he was thrown into the sea with a stone tied to his neck (but, as the Akathist says, he stood on the sea as on the shore), and he was thrown into a lime pit and left for three days, but he emerged unharmed.

God endows His martyrs with a certain spiritual strength, and I have seen this also in prison. Namely, very weak men, sick men, barely breathing, like Valeriu Gafencu, had an extraordinary strength. Even when they were tortured, even when they were starved, they did not feel pain but continued to confess God and bless those that tortured them. Gafencu was like this, he who died as a saint; this is what happens to the martyrs. God gives them strength, and often they do not feel the physical pain. The skin of their bodies was torn apart with metal claws, they were nailed through their palms and feet, they were burned with torches, and they did not feel the pain. God gave them this strength in order that they might overcome their suffering. But the fact that they did not renounce God, that after they were burned they would appear unharmed before the people, this caused many who witnessed their sufferings to repent and become Christians. This was the greatest glory of the martyrs. This is why our Church says that the blood of the martyrs is the seed of the Church. The more martyrs were tortured and killed, the more Christians sprang from their blood, because they witnessed their strength, the power of God, and the miracles that were accomplished, and they would repent. Right then, during the time of the tortures, the witnesses would come forth and confess before the emperor that they were Christians. Often scores of them were thrown in the arena, lacerated by wild beasts or killed by the soldiers.

THE FEAST OF THE HOLY GREAT-MARTYR GEORGE

St. George was the patron of the Romanian Army. You can see how venerated a saint he was for us: even St. Stephen the Great[2] had him as a protector. A flag sent by St. Stephen to Zographou Monastery[3] on Mount Athos has St. George depicted killing the dragon. And on the flag the following inscription is found:

"O warrior and victory-bearer Great George, quick helper and warm protector to those in needs and sorrows, and untold joy to those in sadness, receive from us this prayer of thy humble servant, of thy lord, me, Stephen Voivode, the lord of the Moldavian land by the mercy of God. Protect me untouched in this world and in that to come, through the prayers of those who venerate thee, glorifying thee unto the ages. Amen. This was carried out in the year 7008, namely in 1500, in the forty-third year of my reign, by me, Stephen Voivode, the lord of the Moldavian land."

I wanted to present this historic confession in order to demonstrate how greatly venerated St. George has been in our history. Even the Voivode, the Great and Holy Stephen himself, dedicated and wrote this prayer to St. George and placed it on his flag of victory.

There is a very strong relationship between St. George and me. When I was in prison, I constantly called on him, and in many situations he helped me. From then until this day, I have never failed to address a special prayer to him each day. I am sure that a strong relationship develops between a saint and a person who prays to him. Often the characteristics of a saint—if you have a spiritual relationship with him—will also be manifested in you. In my case, for example, just as St. George passed through prisons, so did I; just as St. George was strengthened by God in difficult situations, so was I strengthened in the most difficult moments, where I could have perished, not just physically but also spiritually. But the presence of the saint made me stronger,

---

[2] King of Moldavia, reposed 1504. He is commemorated on July 2.—ED.

[3] Zographou is the only Bulgarian monastery on Mount Athos. It is dedicated to Great-martyr George.—ED.

because he sent me, who prayed to him and carried his name, great strength of faith and spiritual protection bestowed on us by God through him.

Address yourself to the saint whose name you bear, and he will help you. Address him in time of sorrow, in times of sickness, in difficult situations, and in moments of joy: "St. John, my protector!" or, "St. George, pray to God for me, a sinner!" Address him and he will listen to your prayer! He is the advocate for those who bear his name, before the face of God. He brings his prayer before God and intercedes for us. And at the end of our lives, when we pass to the other world, our patron saint will stand beside us. If we honor him and pray to him, he will remain close to our guardian angel, defending us from the accusations of Satan. This is because, at the particular Judgment, the devil brings forth all our sins, which we cannot even remember. He brings them into the light, and he places them on the scale. And so, we need a defense lawyer, who can bring forth our good deeds also. We will be so ashamed that we might not even remember our good deeds, just as we have forgotten our sins. But our guardian angel and our patron saint will come and place our good deeds onto the balance. And often a tear weighs as much as all the bad things we have done in an entire lifetime. Therefore, I beg you, remember the saints whose names you bear, and pray to them to protect you, to protect your family, our people, and the entire world.

AN INTERVIEW ON THE FALL OF COMMUNISM AND THE FUTURE OF ROMANIA

REPORTER: *It is more than one year since your first and only visit to Romania after the fall of the Ceausescu dictatorship. It was, if I am not mistaken, February–March 1990. Did that visit leave you with such a bitter taste that you won't be tempted to return again?*

FR. GEORGE CALCIU: My visit to Romania, a short time after Ceausescu's fall, was made indeed in a context of facts not only unpleasant but also extremely alarming. At that time, under the wide smile of the future president [Ion] Iliescu, the first massive intervention of miners in the capital city took place.[1]

---

[1] Altogether, there were four "miners' interventions" (also known as "mineriads") during the period from February 1990 to September 1991, the most violent being that of June 13–15, 1990. These interventions were used to end the long anti-Communist demonstration in University Square, Bucharest. Fr. George adds: "In 1990 the students began a strike in University Square, protesting that the revolution of the youth against the Ceausescu regime was 'stolen' by the second generation of Communists—the regime of Iliescu. The students asked for freedom, democracy, and free elections; and the majority of the intellectuals joined them. The university dean allowed the students and other speakers to speak from the second-floor balcony of the university, and they asked Iliescu to resign and allow free elections. Iliescu could not force the army to make the students leave the square because they were on the side of the students. He could not have the police torture the students because he was afraid the Western countries would accuse him of violating human rights. So he sent his messengers to the miners, telling them that the youth were under the influence of the capitalist powers in the West and that they wanted to bring American capitalism into Romania to make Romanians the slaves of Americans. The miners, who still had a Stalinist understanding of a movement such as this, came and cruelly beat the students, killing some and arresting others. It was strange to see that civilians had the right to arrest

Now, when I look retrospectively at the events, I realize that it was a prelude of the miners' intervention of June 1990 and that the tactics of the neo-Communist power were clear and united from the beginning. I heard that there were some comments made about my humble person, accusations being brought to light in front of the whole country that were as dangerous as they were unfounded. I had just arrived in the country and, being barraged by relatives and friends, I did not watch the news on television. I knew of the incident mainly from the narration of others. I did not blame the miners either then or later. The guilt belongs to those who used them unscrupulously, consciously compromising for a long time the image of the Romanian people in the eyes of the whole civilized world.

From that time on an extremely dangerous tension was produced in the country, which seems unable to be released even to this day. Do you know what the first question was that I was asked by a journalist when I had just arrived at the airport? "Coming back into the country, don't you feel in any way ... manipulated?" I was startled by this question even more than by all that happened afterwards! This was the reflex of a general psychosis. I answered that obviously I, as a priest, am "manipulated" permanently by Jesus Christ....

The spreading of rumors and suspicions, some actually absurd, is part of the traditional tactics of Communism. I know these tactics from a long experience of life, paid for with hard years in prison. Of course the visit to Romania, which I had dreamed of and waited for for years, under these circumstances left me with a bitter taste. On the other hand, however, the warmth with

---

people and bring them to the police. The prisons were full. Finally, under the pressure of Western governments and human rights' groups, the young men were freed, but no one could bring back to life those who had been killed. Iliescu stated that it was merely a conflict between the intellectuals and the workers, and no one was accused of violating the law or killing innocent people in University Square."—Ed.

AN INTERVIEW ON THE FALL OF COMMUNISM

which I was received by many friends and strangers sweetened this bitterness. No matter how badly I was received by some, I would gladly return to the country, as long as circumstances allow.

Overlooking your personal trouble, what is your opinion about the general development of Romanian society after the events of December 1989?[2]

I don't know if you did it intentionally, but I am glad that you avoided the improper term "revolution." I don't want to start a caustic discussion about the "behind the scene" events. The truth is that, no matter how things were actually happening, the big popular movement represents the decisive factor from both a historic and a mystical point of view. It meant, I think, something more than a revolution, because our "revolutionaries," the young people who came forth on the streets, did not premeditate actions and did not use violence. What was important was the spirit of sacrifice, and not of strife. It was like obtaining resurrection through death. The young—even the children—went like lambs to the slaughter. They should not be named "heroes" but martyrs, so that the mystical dimension of things might not be lost. In this sense one can say it was a "miracle." But only initially. What happened after that—and is still happening today—is another story. You see, throughout history miracles have taken place without taking root. I mean that what is accomplished in a moment of individual or collective enlightenment can be lost the next moment by ignorance or negligence. God asks more of the one who has received more from Him. In vain have you achieved something if you are not able to keep and consolidate what you have achieved—that is, to wisely manage the gift you have received. The danger in which I think we are now, as a nation, is of ignoring that we were the beneficiary of a "miracle," and losing the mystical dimension of reality; of going back, as the

---

[2] In December 1989, the dictator Ceausescu was overthrown in Romania. There was an overwhelming uprising of the youth, who made a stand against the Communist regime.—ED.

holy Apostle Peter says, as *the dog is turned to his own vomit again* (II Peter 2:22). If we forget God, as we did before, then it might be that the latter wrongdoing becomes greater than the first....

We should admit that, in principle, any new order implies a previous chaos, and it is not easy to enter a viable formula of normality after forty-five years of organized disaster. Only now, in the new context, can one see clearly how much evil Communism did, not only at the social and material level but also at the individual and spiritual level. The Communists physically exterminated hundreds of thousands of people, but spiritually several millions....

Yes, we live in a moral and a intellectual crisis....

Exactly. And to overcome this, we should appeal to the Christian foundation of our nation, so that it [the Christian foundation] might be brought up to date and enhanced in value as such. The resurrection from death of the Romanian spirit, under the sign of faith and Christian love, represents the great desire of this epoch. If this "reform" is accomplished, the rest will follow.

We should no longer put the cart before the horse, as Communism did and seems to be willing to do again. We should no longer consider the idea of creating a new world from which a new man emerges, but, on the contrary, we should shape a truly new man able to naturally create a new world afterwards.

I understand that this "new man" should be the Christian man. Some could consider that a paradox: how can something be "new" that is two thousand years old?!

There is no paradox. New, in the Christian sense, means alive and present.

There is no new thing under the sun (Eccles. 1:9), the Bible teaches us. The only true newness was the Incarnation of Christ. Otherwise the "newness" in history is nothing other than an endless updating and enrichment of the old eternal values. That is, if you wish, the ability to live in a new way on the grounds of an ancient experience. In the absence of such grounds, the "newness" is a mere adventure, an illusion indeed.

We are in a position to create the "new man" not out of nothing, but rather out of the ancient Tradition. The Romanian nation is called to rediscover itself as a Christian nation. Christian *in essence,* it should be born as Christian *in fact,* and should consciously live a Christian life. We have to re-link a chain broken half a century ago. To be able to renew ourselves we must first return to our inner self. That is the urgency of this very hour, and not the common "labor"—as the slogan goes. This is labor, too, but a subtler and more difficult one. It is a work within ourselves, in the "mine" of our souls. Let us do the latter and not forget the other, either!

And to whom do you think belongs the mission of this necessary moral-spiritual reform?

Obviously, in the first place to the Romanian Orthodox Church. Only, unfortunately, our Church has undergone in the last decades a serious decline, losing its old and natural prestige. Some, for lack of discernment, have even fallen to accounting this weakness of the Church to Orthodoxy itself or even to the Church as a mystical reality.... The truth is that our Church, as a historical institution, is confronted with an internal crisis; that is why we should not expect everything from the clergy (from the priests and the monastic synaxis) alone. *All* Christians of Romania are called, more than ever, to the *good fight* (I Tim. 6:12), each according to his strength and means, so that no talent should remain buried. The parties, unions, foundations: all Christian organizations should play an important part, as long as they prove to be up to the mark of the Christian position they chose. There is need of a lively missionary consciousness and a sustained campaign for Christian education of young people, especially through the press and schools. It is regrettable that the authorities, which, I heard, are occasionally promoting a shallow Christianization, do not facilitate this process of moral cleansing. For example, the reinstatement of religion in schools is still disputed.[3] As long as people are either abandoned—under the pretext of a misunderstood freedom—to the danger of modern secular information and education, or tempted to join again a narrow-minded "official direction," they won't come out of the unseen prisons of the old mentality, and therefore they won't be truly free.

Do you trust the ability of Romanian people to overcome this historic impasse?

I trust God and our national tradition and the young people of this country. I do not expect the impasse to be overcome overnight. We need to make efforts, to keep vigil and to pray, guarding our hope even in times of confusion and suffering, since it [our hope] is from the One Who has *overcome the world* (John 16:33). It is not easy to advance through all the obstacles and traps laid by the more or less occult powers of this century. The battle is fought on a much larger plane, and at a much higher level, than we usually imagine. The whole world is nowadays haunted by the forces of darkness, even if not everywhere in the same way. The faces of evil are multiple and deceptive. You know, Romanians have a saying: "Do not make the sign of the Cross until you know who the saint is!"[4] We should preserve this wisdom more than ever. And we should be united in the spirit of endurance. The world began from God and it will end in God.

What would the Romania you are dreaming of and hoping for look like?

I will express myself completely, not in political but spiri-

---

[3] Since this interview, religion has been reintroduced in the schools, but with a more inferior status than anticipated. Orthodox Christians in Romania are laboring to improve this situation.—ED.

[4] I.e., do not commit yourself until you know to what you are making a commitment.—ED.

tual terms. The Romania I am dreaming of is one which would gather together in her bosom all her sons dispersed by fate throughout the world, so that we would all be one, upon the ancient land of our suffering and also of our rejoicing, under the sign of the Cross of Christ.

May God hear you.

Translated from "A Conversation with Fr. George Calciu-Dumitreasa," Puncte Cardinale *(Cardinal Points), vol. 1, no. 6 (in Romanian) (June 1991), p. 4.*

AN INTERVIEW ON ECUMENISM

QUESTION: *Regarding compromises within the Church: the idea that ecumenism is a necessity in the ecclesiastical space is very much promulgated today. What are your thoughts on this?*

FR. GEORGE: If we submit to the devil, does that mean it is a necessity? This is not a need, but a sin, a great temptation, a heresy. I think that the Orthodox Church should mind its own business, and not take an interest in ecumenism and so on. The Church should live in Christ as it has lived until now.

What do you think the strength of Orthodoxy consists in?

The power of Orthodoxy lies in the preservation of the canons confirmed by the Holy Ecumenical Councils ..., while Catholicism's power consists in number and organization. Today the power of Catholicism has faded, but the strength of Orthodoxy remains. If Orthodoxy falls, it's through the sins of the people inside her, not by any other means. Because Orthodoxy in itself is invincible.

So we wear down from the inside ...

Yes. The problem is that we ourselves have become corrupted; we have not been influenced by others. Even now, in the European Community, the Church could retain its full identity, without compromise or diverging from its religious doctrine, if she had the awareness that she (the Church) must keep her identity.

So, we have to work on the mentality ...

Well, that's the problem. If we lose our attachment to the Orthodox tradition and start to dilute ourselves in this absurd and criminal movement of ecumenism—and if it's not criminal, it's at least anti-Christian—then we'll certainly be lost. It's a great

AN INTERVIEW ON ECUMENISM

Fr. George talking with monks on his last visit to Romania, in 2006.

tragedy! I wonder if they really don't understand its danger? Or perhaps they are bribed? I don't know, I don't get it ...

What is the relationship between the hierarchs and the monasteries?

Generally the monasteries obey their hierarch. But only to the limit of heresy. Because of this, the hierarchy, especially in some areas, is upset. It persecutes monks, creates all sorts of stories about them, all sorts of lies, such as their obedience to the Russians, etc. All this is aimed to justify their ecumenist actions ...

If you were to meet the Patriarch of Romania, Teoctist, what would you say to him?

I have met him many times. And I professed everything that I thought. And I was surprised that he was open to listening, that he passed many things on to me, and that he did not get offended. He has balance! I am a little worried and troubled at the thought that the patriarch will die. For he maintains a balance where he is.

How do you see the current state of our Church?

Like the story that my mother used to tell us children ... about the legion of devils gathered at the house of the widow with seven children who were always praying. Even today, the Church is surrounded by legions of devils. I mean not only our own but every Orthodox Church in the world: millions of devils surrounding them.

Tribulations have taken place at all times, but now they seem to multiply. There are many disobedient priests and many wandering monks, which should not be the case. Many monks are wandering to the West. Why?! They should remain in the monastery. If they do not like their monastery, because it is ecumenist and so on, they should choose another monastery....

I mean we must impose upon ourselves a discipline to respect the Church's authority, as far as it is worthy of Christ to be respected. But you must be steadfast before Satan! Steadfast as a pillar! So that he knows that when he faces a monk, a priest, or a bishop, he will be defeated!

Translated by Elena Chiru from Diaconesti Monastery, ed., The Life of Father George Calciu *(in Romanian) (Bucharest: Christiana Press, 2007), pp. 131–32.*

APPENDICES

Fr. George with his close friend Demostene Andronescu, who spent many years in prison.

APPENDIX ONE
FR. GEORGE'S
LETTER TO THE CIEL

This letter was written by Fr. George to the CIEL (Comité des intellectuels pour l'Europe des libertés) in 1978, during a time of intense persecution, after delivering his sermons to the youth and right before his second arrest and imprisonment.—ED.

DEAR FRIENDS,
First of all I thank you for the letter of September 13, 1978, which reached me miraculously, and in which you shared the news that I have been accepted as a member of the Committee of Intellectuals for a Free Europe. As far back as when I, as a priest and teacher, began my battle for the religious rights of man, I considered myself to be a member of this Committee. The official acceptance certifies something that I had chosen long ago. Thank you for your brotherly assistance and protection, for your solidarity of which I am now, and will be, in need.

I have been pushed to the edge of society, left as prey to all attacks and defamation, at the mercy of all. It was not enough that I was expelled from the Theological Institute of Bucharest, where I was professor, and was deprived of all human rights. It was not enough that I was forbidden to speak and that my theology pupils and students who were on my side were hunted. Now they want to fire my wife, and my eleven-year-old son is subjected to all kinds of mockeries. They want to let us starve to death. What seems to me to be most frightening is that the Church hierarchy itself asked the authorities to take all these actions!

Why? Because I asked for the freedom to preach unrestrictedly. Because I have protested against the demolition of churches, in place of which they now build taverns, as is the case with the Enea Church in Bucharest and Voivode's Church in Focsani. Because I asked for exemption from military service for theology students—for the spiritual purity and sensibility of these young theologians should be protected. Because I intervened in favor of religious liberty for Romanian young people, no matter what confessional denomination. Because I demanded that any Christian, young or old, should have the right to enter the monastic life, which the government forbids. Because I have drawn attention to the dignity of the priesthood, which is above any other human dignity, insisting that the priests be freed of the obligation to expound political propaganda from the altar, since for a priest there is only one great theme for a homily: Jesus Christ.

All these assertions were imputed to me as offenses. But I did not consider myself for even a moment to be unhappy. And I consider myself neither victorious nor vanquished. I am merely a fighter among many others in this battle of man to regain his dignity.

When will the threats against "the parasites of society" really cease, the sending of anonymous letters—a method learned in the school of the Soviet Union which has now spread to us like a plague? When will the tactic come to an end of confining those who fight for human rights to psychiatric hospitals?

Fr. Costica Maftei suffered many months, together with his wife and children, and was finally exiled, because he committed the crime of wishing to build a church!

Fr. Gavrila Stefan had to endure years of suffering because he dared to refuse to utter political slogans in church!

The monks who do not want to abandon their monastic life are expelled from theological education!

Members of the "Christian Committee for Defending Religious and Spiritual Rights in Romania" are driven away from church and are constantly molested by the police, forced to pay ridiculous fines and even arrested on the pretense that the founding of associations is forbidden!

We ask that these persecutions be put to an end! The endangering of human and religious rights should stop! We appeal to all international organizations to defend human rights and to help us! There is only one righteous battle to which the whole of Christianity is called: the battle for the freedom and dignity of man.

Fr. George Calciu-Dumitreasa
Bucharest
October 17, 1978

APPENDIX TWO
FR. GEORGE'S PREFACE TO *PITESTI* BY DUMITRU BACU

Fr. George's preface to Dumitru Bacu's Pitesti: Centru de Reeducare Studenteasca *(Pitesti: Center of Student Reeducation) was printed in the second (Romanian) edition of the book, published in Hamilton, Ontario in 1989, and in Bucharest in 1991. The first edition was published in 1963 in Madrid. An English translation of this first edition was published as* The Anti-Humans: Student Reeducation in Romanian Prisons *in Englewood, Colorado in 1971.—*Ed.

THIS BOOK IS a book of facts. Their shocking accumulation creates a history, a tragic one, inconceivable and absurd. But this book is meant to be a spiritual phenomenon. Suddenly, struck by the concreteness of the events, the spirit of the reader rears up in an attempt to rise above the circumstances, because everything that was suffered in the material world, in the flesh, is nothing other than the later reflex of what was long before consumed in spirit.

The subject, Pitesti, with all its train of consequences, will never be exhausted, because this history is inscribed in the human spirit forever and will not be concluded even when the last survivor of these events shall pass away. It is a Golgotha bearing general human significance, a Mount of Olives where we, who were there, drank the cup of despair, of abandonment, and of self-denial.

It is interesting that not one of those prisoners with whom

PREFACE TO *PITESTI*

I was in Pitesti has written a book about it.[1] Books have been written only by some of those who were in other prisons and saw the phenomenon [of Pitesti] from outside, not as sentimental non-participants, but as those who found it impossible to integrate the phenomenon of Pitesti; because it was not only something anti-human—like a war, a plague, or a Communist revolution—but it was also something superhuman, an infernal war against God, the battle of devils against angels, an upside-down liturgy, aiming to invert the vertical order of heaven and to replace the heavenly hierarchy in the victims' souls with a diabolic one.

There were books about Pitesti written by people who did not even see the Communist prisons and who thought that by using aesthetic criteria or laboratory psychology, they were solving a problem which was, in fact, metaphysical. The antidote is wrong, the solutions are false, the feelings are unjust, and the criteria are absurd.

There was something there that is beyond human comprehension, because it was a war between two superhuman armies. Seen from outside, there was a space in which the war was won by Satan, because psychologists and aestheticians confuse appearances with the reality of the spirit and ignore the fact that this world is an interval given to attain salvation—the only time given for a person to attain salvation.

The depth of our soul's enrichment is difficult to apprehend, for its defeats are spectacular, the deaths are dreadful, madness is logical. But the wisdom and spiritual martyrdom of the survivors, as well as the immeasurable vibration of the spirit, represent something too subtle for the dull sensitivity of the aestheticians, too mystical for the perception of a psychologist and of any human being who has not lived in madness but only within the

---

[1] Please note that this text dates from 1988. In the meantime, many books have appeared by former Pitesti prisoners. [See p. 377, note 5 below.] At that time, there was only one book, *The Unmaskings* by Grigore Dumitrescu (1978), printed in Munich and not widely known.—ROM. ED.

limits of common sense. Only he who possesses a dose of madness can understand somewhat, although not all. Not even we who lived through it can understand everything. And this is because God cries shame upon the wisdom of this world. We need an apocalyptic sensitivity.

In 1948, at Jilava Prison, Stanescu, at that time a young man possessing a rare intuition of future events—and I am talking not only about what was happening at Pitesti, but about the whole historical absurdity from that time until now, there [in Romania] and in all the world—said that humanity had begun to live the Apocalypse and that anyone who does not develop an apocalyptic consciousness will not survive either physically or spiritually.

We have not succeeded in forging this type of consciousness yet. None of us. We still live according to the same human logic which bows down before the formal perfection of syllogism. We fabricate major and minor premises and draw serene conclusions, well established in accordance with human wisdom, forgetting that the battle is fought in a space in which not only logic or reason, but even concrete facts have no significance.

In 1958 we were on a death ship: sixteen people placed in four blind cells at Jilava. It consisted of four cells built out of one larger cell, in the shape of a horizontal semi-cylinder. It was a ship with death as its destination—sixteen people, each with his own madness and wisdom, sickness and tragedy. Most of the prisoners had passed through Pitesti, more than two thirds of us had been imprisoned there. We were sick in body and wounded in soul, hungry and trembling from cold in those cells with water seeping through the walls, where the moisture would penetrate into our bones. We were a hodgepodge, scientifically doled out according to all the knowledge of the Kremlin, to determine how long a man can resist terror, famine, torture, brawling in the cell, and diseases which infested every cubic centimeter with millions of germs.

It was then, in my cell, that the best among us died. He was so sick and weak that death itself was more present for us than the wet walls, and even more real than the hand of the guard which would hit us or would open and lock the door. His death was more real than our daily bread and water. The tubercular cough of Constantine [Costache] Oprisan, the abundant and fetid matter expelled from a lung almost completely eaten away by bacteria turned our stomachs in spite of the immense love all three of us had for him. However, he, Costache, the dying man, was our axis and support, our justification for being there, the angel defeating the devil for us. The moment he died, our universe lost its meaning; the world collapsed, groaning. A cataclysm had been produced, and we remained three people in a desert of despair. There were no guiding arrows. The one who guided us had died; we were surrounded by a hostile world of six square meters oozing death and hopelessness from every atom of matter.[2]

---

[2] Constantine Oprisan had been the president of "The Brotherhood of the Cross." Being extremely ill with tuberculosis, he was refused medical assistance. Following is a portion of the scene of his death, as described in Marcel Petrisor's book, *The Secret of Fort 13*, pp. 127–33, where George Calciu appears as "Gore Bolovan" and the author himself as "Mircea Petre": "For him, forcing the impossible, Gore Bolovan would open his own veins: 'O God!' said Mircea, jumping toward Gore. 'What are you doing?!' 'Be quiet!' ordered Gore. 'I am squeezing a kettle of blood from my arm to give Costache some lymph. Don't you see he lost so much blood that he will die if we do not do something?...' In the meantime, Gore had filled half of the kettle with blood and put it on the water canister, covering it with a rag. 'I will let it sit for a while for the red cells to form sediment and then I will give him only the lymph,' he explained to Mircea, whispering as he summarily bandaged his arm joint from where he had drawn blood.... They understood quickly when they saw how he poured off the lymph from his kettle into Mircea's. 'Drink!' he said to Costache, with a commanding tone. But Oprisan was smiling motionlessly. He answered with an unearthly grin at everything around him. 'Costache, drink this!' Gore tried to make him drink the lymph at any cost.... 'Too late!' exclaimed Joseph. 'Costache is far away now; so far away that nobody can do him any harm.... Leave him alone!' 'Costache! Costache!' cried Gore, as if he wanted to make him return with a kettle of blood. 'It is mine, mine, I have more!' he murmured. 'And they ... will give you theirs.' But he did not finish his word, when Oprisan quivered three times, as if he saw something unseen,

Fr. George with Marcel Petrisor: the two had been imprisoned in Jilava Prison with Constantine Oprisan.

It was July of 1958. At about sunset, ten hours had passed since Costache's death, time in which we tearfully and desperately prayed: "With the saints give rest, O Christ, to the soul of Thy servant who hath fallen asleep, Costache ... Costache ..." After we had washed his body so he would enter clean into the earth of which he was made, we took him naked on a litter into the prison courtyard. The sun was setting and its golden light fell upon a luxuriantly wild and overwhelming vegetation. The world did not care about us. The universe did not vanish into non-existence, the sun did not darken its light, the earth did not split to its depths, nor had the flowers lost their beauty. Once again, nature did not care about us. Our universe—the locked-up cell! To the world—unknown and indifferent....

We came back into the cell overwhelmed, hating the flowers and trees, the pure blue sky and the golden sun. There was the

---

and gave up his spirit in Gore's arms. The kettle with lymph had fallen down, and he [Gore/Calciu] hugged Costache as if he wished to stop him from going...."—ROM. ED.

naked body of Costache on the dirty little litter in the middle of the immense courtyard, guarded by a watchman in uniform. Thin, only skin and bones (it was incredible how that could be a human body!), under the hard light which emphasized the weakness and ugliness of an emaciated body, it rested there like a monument of Death. And no angel with a fiery sword was guarding him against future profanation. No one. Only a watchman in uniform.

On his naked and fleshless chest shone two blue flowers, big and unknown—all flowers became unknown for us. Joseph had put them there, taking advantage of the watchman's moment of confusion. He picked them hastily and placed them on the bony chest, thrown askew, but sincerely and decisively. The watchman yelled at Joseph, "Take them out of there, take them quickly!" (He was afraid to touch the dead.) Joseph did not listen. "I will teach you a thing or two, you and him!" yelled the watchman again. For the first time, Joseph answered back—since Costache had died, except for tears and prayers, we had not exchanged even a word; not with each other, not with the guards. "You can show us even more, but to him you cannot; he has escaped from you forever."

You see, they, the watchmen—the angels of matter—thought that they had power over us, even after death!

Since then, years later, I have kept calling Costache Oprisan, day and night, to give me a sign, to tell me something about death and everlasting life ... and he has never answered. Since then I have wondered and I keep asking myself: "What is the boundary between death and life, who is dead and who is alive—we or Costache Oprisan?"

Let us remember the verses of Sergiu Mandinescu:

> Of those who passed that way,
> the dead only are alive.
> Like him, like you.
> I, for instance, walk and talk,

but my life is not;
friend, it is nothing but a living death....[3]

In 1977 I started to write a kind of journal of my memoirs of the spiritual history of Pitesti. I tried to avoid the facts and to decipher the meaning of the infernal and the Divine Providence in our lives and deaths. I tried to avoid passion and to write impartially about friends and about enemies, about prisoners and about guards, about those who had died and those who had fallen, so I could extract the oppressive and delusive dross of a solidified reality from the fiery core of the senses, to reveal the divine or the diabolic unseen mystery. After writing around eighty bloody pages I was suffering terribly because I was no longer under the vertigo of madness and I could no longer understand what had happened at that time, how all those things could have happened. I was no longer under the alternate or concurrent influence of the beast and the angel who lived in me, but I was authentically and painfully reviving life and death—Pitesti, the unmaskings.

Nevertheless, my memory was a sentimental one. Sometimes I was hammering at one word, timidly, then persistently, then intensely, to madness. The word became nothing other than a sequence of letters or sounds. It had no meaning. It didn't tell me anything. I would say, "beating" or, "pain" or, "prayer" or, "curse" ..., and I would substitute one for another without any change; none told me anything! I would say "cell" and the word would not speak. I could say instead, "lelc" or, "clel" or, "ellc" with the same result. Everything was mute and absurd. And suddenly a curse from that time would resound in my mind, or a song somebody sang during the unmaskings, and the whole atmosphere would install itself with a painfully striking character and with a reality more real than it was then.

---

[3] From the poem, "Amen," Pitesti, 1949. This author died while being cruelly tortured.—ED.

Affective memory! Proust was a genius in his intuitions, a part of the literature he wrote.

Shortly after I had started my memoirs, events changed and came tumbling rapidly one upon another. God had called me to an intense preaching, to an awakening of young Romanian souls to the Christian truth, toward human dignity and the supreme Christian dignity. The memoirs were put into the shade, the passion died out. They became unimportant; the value I had given them was only a sentimental one. Their importance was nothing other than a form of my selfishness.

Then events precipitated once again. God rewarded me for obeying His call, and I was arrested and convicted.

I am not just writing a beautiful story when I affirm that which I have said, and I am not boasting of my heroism in a romantic view of a triumphalist Christianity, like heroes that come forth after the war is over.

God did reward me. Out of my sickness He made me sound, from the vainglorious temptation which had begun to make itself known. He cast me out into the deepest darkness, where there was weeping and gnashing of teeth, so that I would remember that He is the only One who decides everything.

The manuscript was confiscated by the Securitate when I was arrested. The rest of the story is known.

Now I am reading the books about Pitesti and making an attempt to draft a preface. Anything one could write about these things is insipid for us, for those who were there—trying to explain what is inexplicable, what is not to be explained. And I am afraid that I will end up adding to cheap literature, like certain leading intellectuals who think that literature can save a nation which is dying of cold and famine.

I wrote a long and incomprehensible introduction. I did not take into account the words of the Apostle to the Gentiles: *Where is the wise? Where is the scribe? Where is the disputer of this world?* (I Cor. 1:20).

After we were set free from prison, we (Marcel Petrisor and I, as well as many others) were summoned from time to time to come to the Securitate. It was the same blackmail practiced for seventy years by the Soviet Union, and for forty years by the satellite countries. Each call to go there scared us terribly, and after each trip we met and told each other, "From now on we should behave! They will send us to prison again and this time we won't escape alive!"

In fact, we didn't make much trouble—a meeting now and then to reminisce about the time spent in prison and to recast the poems learned there for a possible future edition,[4] discussions about people who had died and people who had survived, about the Canal[5] and its victims, so that we would not forget anything and would be able to reproduce them at times. We could not live outside the prison spectrum or without meeting with those who had been there.

A month later, Marcel told me: "Ghitsa, these people want to make us wise in a worldly sense, in their world. They want us to be quiet, to sit like an obedient dog on his tail with his head

---

[4] We owe to them, among others, the reconstitution of the poetry of Constantine Oprisan, especially of the "ontologic poem" *Psyhaion*, a vast lyric-philosophic panorama of the spiritual development of the human being, which can be compared in many ways with *Faust II* by Goethe, or *Panorama of Vanity* by Eminescu, or *The Tragedy of Man* by Imre Madach. A modest edition was issued in 1995 by Majadahonda Publishing House in Bucharest, under the aegis of the Professor George Manu Foundation. (Fragments of *Psyhaion* appeared also in *Puncte Cardinale* [Cardinal Points], vol. 2, nos. 8–9/20–21 [Aug.–Sept. 1992], p. 7, accompanied by a note by Fr. George Calciu and an article signed by Demostene Andronescu.)—ROM. ED.

[5] A Communist labor camp for digging a canal between the Danube River and the Black Sea. According to the official statements of Gheorghe Gheorghiu-Dej, the chief of the Communist party in Romania, the Canal was to be the cemetery of the Romanian bourgeoisie. The Communists exterminated there—by hunger, torture, and forced labor—peasants, workers, intellectuals, members and leaders of the former political parties, women, and teenagers.—ED.

on his paws, and to howl at the moon, only at the moon [i.e. to speak futilely without anyone paying any attention to you]. I can't be such a philosopher!"

We started meeting again, looking for those who had been in prison, and remaking the old connections and memories, until the Securitate summoned us again and the story repeated itself, like the ring "of the eternal return" from *Thus Spake Zarathustra*.

I remember that a group of poets from the period between the two world wars decided that the ultimate and supreme form of poetry was its own negation....

Perhaps, from the whole story about Pitesti only this should remain: *And forgive us our trespasses, as we forgive those who trespass against us.*

And, on our human plane, the finale of Sergiu Mandinescu's poem:

> O Lord, here I am, at this precious hour,
> under the heavy tombstone of passions and
>   pain, embracing my affliction, I await the
>   Archangel of Dawn,
> I await the Resurrection,
> In the name of the Father, and of the Son, and
>   of the Holy Spirit, Amen!

Fr. George in Chicago with the religious historian Mircea Eliade and his wife, Christinel, shortly before Mircea's death in April 1986.

APPENDIX THREE
A REDEEMER OF THE TIME:
RAZVAN CODRESCU'S INTRODUCTION TO THE ROMANIAN EDITION OF FR. GEORGE'S *SEVEN HOMILIES TO THE YOUTH*

> *The only chance of survival for Eastern Christianity is that of a war within the Word. Our solution is that of Calciu-Dumitreasa....*
>
> Nicolae Steinhardt[1]

FATHER GEORGE CALCIU-DUMITREASA (born in 1925) is the priest whom Nicolae Ceausescu declared as his personal enemy. In an epoch in which the Romanian Orthodox Church appeared overwhelmed by the times and ready to make any compromise with the atheistic and materialistic political regime, a teacher at the Theological Seminary, ordained not long after encountering the most radical experiments of the Communist inferno, dared, in the very heart of Bucharest, to raise the Cross and defy, almost alone, both the destructive madness of the authority and the cowardliness of his ecclesiastical superiors.

Apart from other forms of Christian struggle or resistance, about which his students of that time will possibly more extensively confess in much more detail, Fr. George Calciu delivered during Great Lent of the year 1978 a number of sermons of great courageous confession.[2] Addressed to young people eager for the

---

[1] *Journal of Blessedness* (Cluj-Napoca: Dacia Publishing House, 1991), p. 417 (quoted in Virgil Ciomos' afterword).—ROM. ED.

[2] One could even talk about "the suicidal measure of the incendiary

truth, they were pronounced forcibly against official atheism and materialism, against the demolition of churches and consciences, as well as against those who were (often despite their intimate beliefs) in an old and implicit conspiracy with the Communist power. The sermons were delivered either inside the Radu Voda Church or on its outside staircase (when his superiors locked the church and confined the seminarians to their dormitories to prevent him from preaching anymore).[3] In spite of all the harassment by the civil and religious authorities, the audience became more and more numerous. In addition to the high school students, seminarians, and theology students, every week more and more youth from the general lay community came, mainly students of other institutes and faculties from the capital city [Bucharest]. Many of the "calcistii"[4] themselves had to face the pressure of the Securitate; some of them were even expelled from their universities. Fr. Calciu was first subjected to the usual criticisms, persecutions, threats, and slanders. Finally he was arrested on May 10, 1979, tried and condemned to ten years in prison for several ridiculous and fictitious counts of indictment, his "guilt" being in fact that he spoke the whole truth straightforwardly and bluntly. The Church itself, panicked by the reaction of the authorities and trying to accede to their request, expelled him—[the very one] who defended its foundation and whose sermons, translated into many languages, gave the world the true measure of our Christianity.

Before becoming a priest, this man experienced the depths of hell. In all he spent twenty-one years in prison under the Communists (1948–64; 1979–84), even going through the wave of terrors in Pitesti (1949–51). It is to Dumitru Bacu that we owe the first substantial disclosure of the monstrous experiment named "reeducation," unique in its degree of terror and perversity in the

---

sermons uttered by Fr. Calciu-Dumitreasa" (Sorin Dumitrescu, in *Transylvania*, 1992, nos. 1–2, p. 17).—ROM. ED.

[3] As occurred, for example, on April 12, 1978.—ROM. ED.

[4] Derived from the name Calciu, meaning Fr. George's followers.—ED.

whole Communist universe of detention. For a subsequent edition of D. Bacu's book, prepared in 1988 and published in 1989 (in Hamilton, Ontario, Canada),[5] Fr. Calciu agreed to write the preface. "Now I am reading the books about Pitesti and making a draft for a preface.[6] Anything one would write about these things is insipid for us who were there—trying to explain what is inexplicable.... I wrote a long and incomprehensible introduction," he declared with too much modesty. And, toward the end: "Perhaps, from the whole story about Pitesti only this should remain: *And forgive us our trespasses, as we forgive those who trespass against us*."[7]

---

[5] With Bacu's book, *Pitesti* (published in the West in 1963), the bibliography of the "Pitesti phenomenon" was substantially enriched. Besides D. Bacu (whose book was translated into English in 1971), others presented the facts without knowing them directly. Paul Goma (*Les chiens des morts/The passions after Pitesti*, 1981, in French; 1990, in Romanian); Virgil Ierunca (*The Pitesti Phenomenon,* 1990); Marcel Petrisor (*Fort 13: Talks from Detention,* 1991, and *The Secret of Fort 13*, 1994, where Fr. Calciu appears under the name "Gore Bolovan"), etc. Among those who wrote about Pitesti from their own experience, it is worth mentioning especially Grigore Dumitrescu (*The Unmaskings,* 1978); Viorel Gheorghita (*Et ego. Sarata-Pitesti-Gherla-Aiud*, 1994); Dumitru Gheorghe Bordeianu (*Confessions from the Mire of Desperation,* 2 vols., 1995); Octavian Voinea (*The Massacre of Romanian Students in the Prisons of Pitesti, Gherla and Aiud,* 1996). The volume *Memorial of Horror: Documents of the Reeducation Process from the Prisons of Pitesti and Gherla* (issued in 1995 by Vremea Publishing House) contains declarations extorted under terror (taken from the Securitate Archives), which are far from the truth. (See also the speech of D. Bacu: "The Reeducation Process: Why and What Were the Unmaskings in Pitesti and Gherla," recently published in the magazine, *Puncte Cardinale* [Cardinal Points], the issues from April, May, and June 1996.)—ROM. ED.

[6] An English translation of this preface appears on pp. 364–73 above.—ED.

[7] D. Bacu wrote in the preface of the second edition of his book: "I gave Fr. George the difficult task of writing a new introduction.... In his sufferings is projected the suffering of the whole nation. His passing through that inferno is our passing, all of us. His resurrection from the tomb of Pitesti strengthens our faith that no matter how heavy the stone of our sins is, the resurrection of the whole nation is possible."—ROM. ED.

The whole life of this man after the Pitesti episode was a life of *confession* and *sacrifice*. He crossed, in both soul and flesh, the distance between hell and heaven. Perhaps there is no one else who succeeded *after Pitesti* in a moral victory so exemplary and steadfast. Because there is the case of "George Calciu," one can say that the "Pitesti experiment" failed. It crushed men, but it could not completely destroy man.[8]

Fr. Calciu did not save himself alone: he redeemed, in the long run, *human dignity* in the face of what Mircea Eliade named "the terror of history."

After the Pitesti episode, the medical student George Calciu lay in Communist prisons twelve more years, being known as one of the most "stubborn" prisoners and as a dreaded "hunger striker." Set free as a result of the general amnesty of 1964, he had the strength and grace to rebuild his life, devoting it to Christ. He attended classes in philology and theology, becoming a priest and one of the most beloved teachers of the Orthodox Theological Institute in Bucharest (where he taught French and the New Testament). He married Adriana Dumitreasa, the sister of another political prisoner, and had a son, Andrei. But having a wife and child did not present to the struggler and confessor George Calciu a justified reason to obey [the Communist authorities]. No risk was too big for him in his service for Christ.[9] While the Enea Church was

---

[8] Those who went through the hell of Pitesti cannot be judged by current criteria. Those who did not undergo the experience of Communist prisons have by no means the moral right to pass judgment on them. Even among former political prisoners who went through other penitentiaries and camps, I often heard the statement: "We do not have the moral right to judge those from Pitesti. No matter how long and hard we suffered, we were not destined to undergo even a little of what those from Pitesti did. Judgment should search out the initial assassins, the diabolic minds who plotted the 'experiment,' not the subsequent victims."—ROM. ED.

[9] "He who guides his conscience with the statement, 'I have children to bring up,' or justifies his action by saying, 'The dean forced me to take declarations,' has a remote-control machine rather than a soul.... Be most diligent

being demolished in the heart of Bucharest (May 1, 1977),[10] in place of which a tavern was to be built,[11] Fr. Calciu commenced an outspoken fight against the wicked political regime and its accomplices within the bosom of the Church. In 1978 he became more and more troublesome, particularly because he gathered around him groups of young people full of Christian and national zeal. His sermons held at Radu Voda Church were equivalent to a spiritual earthquake against the gray and fearful background of the epoch. They bear witness up to today that under the red dictatorship more could be done for Christ and His Church than we usually dared to do.... The unjust sentence of 1979 roused a wave of reactions abroad; the prominent representatives of Romanians in exile (Mircea Eliade, Eugene Ionescu, Virgil Ierunca, Monica Lovinescu, Paul Goma, etc.) came forth to his aid, making the international forums and organizations sensitive to it. As a consequence, he served only five out of ten years of imprisonment. The international pressure (his name was mentioned even in the negotiations for most-favored-nation status) made it possible for him to be set free in 1984 (April 20). Perhaps if there had not been such commotion surrounding his case from so much international notoriety, Ceausescu would have resorted to murder. (Ceausescu was gripped by a blind rage by the mere mention of the name in question.) An army of Securitate men followed every step of Fr. George and of his family members, devising a concerted psychological terror. After less than a year they imposed on him

---

harvesters yourselves. Forget your instincts, which are overpowered by your teachers, whose principles are: 'I have a mother, father, sons, and daughters, too large a salary to accept the sacrifice and suffering of Christ and His Church,'" he wrote to the young theologians in the "Additional Homily."—ROM. ED.

[10] See the collective volumes, *The Churches Doomed by Ceausescu, Bucharest: 1977–89* (Bucharest: Anastasia Publishing House, 1995), pp. 13–21.—ROM. ED.

[11] See, especially, the "Fifth Homily to the Youth," pp. 175–80 above.—ED.

the "solution" of leaving the country. He settled with his family in the United States, where he had already been granted "honorary citizenship" and where he lives up to today. In these more than ten years of exile, he has returned to his homeland, Romania, only once, at the time of the first miner's rebellion.[12] Fr. Calciu strove, as much as was in his power, to continue the fight for God and the Romanian people. Besides the usual preaching (in Washington), he defended the interests of the oppressed Romanians at many international forums. He was received by Presidents Francois Mitterand and George H. W. Bush among others, as well as King Michael of Romania. He was a central presence at almost all the important meetings of the Romanian "diaspora." He is to this day the honorary president of Romfest.[13] He has facilitated numerous contacts and much humanitarian aid (especially immediately after the events of December 1989[14]); he has written constantly in the *Exile's Press,* but also in some of the post-December publications in his country, always with the same missionary and confessional pathos, which recommends him as the most significant figure of the Christian and national resistance in Romania of the last decades.

From 1978 until 1989, the "Seven Homilies to the Youth" had a clandestine circulation in Romania through hand-typed copies. In Romanian, or translated into other languages, they were broadcast by several radio stations and were partially reproduced in foreign journals. In 1979 the only edition in Romanian was issued in Munich (Ion Dumitru-Verlag), with a limited number of printed copies. In 1984 the entire text came out in German (translated by Johannes Zultner); the small volume contains also the petitions made in behalf of Fr. Calciu by Mircea Eliade (to the "Religious News Service," May 21, 1979) and Eugene Ionescu (in

---

[12] See p. 349, note 1 above.—ED.

[13] Abbreviation of Romanian Festival. Romfest is an organization of Romanians in exile.—ED.

[14] I.e., the overthrow of the Ceausescu government.

Fr. George being greeted by President Ronald Reagan.

Le Monde of July 26, 1980), as well as a letter which the persecuted one (Fr. Calciu) succeeded in sending in the fall of 1978 to the CIEL (Comité des intellectuels pour l'Europe des libertés).

Beginning in 1990, some of the sermons were also published in Romanian journals (such as *Transylvania* or *Cardinal Points*). A complete edition in the Romanian language has not been published in Romania until now. The Anastasia Publishing House felt obligated to fill this gap, offering all the texts in the present edition to the larger public as part of its "Homiletics" collection. Obviously, the readers should take into account the timing and intent of these sermons; this does not mean that their message is not one of present interest. Apart from their "documentary" interest, their inner value (spiritual, moral, catechetical) remains indisputable. Their spirit and language constitute to this very day a model of the Orthodox sermon—full of life, and adapted, without any essential compromises, to the receptivity of contemporary youth.

Fr. George walking with Marcel Petrisor at Prislop Monastery.

INDEX

Page numbers for illustrations are in boldface italics.

abortion, 121
Agapia Monastery, 178
Aiud Prison, 34, 39–40, 79, 138, 227, 241–42, 258, 272
Alexandra, Mother (Princess Ileana), 41, 238
American Orthodox Christians, 320
Andrew, Apostle, 216
Andrew, Monk, *298*
Andronescu, Demostene, *360*, 372
anger, 304, 308–13
Antim Monastery, 269
Antonescu, Ion, 115, 135, 137, 138n
Antonie, Bishop, 236
Arghezi, Tudor, 88–89
Army of the Lord, 28, 98, 141–42, 199–200, 220
Athanasius the Great, St. 167n
atheism, 157–58, 173–74, 176–77, 181–87, 190, 200, 202, 342

Bacu, Dumitru, 364, 376–78
Barlaam, 268
Basil (Essey), Bishop of Wichita and Mid-America, 10
Basil of Poiana Marului, Elder, 30

Basil the Great, St., 232, 318–19
Benedict (Ghius), Hieromonk, 269–70, *271*, 323
Bratianu, Ion, 227
Brincoveanu Church, 72
Brotherhood of the Cross, 133–35
Bruno, Giordano, 158
Bucharest Theological Institute, 66, *154*, *156*, 193, 199, 361
Burning Bush Movement, 30–31, 64, 220, 269
Bush, Barbara, 257
Bush, George H. W., 16, 39, 75, 83, 256, *257*, 286, 380

Calciu, Andrei (son of Fr. George), 15, *38*, 40, 48, *54*, *67*, 259, 378
Calciu-Dumitreasa, Adriana (wife of Fr. George), 15–22, 35, *36*, 37, *40*, 50, 54, 57, *67*, 74, 83, 92, 238, 256, 259, 378
Calciu, Elena (mother of Fr. George), 25n, *27*, 63, 225–26, *226*, 289–90, *289*
Calciu, Fr. George
amnesty of, 35
asceticism of, 11, 45–46, 91, 249–50
autobiography of, 25–42

383

Calciu, Fr. George (*continued*)
  childhood of, 25–29, 63–64, 225–26
  final illness of, 46–54, *49*
  funeral of, *42*, 54–57, *55*, *56*
  homilies and talks of
    "Centurion's Faith and the Healing of the Heart, The," 322–24
    "Divine Light in the Devil's Lair," 213–77
    "From Holy Romania to the Devil's Lair," 215–35
    "Great Supper, The," 334
    "Healing of the Paralytic and the Loneliness of Contemporary Man, The," 329–31
    "How to Battle against Demons," 318–19
    "Inner Church, The," 281–99
    "On the Communion of the Soul with God," 335
    "On the Importance of Holy Tradition," 320–21
    "On the Meaning of Suffering," 332–33
    "Prayer is a Struggle," 338–40
    "Return to the Devil's Lair," 237–80
    "The Church and the Spirit of the World," 341–42
    "Thomas Sunday," 325–27
    "Walking on the Sea of Life," 316–17
    "Word for the Feast of the Holy Great-martyr George, A," 343–48
    "Word on Anger, A," 308–13
    "Word on Pious Prayer, A," 301–7
    "Word on the 'Spirit of the Times,' A," 314–15
  imprisonments of,
    first, 31–34, 64–66, 86–87, 226–28
    second, 37–41, *74*, 75–84, 86–89, 91–92, 238–61, 272–75
  interviews with
    "Interview on Ecumenism, An," 356–58
    "Interview on the Fall of Communism and the Future of Romania, An," 349
  joy of, 11–12, 44, 130
  last days of, 43–53
  love of, 44, 46, 50, 52
  marriage of, 35, *36*
  medical studies of, 29, 64, 67
  ordination of, 118, 141
  pastoral work of, 16–18, 43–46
  persecution of, 197–204
  photographs of, *8*, *12*, *17*, *24*, *27*, *32*, *38*, *40*, *42*, *47*, *58*, *60*, *65*, *67*, *69*, *70*, *119*, *123*, *131*, *139*, *143*, *150*, *156*, *168*, *214*, *229*, *257*, *259*, *262*, *278*, *280*, *289*, *293*, *298*, *300*, *303*, *315*, *321*, *328*, *336*, *357*, *360*, *368*, *374*, *381*
  repose of, 54
  solitary confinement of, 79–87, 91–92, 286
  theology studies of, 35–37, 66–71
  torture of, 14, 102, 105–6. *See also* reeducation experiment; Pitesti Prison; suffering
  Uncreated Light, experience of, 263–77
  young people, work with, 70–72, 93–94, 128–33, 229–31
Calciu, Stefan (Fr. George's father), 25n

INDEX

Carol II, King of Romania, 133, 221
Ceausescu, Nicolae, 16–22, 19, 37–40, 71, 76, 86, 91, 238, 240–41, 256, 349, 375, 379
Cernica Monastery, 269
Chiricutsa, Fr., 29
Chomsky, Noam, 167
Christian dignity, 87, 118, 159, 219, 231, 362, 371
Claudel, Paul, 219n, 333
Cleopa (Ilie), Elder, *123*, 223
Codreanu, Cornel, 137
Codrescu, Razvan, 14
 "Redeemer of the Time, A," 375–91
Comité des intellectuels pour l'Europe des libertés (CIEL), 361
Communion, Holy, 60, 91, 124, 219, 221, 244, 254, 261, 270, 271, 274, 291–92, 334
Communism, 330–31
 capitulation to, 127, 222–23
 creation of new values under, 99–100
 fall of, 349–55
 goal of, 217
 takeover in Romania by, 64, 97
Contemporanul (The Contemporary), 173
Crainic, Nichifor, 292
Crasna Skete, 223
Cyprian of Carthage, St., 329

Daniel, Patriarch of Romania, 53
Danube Delta, 27
Da Vinci Code, The (Brown), 13
death, spiritual, 181–87
deification, 22n, 167n, 187, 191
DeLucia, Fr. Paisius, *262*
demons, 63–64, *241*, 289–90, 311, 312, 313, 318–19, 326, 338, 358. *See also* devil, the

d'Estaing, Giscard, 75
devil, the, 64, 143, 206, 288–89, 302, 304, 339, 348, 365. *See also* demons
Diaconesti Monastery, 57
Diocletian, Emperor, 343–48
Dionysius the Areopagite, St., 263
distraction. *See* thoughts: during prayer
Dormition Monastery, Rives Junction, Michigan, 31

ecumenism, 121–24, 208, 314–15, 356–58
Eliade, Christinel, *374*
Eliade, Mircea, 16, *374*, 379, 380
Enea Church, 71, 164, 177, 198, *200*, 201, 203, 362
Energies, Uncreated, 22n, 265, 268. *See also* Uncreated Light
Euclid, 242
evolution, 118–19, 121, 159, 167–69

faith, 26, 149, 170–74, 178, 184, 186, 190, 200, 201, 219, 252, 284, 287, 288–89, 290, 316–17, 322–24, 325–27, 335, 336
fasting, 17, 318–19
Focsani, 197n, 201, 203, 362
forgiveness, 66, 87, 104, 188–95, 296–97
France, 298–99

Gafencu, Valeriu, 135, 136–37, *137*, *139*, 301, 346
Galati Prison, 40, 91, 252, 257
George, Great-martyr, 343–48
Gheorgiu-Dej, Gheorghe, 221, 223, 372n

INDEX

Gherla Prison, 34, 252
Gnosiology of Paradise, The (Crainic), 292
God the Father, 55, 148, 170–71, 185, 191, 209, 266, 285, 307, 339
Goma, Paul, 379
Grabenea, Priest, 115–16
Graham, Billy, 216
Gregory Palamas, St., 268–69

heaven, 166–69, 285
hesychasm, 267–69
Holy Cross Antiochian Orthodox Church, Linthicum, Maryland, 9
Holy Cross Romanian Orthodox Church, Alexandria, Virginia, 10, 42, 43, 54, **55, 58**
"Homilies to the Youth," 15–16, 71–73, 196–97, 206, 231–35, 375
  "Additional Homily to the Youth, An," 196–204
  Fifth Homily: "The Priesthood and Human Suffering," 175–80
  First Homily: "The Call," 157–60
  Fourth Homily: "Faith and Friendship," 170–74
  Introduction to (Hieromonk Seraphim Rose), 153–55
  Introduction to Romanian edition of (Razvan Codrescu), 375–82
  "New Word to the Youth, A," 205–12
  Second Homily: "Let Us Build Churches," 161–64
  Seventh Homily: "Forgiveness," 188–95
  Sixth Homily: "About Death and Resurrection," 181–87
  Third Homily: "Heaven and Earth," 165–69

Holy Spirit, 55, 72, 135, 148, 232, 234, 234n, 268, 281, 284–85, 302, 305, 307–8, 318, 324, 338–39
humility, 45, 190, 237, 293, 294, 304, 313
Ierunca, Virgil, 379
If You Give, You Receive (Steinhardt), 85n
Iliescu, Ion, 349
Inova Fairfax Hospital, 48, 50
Ioanichie (Balan), Archimandrite, ***123***, 223, ***328***
Ioannou, Iacovos, 43, 44
Ionescu, Eugene, 16, 379, 380
Ionescu, Nan, 133
Irineu, Bishop of Dearborn Heights, 52, 54

Jesus Christ, Lord, God, and Savior
  call of, 157–60
  faith in, 149, 170–74
  freedom in, 171–74
  as Head of the Church, 162–63
  and human suffering, 140, 333
  gifts of, 95
  love of, 77, 81, 172, 185, 291
  man saved by, 317
  as the only friend of man, 170–74
  presence in Holy Communion of, 334
  relationship with, 132, 323–24, 335–37
  Resurrection of, 21, 82–83, 87, 115, 182–87, 194, 210–12
  Transfiguration of, 266
  unity in, 174
Jesus Prayer, 18, 30, 240, 267–70, 275–77, 312–13, 339
Jilava Prison, 33, 66, 85n, 91, 109, ***110***, 241, 258, 366

INDEX

John Chrysostom, St., 194–95
John of the Ladder, St., 304
John Paul II, Pope, 118–21
John the Theologian, St., 130
Journal of Blessedness (Steinhardt), 85n, 297
Judgment, Last, 88
Judgment, particular, 348
Justin (Moisescu), Patriarch of Romania, 67, 122
Justin (Parvu), Abbot, *47*, 53, 54, 57, 126
Justinian (Marina), Patriarch of Romania, 37, 66–68, *70*, 117, 221–22

Kim, Ho (Symeon), 44

Lactantius, 344
Lainici Monastery, 95
Legionnaires, 65, 85n, 115, 133–40
"Letter to the CIEL" (Fr. George), 361–63
Little Prince, The (Saint-Exupéry), 84, 245
loneliness, 329–31
love, 55, 77, 158, 162, 171, 172, 174, 335
 for enemies, 295–96
Lovinescu, Monica, 379
Lutai, Fr. Claudiu, 50
Lyon, John, 44

Maftei, Fr. Costica, 362
Mahmudia, Tulcea County, Romania, 25n, 224n
Makarenko, Anton, 98
Mandinescu, Sergiu, 369
Maniu, Iuliu, 227
materialism, 76, 165, 169, 176, 177, 179–80, 206
Maxim, Virgil, 301

Michaila of Vladimiresti, Nun, 91, 124, 219
miners' intervention of 1990, 349–50
miracles, 322–24
Mitterand, Francois, 380
Moldovan, Ilie, 199
Moses, Prophet and God-seer, 265
Mother of God, Most Holy, 28n, 31, 54, 57, 96–97, 148, 218–19, 224, 242, 264, 288, 303, 307, 322, 339

Nathaniel (Popp), Archbishop of Detroit and the Romanian Orthodox Episcopate of America, 54
Neamts Monastery, *97*
New Age movement, 314–15
Nicodemus, Patriarch of Romania, 67, 221
Nicolae (Steinhardt), Hieromonk, 85, *86*, 296–97, 375
Nicula Monastery, 96
Niculitel, Romania, 345
Nina, Nun, 14, *60*, 63
1907 (Arghezi), 88

On the Deaths of the Persecutors (Lactantius), 344
Oprisan, Constantine, 34, 109–21, *113*, 131, 135–36, 295, 301, 367–69
Orthodox Church, the, 161–64
 persecution of, 142, 216–18, 341–42
 relations of, with other faiths, 356. *See also* ecumenism
 salvation only in, 316–17
 unity through, 331

Paisios, Elder of Mt. Athos, 11, 338–39

INDEX

Paisius (Olaru), Elder, 223
Paisius Velichkovsky of Neamts, St., 30, 223, 269
Pasarea Monastery, 68 n
Pascal, Blaise, 178, 242–43
Pedagogical Poem (Makarenko), 99
Peter, Apostle, 316–17
Petrisor, Marcel, 110, *131,* 367n, 368, 372, *382*
Petru Voda Monastery, 53, *56,* 57
Pitesti Prison, 12–13, 34, 64–66, 84–86, 98–108, 227–28, 287, 364–73, 376–78
Plekhanov, Georgy, 283
prayer, 18–19, 146–47, 301–7, 318–19, 338–40. See also Jesus Prayer
"Preface to *Pitesti*" (Fr. George), 364–73
priesthood, 145–46, 175–80, 319
Prisacaru, Colonel, 211
Protestants, 206–7, 216, 220, 316
Puncte Cardinale (Cardinal Points), 355, 372n, 377n, 381

Radu Voda Church, Bucharest, 55, 71, *154, 191,* 197, *198,* 376
Reagan, Ronald, *381*
"Redeemer of the Time, A" (Codrescu), 375–82
reeducation experiment, 98–107, 226–28, 364–73. See also Pitesti Prison; unmaskings
repentance, 14, 104, 209, 228, 304, 307, 334
Roman, Bishop, 235–36, 238
Roman Braga, Archimandrite, 13, 31, 127, 305
Romania, 215–16
  as a Christian nation, 174, 178, 187, 195, 352–55

Romanian Orthodox Church, 127–28, 353
  persecution of, 216–18
Romfest, 380
Scinteia Tineretului (Young People's Spark), 173
Securitate, definition of, 64
September 11 attacks, 10–11
Seraphim (Rose), Hieromonk, 61, 121–22, 153
Sihastria Monastery, 223, *224*
society, modern, 205–12, 330–31, 341–42
Stalin, Joseph, 217
Staniloae, Fr. Dumitru, 31, 88, 89, 117, 334
St. Antim Monastery, Bucharest, 30
Stefan, Fr. Gavrila, 362
Stephen the Great, St., 347
St. Herman's Spring, Alaska, 298
St. Innocent's Academy, *24, 262, 303*
Stoica, Dr. Maria Rosana, 46–49, 53–54
suffering, 14, 66, 102–3, 175–80, 329–31. See also Calciu, Fr. George: torture of; reeducation experiment; Pitesti Prison
  for Christ, 218–19
  meaning of, 332–33
  of Christ, 140, 183
  purification through, 296
Symeon Metaphrastes, St., 303
Symeon the New Theologian, St., 303

Teoctist, Patriarch of Romania, 53, 357
thankfulness, 330
theosis. See deification
Thomas, Apostle, 325–27

INDEX

thoughts
  of anger, 311, 313
  during prayer, 290, 302, 304–5, 338–39
Thus Spake Zarathustra (Nietzsche), 373
Titulescu, Nicolae, 193
Tradition, Holy, 217, 320–21, 353, 356
Transfiguration, Orthodox Monastery of the, Ellwood, Pennsylvania, 41
Trifa, Fr. Joseph, 28n, 98
Trinity, Divine and Holy, 148, 168, 263–64, 285, 307, 339

Uncreated Light, 19–22, 263–77

Uniates, 215–16
United States of America, blessings of, 297–99
unmaskings, 13, 100–101. *See also* re-education; Pitesti Prison

Vladimiresti Monastery, 218

watchfulness, 302, 305
Way of the Pilgrim, The, 269
Western values, 205–12

Zographou Monastery (Mt. Athos), 347
Zoticus, Martyr, and companions, 345

Saint Herman of Alaska Brotherhood

Since 1965, the St. Herman of Alaska Brotherhood has been publishing Orthodox Christian books and magazines.

View our catalog, featuring over fifty titles, and order online, at

www.sainthermanpress.com

You can also write us for a free printout of our catalog:

St. Herman of Alaska Brotherhood
P. O. Box 70
Platina, CA 96076 USA

Father George Calciu
Interviews, Homilies, and Talks

*Typeset in Adobe Garamond.
Printed on sixty-pound Glatfelter Offset paper
at Thomson-Shore, Inc., Dexter, Michigan.*